BEYOND *the* BATTLEGROUND

BEYOND *the* BATTLEGROUND

Classic Strategies from the **Yijing** and **Baguazhang** for Managing Crisis Situations

Tom Bisio

BLUE SNAKE BOOKS
BERKELEY, CALIFORNIA

Published by
North Atlantic Books
Berkeley, California

Cover photo © iStockphoto.com / Francis Wong Chee Yen
Cover design by Daniel Tesser
Book design by Brad Greene
Printed in the United States of America

Beyond the Battleground: Classic Strategies from the Yijing and Baguazhang for Managing Crisis Situations is sponsored and published by the Society for the Study of Native Arts and Sciences (dba North Atlantic Books), an educa-tional nonprofit based in Berkeley, California, that collaborates with partners to develop cross-cultural perspectives, nurture holistic views of art, science, the humanities, and healing, and seed personal and global transformation by publishing work on the relationship of body, spirit, and nature.

North Atlantic Books' publications are available through most bookstores. For further information, visit our website at www.northatlanticbooks.com or call 800-733-3000.

Library of Congress Cataloging-in-Publication Data

Names: Bisio, Tom, author.
Title: Beyond the battleground : classic strategies from the Yijing and
    Baguazhang for managing crisis situations / Tom Bisio.
Description: Berkeley, California : North Atlantic Books, [2016] | Includes
    bibliographical references and index.
Identifiers: LCCN 2015037865 | ISBN 9781623170066 (pbk.) |
    ISBN 9781623170073 (ebook)
Subjects: LCSH: Taoism. | Yi jing. | Martial arts—China. | Strategy. |
    Military art and science—China. | Conflict management.
Classification: LCC BL1923 .B56 2016 | DDC 303.6/9—dc23
LC record available at http://lccn.loc.gov/2015037865

1 2 3 4 5 6 7 8 SHERIDAN 20 19 18 17 16
Printed on recycled paper

To my brother Joe

Acknowledgments

Endless thanks to my wife Valerie who helped me in so many ways with hand holding, listening, fixing computer problems, and in general putting up with my obsession to write this book. She also helped edit the original text book and critically analyzed some of my ideas. Without her support and encouragement, I would not have written it. Valerie, thank you for being there!

To my son Virgil for his interest in the project and in history in general. He asked questions, gave me input based his own reading, and provided constructive feedback. Virgil also did the great drawing of Zhuge Liang.

To my teachers in the internal martial arts who gave me an appreciation and basic understanding of the Yi Jing. My deepest thanks to Vince Black, Zhang Hua Sen, Li Gui Chang, Song Zhi Yong, Wang Shi Tong, Gao Ji Wu, and Zhao Da Yuan.

Thank you to all of my students for their input and thought-provoking questions.

Wes Tasker helped me to formulate a relationship between the *Yijing* hexagrams and the 64 hands of Ba Gua Zhang. We discussed and shared many of the historical source texts. Wes also helped me with heuristic theory and understanding the OODA loop He is a great friend and a valuable and treasured colleague. Thank You, Wes!

A heartfelt thanks to my good friend Huang Guo Qi. Huang helped me with fact finding, translation, and general advice on Chinese culture. My many trips to China for study and research would not have been possible without him. Huang was invaluable in helping me find information on Zhuge Liang and translating it from the Classical Chinese. He took the time to sit with me in Taiyuan and read through the translations character by character.

I thank Teja Watson for her careful copyedit, and a big thank you to Louis Swaim, who project edited the book. He pointed out inconsistencies and errors that I missed and in general put up with my impatience with the complex process of publishing. Louis, thank you for your patience and persistence.

Contents

Preface to the Second Edition

Soon after publishing a book, I immediately think of all things I wish I had added to make the discussion more clear and more complete. Never has this been more true than with *Strategy and Change*. When North Atlantic Books expressed a desire to republish *Strategy and Change* and asked me to add additional material on the application of strategy and the *Yijing* (*I Ching*) to daily life, I was pleased to accept, because this is exactly what I felt was lacking in the first edition. Furthermore, attempting to apply these strategic principles to my own life led me to look beyond the military and martial applications of strategy to try to understand more clearly how these concepts relate to business, interpersonal relationships, and life in general—hence the new title *Beyond the Battleground*. Researching, discussing, and writing about these aspects of strategy and change has been illuminating for me personally, stimulating new thoughts about my own interaction with life in a constantly changing world. I feel the addition of this discussion on the application of the principles of strategy and change to daily life (Chapter V) brings the book full circle, transforming it from an examination of strategic thought to a meditation on strategy and adaptation to change and uncertainty.

Living is not easy, and life is full of unexpected curves and unforeseen events. Negotiating our own personal circumstances as they change and unfold within the world is a challenge for every individual. Knowledge of strategic thinking, and understanding the patterns of change operating in the world around us, can help us to navigate the uncertainties of life, while maintaining our own inner integrity. This in turn creates the possibility for living in concord with the world, by knowing that we have done everything possible to achieve harmony between who we are, what we do, and the effects and consequences of our engagement with the world. If this book in any way aids the reader in gaining greater insight into how to achieve some measure of this harmony, then it has been a useful and fulfilling labor.

—Tom Bisio, March 2015

Introduction

This book started as a ten-page essay on Ba Gua and military strategy and became an obsession that took me through piles of books, online research, numerous emails to China, and many sleepless nights with *Yijing*, the Classic of Change, hexagrams dancing through my head. The essay gradually morphed into something much larger in scope then I ever intended. Once I began, the possibilities multiplied along with the source material and it became a book. I fear in writing it I have only just scratched the surface of the subject, that my own understanding of Ba Gua, the *Yijing*, and military strategy is inadequate. This book is, on some level, a work in progress. I apologize in advance for any incorrect facts or historical simplifications and look forward to criticism.

Military strategy is to some degree the study of how to shape and manage crisis situations. On a fundamental level, crisis situations stem from a larger dynamic of individuals, groups, or nations attempting to overcome obstacles in their path in order to make manifest the individual's or group's will and intentions. Strategy itself manifests in how the individual or group reacts to changing events in relation to the interests of other individuals and groups, who are also interacting with these same events as they unfold. Martial arts can be viewed as an extension of military strategy, because these arts are largely a development or refinement of techniques and principles that were originally used in waging war. Both the martial arts and military strategy are concerned with methods of surviving and prevailing in adverse circumstances. Over thousands of years both disciplines have developed extensive and diverse techniques and principles of application.

The question of how to achieve success in a seemingly chaotic world is one of the fundamental questions Chinese strategists have grappled with for centuries. Much of Chinese thought advocates understanding the natural order of the world in order to harmonize and flow with it. In the *Sunzi* or *Art of War*, principles of strategy are delineated and applied both to military endeavors and to their wider application in the relationships between states. However, if viewed in a more general way, the *Sunzi* is a text is about

understanding crisis situations and how to adapt to them. In formulating
this approach it is fairly certain that the *Sunzi* draws to some extent on the
Yijing, the Book of Changes, a work that has been commented on by schol-
ars for over two millennia. Although the *Yijing* is often viewed as a book
of divination, it has also been applied to social and political thinking, as
exemplified in the ideas of thinkers like Wang Bi (226–249) and Cheng Yi in
the eleventh century. Wang Bi lived during a period of social and political
upheaval, marked by rebellion and constant warfare.[1] This period, between
the disintegration of the Han Dynasty and the beginning of the Northern
and Southern Dynasties, is generally referred to as the Three Kingdoms
era. During the Three Kingdoms, the great general Cao Cao usurped the
power of the Wei state and made himself dictator of Northern China. Cao
Cao pitted his armies and his wit against both the Southern state of Wu and
the forces of a distant member of the Han imperial family advised by the
master strategist Zhuge Liang.

Wang Bi's commentaries on the *Yijing* reveal his acumen as a political
and social thinker, and demonstrate the *Yijing*'s utility when applied to
strategic thinking. The diagrams of the *Yijing* (composed of broken and
solid lines) serve as a kind of binary code that can be used to describe fundamental forces operating in the world around us. For example, "Heaven"
in the *Yijing,* and in Chinese culture, refers to a natural operating system,
an overarching cosmological order that governs everything and is all-
encompassing. Hence, Heaven has a capacity for action. "Earth," its polar
opposite, is receptive; it responds to the creative force of heaven bringing to
completion its initiating force. These forces both interact and interpenetrate
with each other. The *Yijing* diagrams, particularly the hexagrams (groupings
of six lines), represent specific but fluid situations in which unwise actions
can undermine favorable circumstances, while wise actions can salvage
seemingly hopeless ones. Looked at in this way, the hexagrams signify not
only discrete states of change occurring in moments in time, but also larger,
more global patterns of change, while simultaneously indicating flexible
decision-making strategies that can help one prevail in the midst of these
changing circumstances.[2]

It could be argued that martial arts are fundamentally systems for dealing with chaotic crisis situations (a fight or battlefield encounter). In the

David Mamet movie *Redbelt,* the protagonist, a jujitsu instructor, is asked if he teaches people to win. The instructor, who eschews competition, responds that he teaches them to prevail. In this context, martial arts are not about defeating opponents but about prevailing in adverse circumstances. These circumstances might encompass a fight, but they may also be something else entirely.

Ba Gua Zhang or Eight Diagram Palm is a martial art that references both the *Yijing* and texts on Chinese military strategy, including the Thirty-Six Military Stratagems. The names of some of the individual fighting movements refer to military commanders and strategies that were used in the Three Kingdoms period. One commentator wrote that to understand the *Art of War* you have to understand change[3] (an oblique reference to the *Yijing*). Similarly, Ba Gua stresses movement and constant change in order to negotiate the uncertainty of hand-to-hand combat. Its unique combat theory employs *Yijing* diagrams to describe body principles. Because Ba Gua Zhang relies on constant change and transformation in order to employ its defensive and offensive strategies, it can be used as a vehicle to internalize the principles of change delineated in the *Yijing* and embodied in military strategy. In this way, Ba Gua Zhang is a connecting point through which change and strategy can be experienced in body movement. In Ba Gua Zhang, specific body movements are ideally not techniques or postures, but potentiated states of change, fluid situations that contain an inherent dynamic potential. The reverse is also true—the diagrams of the *Yijing* can also be applied to understand the principles of change within Ba Gua's endless "palm changes."

This book, then, is an attempt to draw together Ba Gua Zhang, the *Yijing,* and military strategy. In some ways this is an impossible task, for the more one says about any one of these three subjects, the more is left unsaid. To get around this difficulty I have tried to come at the subject from various viewpoints. Chapter I correlates relationships between Ba Gua Zhang and military strategy. In Chapter II, the much broader scope of strategy and grand strategy is examined and connected to principles of adapting to change expressed in the *Yijing* diagrams. Chapter III looks at the structure of the *Yijing* diagrams and their manifestation in the physical movements of Ba Gua Zhang. Chapter IV examines the order of the Hexagrams as a means of gaining insight into larger patterns of change in the world around us, while Chapter V discusses the application of strategic principles to business, personal relationships, and self-fulfillment. The appendices fill in gaps in the larger discussion. Appendix I analyzes three of the hexagrams in greater detail to gain a better understanding of the potential and uncertainties inherent in conflict, warfare, and peace. Appendix II discusses the strategies of Zhuge Liang, a strategist-general of the Three Kingdoms era, whose principles of crisis management are still used today in business; and Appendix III presents the Thirty-Six Military Strategies of ancient China and their correspondences with *Yijing* hexagrams and Ba Gua movements.

Many teachers of Ba Gua Zhang (some of my own teachers included) do not believe that the diagrams of the *Yijing* have much to do with Ba Gua as a martial art. Nor do they feel that the study of the *Yijing* or military strategy have much value in attaining applied skill in martial arts. Because some of them can demonstrate a high level of ability in fighting, it is impossible to argue with them and their position. Many of the Ba Gua masters I spoke with in Beijing credit Liu De Kuan with the creation of the Sixty-Four Hands—the straight-line Ba Gua forms. Some teachers say Liu created the Sixty-Four Hands to teach the army; others, that the forms are just meant to be examples of Ba Gua combat applications. However, I feel that there is much more to these forms than meets the eye. I believe they have profound relationships with Ba Gua's eight palm changes and with the hexagrams of the *Yijing*. The correspondences between the *Yijing* hexagrams and the Sixty-Four Hands presented in this book are based on my own analysis and research. This correlation is consistent with my interpretation of the internal structure of the Ba Gua ding shi (fixed postures) and their relationship to the trigrams. However, because each of the ding shi can manifest internally and can transform without visible external manifestation of the internal change, other interpretations are not only possible, but likely, and, to some extent, will depend on one's viewpoint.

In a similar vein, most students of military strategy do not feel that hand-to-hand combat has much to do with the movements of larger military forces and the interactions of armies or states. Yet there are strategists like the famous swordsman Miyamoto Musashi, who contend that the principles of defeating a single person are the same as defeating ten thousand. There are also many ways of interpreting battles, military operations, and conflicts between states. It is clear from the many books on the subject that analysis of strategy by soldiers, generals, military historians, and statesmen do not necessarily agree. Yet, there is a thread running through Ba Gua Zhang, the *Yijing*, and military strategy, and that thread in turn can connect one to a larger picture of the world and its potential interactions and changes. Though I am not an *Yijing* scholar, and am at best an amateur student of military history, I feel that study of these three areas brings one in touch with something larger than, yet inextricably linked to, defeating an opponent in hand-to-hand combat, the movement of troops on the field of battle, and negotiating the uncertainties of life. As one Chinese martial arts instructor pointed out to a colleague of mine, strategy is life—we have the opportunity of engaging with it and perhaps profiting from it, or ignoring it, perhaps to our detriment. This is true whether one is a general, a martial artist, or a politician, whether engaged in a business enterprise or a social interaction.

One's strategy and the ability to apply it is to some degree influenced by one's orientation, which in turn stems from one's cultural background, experiences, and training. Therefore, I feel it is important to talk about my own orientation. I have little interest in the *Yijing* as a method of divination. My approach to the *Yijing* has more to do with its structure, and understanding the movements inherent in the lines and their configurations. This approach includes martial arts methods of *Yijing* analysis that employ the *Yijing* diagrams to illustrate the subtle movements of the body's internal energy.

My simultaneous and overlapping studies of Chinese medicine and Chinese martial arts have greatly influenced my outlook on how, by knowing one thing, it is possible to immediately know other things. The principles of learning anything are the same, and doing or knowing one thing well facilitates doing or knowing many things. Much of my ability as a practitioner of traditional Chinese medicine flows from the practice of the martial arts. What is true about the body in martial arts is true in medicine as well, and principles realized in one discipline can be accessed in the other. In short, there is interpenetration between the energies and principles underlying any form, the form itself, and other forms. This kind of thinking permeates the martial arts, traditional Chinese medicine, and Chinese thought, and is part of my thinking in writing this book.

The famous philosopher and mathematician Gottfried Wilhelm Leibniz saw the *Yijing* as a kind of binary computer, with the broken and solid lines representing 0 and 1. Some martial arts teachers use this analogy in relating Ba Gua Zhang's principles of change to the *Yijing*. I see the *Yijing* and Ba Gua more as a map of exponential potential for change, and the changes and hexagrams as diagrams of intrinsic energies inherent in situations and movements. Viewed in this way, martial arts movements are templates through which one can flow with the changing circumstances, rather than discrete techniques or specific movements. Forms then become a vehicle for internalizing movement. Once internalized, the form can be dissolved. The *Yijing* provides us with useful images for understanding movement, posture, alignment, and change, but the images are not the thing itself.

> [Wang Bi] steadfastly maintained that images, like words, were only a means an end, not to be confused with the end itself. A person who remained fixed on words would not be able to grasp the images, and someone who stayed fixed on images would not be able to get the ideas. Thus he argued that since words are the means to explain the images, once one gets the images he forgets the words, and since the images are the means to allow us to concentrate on the ideas, once one gets the ideas, he forgets the images.[4]

If we strip the *Yijing* diagrams down to their most essential component parts, they are about yang (solid) lines and yin (broken) lines. The lines represent movement and transformation that are occurring, or are about to occur, in a variety of changing situations. The yang lines represent dynamic directed movement, and the yin lines either receive and respond to the movement, gathering and channeling its force, or, depending on the configuration, the yin lines may block, retard, or modify movement. Following this line of thought, it might be argued that on a fundamental level, military stratagems and martial arts are reducible to principles of movement and patterns of change.

Although in modern times the focus of the martial arts has become more narrow (i.e., winning matches or preparing for the proverbial "street fight"), the fighting strategies and tactics of Chinese martial arts are much broader in scope. They originate directly from the principles of the art of war, which are in turn derived from the *Yijing*.[5] In China, martial arts traditionally were an extension of warfare, and thus the great military commanders were noted for accomplishments and knowledge in many areas, including hand-to-hand combat, horseback riding, archery, use of the eighteen traditional weapons (which included missile weapons, short and long weapons, double weapons, and flexible weapons), military strategy and tactics, and a working knowledge of Chinese medicine. The famous General Yue Fei of the Song dynasty demonstrated proficiency in many of these areas, and is credited with the creation of several styles of martial arts and at least one method of qigong. In the Three Kingdoms period, Zhuge Liang is the exceptional general who combines knowledge of war with highly developed political and leadership skills, psychology, and an understanding of the heavens: astronomy, astrology, meteorology, and knowledge of wind-water (feng shui). This knowledge enabled him to predict weather patterns, understand the terrain, and calculate the influence of these factors on military operations. Even less-skilled strategists, like the hot-headed Zhang Fei, demonstrated proficiency in horsemanship, archery, a variety of weapons, strategy and tactics, leadership, and logistical and organization skills. My own perception is that the scope of knowledge contained in the martial arts is necessarily broad, and therein lies its flexibility to adapt. This is neatly summed up in the saying "Quan" ("fist"; i.e., martial arts), originated from the *Yijing*, and Wu Shu (武术: literally, "military arts") theory was completed through traditional medicine theory.[6]

My preference for the underdog has probably influenced my take on strategic thinking. Hence, my fascination with Belisarius and Zhuge Liang, strategists who usually fought against larger, more powerful adversaries (which in of itself might be considered not very strategic!), triumphing again and again only to lose in the end. Similarly, I have been influenced by some of my teachers in martial arts who used skill born out of strategically oriented training, rather than aggression, physical wherewithal, and innate ferocity, to overcome larger, stronger, and faster adversaries. Finally, as a teenager I was introduced to Liddel Hart's classic military book *Strategy*, which connected me with the *Sunzi: The Art of War* and gave me a reverence for the Chinese approach to strategic thinking, or what Hart terms the "indirect approach."

This book does not follow the standard format of presenting a thesis, defending it with examples, and summing up at the end. Instead, I choose to employ a nonlinear approach, presenting related and similar ideas in juxtaposition, so that comparisons can be made and relationships explored. This approach aims at creating cross-currents of ideas that interpenetrate and inform one another. In discussing subjects as diverse and deep as strategy, the *Yijing,* and Ba Gua, there is no one starting point or end point. I feel that this kind of interweaving of ideas will be more useful, as it allows for points, assertions, and ideas to be revisited again and again. In this way I hope the book will serve as a resource for the reader to seek out his or her own answers.

CHAPTER I

Ba Gua Zhang and Military Strategy

Know your enemy and know yourself and you can fight a hundred battles without peril. If you are ignorant of the enemy and know only yourself, you will stand equal chances of winning and losing. If you know neither the enemy nor yourself, you are bound to be defeated in every battle.[7]

—Sunzi

Even if we show people the flexible tactics we used to gain victory in conformity with the changing enemy situation, they still cannot comprehend them. The enemy may know the tactics by which we win, but he does not know how we use the tactics to defeat him. Following each victory, we do not repeat the same tactics, we change them constantly to suit the changing circumstances.[8]

—Sunzi

The Art of War and Ba Gua Zhang

The principles of military strategy and Chinese boxing are in many ways the same. The stratagems and principles of the Chinese martial arts are congruent with those of military strategy set out in *The Art of War*, also known as the *Sunzi*. Sunzi (Sun Tzu), the author of *The Art of War* (probably written in the Warring States Period: 453–221 BC), detailed many principles that reference deployment or *shi*, and were adopted by exponents of the martial arts in general, and Ba Gua in particular. Two of Sunzi's most famous statements are particularly interesting to practitioners of the internal arts:

And therefore the victories won by a master of war gain him neither reputation for wisdom nor merit for valor. For he wins his victories without erring. "Without erring" means that whatever he does insures victory; he conquers an enemy already defeated. Therefore the skillful commander takes up a position in which he cannot be defeated and misses no opportunity to master his enemy.[9]

It is because of disposition (shi) that a victorious general is able to make his people fight with the effect of pent-up waters, which, suddenly released, plunge into a bottomless abyss. The nature of water is that it avoids heights and hastens to the lowlands. When a dam is broken, the water cascades with irresistible force. Now the shape of an army resembles water. Take advantage of the enemy's unpreparedness; attack him when he does not expect it; avoid his strength and strike his emptiness, and like water, none can oppose you.[10]

Dong Haichuan, the founder of Ba Gua Zhang, stressed the importance of walking in a circle as a basic form of martial arts training. He is quoted as saying that "training in martial arts ceaselessly is inferior to walking the circle. In Ba Gua Zhang the circle walk practice is the fount of all training."[11] When confronting an opponent, the walking practice and the use of a curved step allow for quick changes of direction. The body postures and the steps must be in accordance with the opponent's movements, changing freely and appropriately like flowing water. The walking method in Ba Gua is described as follows:

This skill comes from the curved step. Changes in the hands take place with the step. Hitting upward and holding the lower position, blocking across and evading, pushing, upholding, taking and leading, don't leave the two arms.[12]

François Jullien describes shi as the potential born of disposition. In a military strategy this refers to the general's ability to exploit, to his own advantage and to maximum effect, whatever conditions he encounters.[13] Using walking and change as the basis of one's strategic disposition prevents one from being immobilized or blocked, while allowing for spontaneous reaction to the opponent and the situation. Li Zi Ming, a famous Ba Gua practitioner from Beijing, describes Ba Gua as a form of guerrilla warfare and emphasizes the need for mobility and spontaneity, which in Ba Gua is developed and determined by circle walking:

But it should be obvious that in practical application the circle walking doesn't proceed in a fixed pattern. It should proceed according to the situation and the movements of the opponent, changing and transforming ceaselessly. Whether training or in combat, one moves according to one's opponent. We could decide to attack either the lateral side of the opponent by first moving straight in, or vice versa, in order to induce the opponent to enter an empty position and then defeat him. This is exactly the method of "evading and advancing to win." The strategy of the Eight Diagram Palm may be summarized as attack, defend, advance, retreat. Therefore, it dictates to: "move before the enemy is going to move, be still as the enemy comes to rest, avoid the enemy when he strains, be supple when the enemy is strong and rigid, advance when the enemy retreats, retreat when the enemy advances, move when the enemy moves, and also move when the enemy does not move."[14]

These strategies outlined by Li Zi Ming and Sunzi sound remarkably similar to the kinds of tactics Mao Zedong employed in his guerrilla war against the Japanese Imperial Troops and the Guomindang. Mao coined a short sixteen-character jingle to describe the tactics of his troops:

When the enemy advances, we retreat!
When the enemy halts, we harass
When the enemy seeks to avoid battle, we attack!
When the enemy retreats, we pursue![15]

Orthodox and Unorthodox Strategies

B. H. Liddell Hart, whose book *Strategy* is considered one of the modern classics on the art of war, pays homage to the ideas of Sunzi and their application by Mao Zedong. Liddell Hart categorizes this type of strategy as the "indirect approach" to military strategy. He adds:

With deepened reflection, however I began to realize that the indirect approach had much wider application—that it was a law of life in all spheres: a truth of philosophy. Its fulfillment was seen to be the key to practical achievement in dealing with any problem where the human factor predominates, and a conflict of wills tends to spring from an underlying concern for interests. In all such cases, the direct assault of new ideas provokes a stubborn resistance, thus intensifying the difficulty of producing a change of outlook. Conversion is achieved more easily and rapidly by unexpected infiltration of a different idea or by an argument that turns the flank of instinctive opposition. The indirect approach is as fundamental to the realm of politics as to the realm of sex. In commerce, the suggestion that there is a bargain to be secured is far more potent than any direct appeal to buy. And in any sphere it is proverbial that the surest way of gaining a superior's acceptance of a new idea is to persuade him that it is his idea! As in war, the aim is to weaken the resistance before attempting to overcome it; and the effect is best attained by drawing the other party out of his defenses.[16]

Hart's application of the principles of military tactics to other areas of life is not unique. The Chinese and Japanese long ago appreciated the potential for universal application of principles of military strategy. Hence, the adoption of Miayamoto Musashi's *Book of Five Rings* and the *Sunzi* to modern business practices. Musashi implied that correct learning in one area can be applied to other areas: the spirit of defeating a man is the same as defeating a million men. The strategist makes small things into big things, like building a great Buddha from a one-foot model. The principle of strategy is in knowing one thing, knowing ten thousand things. This is similar to a saying among Ba Gua practitioners: "from one change, a thousand changes." From one technique, a thousand techniques.

In China, especially among martial artists, there arose the idea that life is strategy. Metaphors involving military strategy are common in many areas of Chinese culture, including common expressions, politics, and traditional Chinese medicine. In his wonderful book, *A Treatise on Efficacy,* Francois Jullien discusses the application of these ideas to politics and diplomacy. He echoes the words of Liddell Hart when he says that when the potential of a situation is deduced, one can deduce how to profit from it. Therefore, rather than following a predetermined, fixed course of action, the ancient treatises on strategy advise dealing with the inevitable unpredictability of constantly changing circumstances by observing the potential emanating from the situation.[17] This can be applied to any situation in life, just as Liddell Hart suggests. Strategist-philosophers like the late Colonel John R. Boyd, who lectured to America's modern military leaders and White House advisers, relate ideas about military strategy to the basic components of human behavior:

> In a real world of limited resources and skills, individuals and groups form, dissolve, and reform their cooperative or competitive postures in a continuous struggle to remove or overcome physical and social environmental obstacles. In a cooperative sense, where skills and talents are pooled, the removal or overcoming of obstacles represents an improved capacity for independent action for all concerned. In a competitive sense, where individuals and groups compete for scarce resources and skills, an improved capacity for independent action achieved by some individuals or groups constrains that capacity for other individuals or groups. Naturally, such a combination of real world scarcity and goal striving to overcome this scarcity intensifies the struggle of individuals and groups to cope with both their physical and social environments.[18]

The ideas of military strategists like Sunzi, and his ancestor Sun Bin, did not develop in a vacuum. These men wrote in the Spring and Autumn period (722–481 BC) of Chinese history, and based their ideas on those of earlier thinkers. Later, other famous strategists like Zhuge Liang expanded upon them. Warfare in China increased in scope during the Spring and Autumn period. In the earlier Zhou period (1046–771 BC), warfare had been more sporadic and smaller in scope. Now battles were frequent and armies increased in size. In the Warring States period (beginning in 481 BC), small states were swallowed up by larger, more powerful states. By 403 BC there were seven states left. The Qin state, which eventually defeated the others and unified China, was the largest of the survivors, with an army estimated (by some) of one million men.[19] In this period, larger campaigns involving hundreds of thousands of men were not uncommon. Battles involved engagements, offensives, and counter-offensives that went on for days, and sieges could last a year or more. As a consequence, the training of professional soldiers, sophisticated strategy and tactics, as well as the ability to control and direct large bodies of troops became not only more complex, but of vital importance for survival. Additionally, the use of crossbow (invented by the Chinese around 400 BC) became a widespread and important feature on the battlefield. For the Chinese, the activation of the mechanism of the crossbow was symbolic of the sudden unleashing of an army's energy.[20]

Francois Jullien, expanding on Sun Bin's mention of the crossbow, points out that "with a crossbow, one can kill people more than a hundred paces away without their companions realizing from where it was fired." The same applies to the good general, who by using shi ("disposition"; "potential emanating from a situation"), manages with minimum effort to achieve the maximum effect from a distance (either temporal or spatial), simply by exploiting the factors in play, without common knowledge of how the result was achieved or by whom.[21]

As orthodox strategies and tactics evolved, methods of combating them with unorthodox tactics also developed. Sunzi stresses the importance of both kinds of tactics. *Zheng* refers to normal, orthodox, or direct force and *qi* to the indirect, unorthodox, or extraordinary. They are interlinked concepts, like links in a chain. Zheng can be a fixing or holding operation, while qi is a flanking or encircling operation. A qi operation is strange and unexpected, while a zheng operation is more direct, more obvious. Often the engagement occurs with zheng, while the decisive stroke, coming where the enemy least expects it, is qi.[22]

The orthodox and the unorthodox can be employed in countless variations. Sunzi points out that although there are only five colors, one can make from them innumerable hues; though there are only five flavors, they can be combined in endless varieties. Similarly, in military strategy there are only two types of operation, qi and zheng, yet their variations are limitless. They constantly change from one to the other, like moving in a circle with neither beginning nor an end. Who can exhaust their possibilities?[23]

An interesting example of effectively combining zheng and qi occurred in the Spring and Autumn period, when Yue attacked Wu. The armies of both states were deployed on either side of a river. At night, Yue had the left and right flanks of its army attack across the river, accompanied by the clamorous beating of drums. Wu was forced to divide its army to meet these threats. Then Yue's central force crossed the river in silence, and only after the crossing attacked to the beating of drums. Confused and split in two, Wu's army was defeated.

Unorthodox strategies have long fascinated Chinese writers and thinkers. The famous fire oxen of Tian Dan were used to overcome a large army besieging a city. The defenders, led by Tian Dan, attached sharp blades to the horns of the oxen and fire brands to their tails. Released at night, through gaps in the city walls, the crazed oxen surged through the enemy camp, followed by several thousand warriors. The psychological and physical shock of the attack routed the besiegers.[24] The great Carthaginian General Hannibal used similar tactics in 217 BC when trapped on the Falernian plain by the Roman general Fabius, who placed crack troops blocking the defile through which Hannibal had entered the valley. Hannibal realized the Romans would not expect him to attack the defile, as to do so would leave him vulnerable to the rest of Fabius's army. He had pitch-pine torches attached to the horns of several thousand cattle. Released at night near the defile, and maddened with pain and fear, the cattle scattered over the slopes of the hills surrounding the defile. The Roman troops in the defile thought the torches were the Carthaginians escaping through the woods, so they abandoned their positions to attack. Hannibal's army promptly occupied their now empty position and escaped.[25]

Ba Gua Zhang actually defines itself by its unorthodox approach. The "Eight Contraries" specifically delineate how its methods differ from other approaches to hand-to-hand combat:

1. Everyone uses the ends of their limbs, but we use the root first when we want to use the ends.
2. Everyone likes to use varied fists, but we just use the straight pushing palm.
3. Everyone likes to turn the whole body around to face the rear, but in a single step we can move to deal with the eight directions.
4. Everyone advances straight forward with an erect body, but we strike with our palm and the feet follow.[26]

Ba Gua Zhang is characterized by change and transformation, therefore it employs zheng and qi interchangeably:

There are obvious functions and there are obscure functions. They are used to strike and break the body. They can transform and open the enemy's methods. Maybe a hard advance is used. Maybe a soft advance is used. Maybe advancing is used and maybe retreating is used. Maybe inducing is used. Maybe I point up and they are used downwards. Maybe I point down and they are used upwards. Maybe I point left and strike right. Maybe I point to the front and strike to the rear. Maybe I point at this and strike it. Maybe he is hard and I am soft. Maybe he is soft and I am hard. Maybe he is low and I am high. Maybe he moves and I am still. Maybe he is still and I move. Observe the terrain. In expanding and contracting, coming and going, distinguish the terrain: the distances and defiles, whether it is broad and narrow, whether it contains dead or alive things. The body form contains movement and non-movement. Combine the inner and the outer into one Dao. Examine his body to see if it is high or low. Estimate his emotional form, is it full or empty? Examine his qi. Is it substantial or thin? You get his thinking. At your convenience consult the usage and be able to arrange what is appropriate. As for the inner functions of the fist, they are numerous. Then, whatever happens, the actions are transformed.[27]

A preference for using the indirect or unconventional approach does not mean it can be used exclusively. Qi and zheng are interdependent and rely upon each other. As Edward Luttwack points out, when he compares what he calls Relational Maneuver (essentially qi) with Attrition Warfare (essentially zheng), the avoidance of the enemy's strength and the potential for surprise that occurs in Relational Maneuver creates the possibilities of results that are disproportionately large in relation to the resources applied. Attrition Warfare, on the other hand, virtually guarantees results in proportion to strength expended and resources applied. In Relational Maneuver, if one cannot achieve surprise and apply strength against the opponent's weak points, one is bound to fail and may fail quite spectacularly. One has only to look at some of the elaborate and delicately balanced stratagems of the Three Kingdoms period found throughout this book to see that if one thing goes wrong, disaster can follow. Attrition Warfare, on the other hand, has a high cost but a lower risk factor. Additionally, a high level of skill is required in employing Relational Maneuver tactics.[28] Therefore, although Chinese strategists appear to have a preference for the unconventional, there is a tacit recognition that the conventional and unconventional are two sides of a coin that not only operate as extensions of each other, but can transform into each other. If an unconventional operation is expected and one instead does something conventional, that catches the opponent by surprise, then what was normally zheng in effect becomes qi.

Deception in Warfare

Deception is a part of warfare. To some degree, whether engaged in guerrilla warfare or more conventional combat, all warfare employs deception. One of the most quoted passages in the *Sunzi* discusses this aspect of conflict:

> War is a game of deception. Therefore feign incapability when in fact capable; feign inactivity when ready to strike; appear to be far, when actually nearby, and vice versa. When the enemy is greedy for gains, hand out bait to lure him; when he is in disorder attack and overcome him; when he boasts substantial strength, be doubly prepared against him; and when he is formidable, evade him. If he is given to anger, provoke him. If he is timid and careful, encourage his arrogance. If his forces are rested wear them down. If he is united divide him. Attack where he is least prepared. Take action where he least expects you.[29]

The Three Kingdoms period of Chinese history began when the generals assigned to put down the Yellow Turban rebellion became stronger than the throne and fought among themselves for supremacy. By 205 AD, Cao Cao, who eventually won the conflict, had made himself dictator of Northern China. Cao Cao carved out huge state farms from land laid waste by war and settled landless, poor, and captured rebels to work them, thus making the state the greatest of all landlords. He established military colonies for hereditary military households, whose men would both farm and fight. For his cavalry he recruited the nomadic Xiongnu tribesman in large numbers, settling many in southern Shanxi. Two rival claimants to the throne attempted to thwart Cao Cao and his son. In the central and lower Yangzi valley and further south, the brothers Sun Ce and Sun Quan established the state of Wu. In the West, in Sichuan, a distant member of the Han imperial family, Liu Bei, guided by the legendary strategist Zhuge Liang, established a stronghold.[30] The story of the Three Kingdoms comes down to us in the form of a historical novel, but it *should not be underestimated in its role as a source of military wisdom and tactics applicable to the contemporary martial environment.* Strategists from the Peoples' Republic of China (PRC) have studied it avidly for useful lessons.[31]

The strategists of the Three Kingdoms use many ruses, traps, and tricks in a world marked by treachery, deceit, and unending warfare. Although Cao Cao is a clever and ruthless leader of vast forces, it is Zhuge Liang who is most remembered for his brilliant use of unconventional tactics. Using what has come to be known as the "Empty City Ploy," Zhuge Liang and a few thousand men stayed in Yang Ping while the rest of the army went on to combine forces for other operations. The enemy arrived unexpectedly with many thousands of troops. Their scouts reported that the city was weakly defended. Zhuge Liang commanded that the battle flags be hidden and the military drums silenced. The streets were swept and sprinkled with water and the gates left open. Zhuge Liang then went onto the battlements and, in a relaxed mood, played the zither. The enemy, knowing his reputation, thought this was a ploy to deceive them, and that other troops must be lying in wait nearby. They withdrew without attacking.

Another example of Zhuge Liang's strategic prowess was his method of borrowing arrows from the enemy. With his army short of arrows, Zhuge Liang employed boats with straw dummies dressed like soldiers to pass down the river in front of Cao Cao's army. In the fog, with drums beating, it seemed as though Zhuge Liang's men were attacking. Cao Cao's archers feathered the straw dummies with thousands of shafts. By the time the enemy realized their mistake the boats had passed downstream and the arrows had been gathered.

These examples exemplify the idea of the insubstantial appearing substantial, or, in the case of the arrows, the insubstantial transforming to become substantial.[32] Sunzi describes it as follows: "Subtle and insubstantial; the expert leaves no trace; divinely mysterious, he is inaudible. Thus he is master of his enemy's fate."[33] This yin-yang dynamic is an important feature of the internal boxing arts. In Xing Yi Quan (a martial art that, like Ba Gua, is considered "internal" or of the *nei jia* or "inner school"), boxers say:

It is advisable to respond to exactly what the opponent is going to do. It is necessary to punch the fist without the fist, to have the intention without showing it, to have the real intention in no intention. In the alternations of the false and true, I am always in predominance. It is at my convenience to change unendingly and to make the enemy just parry the blows, so that it is difficult for him to ascertain how to dodge and guard against me. No matter what methods are used, head, shoulder, hand, hip, knee, or foot, the fist must punch the three sections without showing the form. Success is not possible if the form and its shadow can be spotted.[34]

Song Zhi-yong, a disciple of the famous Xing Yi boxer Li Gui-chang, is a master of the substantial and insubstantial. Try to punch him and his flesh literally seems to shrink from your hand. When you attack, he disappears, only to reappear inside your inner gate, your feet already leaving the ground as he uproots you. When he attacks, it is light and deceptive until the last instant of the strike. You don't feel him coming, then he is there.

Deception is not just the use of traps and ruses, but of shaping and controlling expectations and intentions. In this way the opponent's ability to detect and take advantage of developing opportunities is impaired, while his actions and intentions become more obvious and take on a concrete form. Once they take on form, they can be guided more predictably. Deception in strategy can take many forms: feeding the enemy false information, using spies and defectors to delude and confuse the enemy, making him see what he expects to see, or telling him exactly what he wants to hear.

Many of the most famous deceptions, like the Empty City Ploy or Operation Fortitude in World War II Normandy, involve leading the enemy's mind. In Operation Fortitude, the allies deceived the Germans into believing that the main invasion of France would take place at Pas de Calais rather than Normandy. This was accomplished through a variety of means, including creating fake equipment and radio traffic that simulated an entire army and led Hitler to position key units in the wrong place. Hitler was deceived because the false invasion conformed with his expectations of what the allied forces might do, just as Zhuge Liang outwitted his opponent with the Empty City Ploy because he understood how his opponent would interpret his actions.

By creating disorder and confusion, Zhuge Liang was able to lead the mind of Cao Cao during the Three Kingdoms period. At the battle of the Han River he took advantage of Cao Cao's suspicious nature by presenting him with events that were unusual, thereby creating doubt and hesitation. Upon observing the terrain, Zhuge Liang hid troops with drums and horns in hills by the headwaters of the river. The two armies squared off across the river. Cao Cao's troops attempted to offer battle but Zuge Liang's army held their positions and refused engagement. At night, as Cao Cao's troops encamped and the lights of their fires died out, Zhuge Liang fired the signal bombard. The troops in the hills began to bang drums and sound their horns. Cao Cao's men, fearing attack, came out to scout the area. Finding no one, they settled down again only to be roused a second time. Their rest was denied for three nights by these stratagems, so finally they retreated. Zhuge Liang now had his troops cross the river and set up positions with their back to the river. This bewildered Cao Cao, who sent a written challenge to do battle, which was accepted by Zhuge Liang. When attacked by Cao Cao's troops, Zhuge Liang's men retreated in apparent disorder across the river, leaving equipment, horses scattered on the ground, and their camps empty. Cao Cao called his troops back as they started to scoop up this booty. He was suspicious of all that had occurred: the enemy taking a position with their backs to the river, and the fact that they had left so much equipment behind. Cao Cao ordered a retreat in order to avoid what seemed to be a trap, but at that moment the army of Zhuge Liang attacked, throwing Cao Cao's troops into disorder.[35]

In another example from the Three Kingdoms period, the hot-headed Zhang Fei was charged with capturing Liu Dai, the leader of Cao Cao's vanguard. He initially tried to taunt Liu Dai into single combat. When that failed, Zhang Fei attempted a deception by feeding Liu false information in order to capture him. Zhang first planned a raid on Liu Dai's camp. Then he spent the day drinking heavily and found fault with one of his men. He had him beaten and tied up and then threatened to execute him, only to secretly release him. As he anticipated, the man fled to Liu Dai's camp and reported the impending raid. The marks and bruises of the dreadful beating convinced Liu that the man was telling the truth. Liu Dai evacuated his camp and posted his men outside it to await the attack. Zhang Fei divided his forces into three parts. One part attacked the camp and the other two circled around. The group attacking the camp fired the tents and this was the signal for Zhang's other forces to attack from the sides and rear, surrounding Liu Dai's forces as they converged on the camp.[36]

Themistocles employed deception at the battle of Salamis. In discussing strategy, he argued with fellow Greek allies that fighting at the isthmus of Corinth in the open sea would put them at a disadvantage against the larger Persian fleet and, worse, it would lead the Persians into the Peloponnese. Fighting at Salamis, on the other hand, had certain advantages based on the terrain and the configuration of the straits around the island. When it became apparent that he would lose the argument, Themistocles secretly gave instructions to his slave Sicinnus. Herodotus tells us that Sicinnus carried a message to the Persians informing them that the Greeks were leaving Salamis. As the Persians had already decided to battle at Salamis, they were given the story they wanted to hear—that the Greeks did not want to fight at Salamis. This made them want to attack even more quickly. Sicinnus also told the Persians that Themistocles's preference was to join the Persians, thereby again telling them what they wanted to hear: that a traitor wanted to ally with them. This fit with the Persians' impression of the alliance of Greek States. The Persians had been aided before by Greek traitors, so they had no reason to suspect Themistocles.[37] The Persians forced the battle at Salamis, requiring the Greeks to employ Themistocles's strategy, and the Greeks won the day.

Ba Gua employs deception through the nature of its continuously changing movements. The goal is to let the opponent see the shadow, but not the movements themselves—to hide the intent until the last moment. Therefore, in Ba Gua one attempts to close in and then suddenly retreat, retreat and then change to attack, appear and disappear unexpectedly. By constantly stepping and turning, stepping in arcs rather than straight lines, and always changing, the opponent can be kept off-balance and confused. One interesting example of this is Li Zi Ming's ability to lead the opponent's mind and body in the Changing Palms form. Li moves in, attacking high, anticipating the opponent's strong resistance. When countered, he retreats, converting the high attack into a low kick to the knee as the opponent follows him, then when the opponent hesitates, he quickly turns back to pierce and enter. This parting shot to the opponent's knee is similar to the famous "Parthian shot." The Parthian shot was a tactic used by many nomadic steppe peoples like the Huns and Mongols, but made famous by the Parthians, whose empire (247 BC–224 AD) occupied all of modern Iran, Iraq, and Armenia as well as parts of Afghanistan and Central Asia. The Parthian horse-archers would feint retreat and then at full gallop would turn in the saddle and shoot at the pursuing enemy.

Terrain

Understanding the terrain and how to use it to one's advantage is an important feature of strategy and tactics. In the *Sunzi* there is a lengthy discussion of the different types of terrain and how to best employ them to gain victory.

> Advantageous terrain can be a natural ally in battle. Superior military leadership lies in the ability to assess the enemy's situation and create conditions for victory, to analyze natural hazards and calculate distances. He who fights with full knowledge of these factors is certain to win; he who fights without this knowledge is certain to lose.[38]

During the Song Dynasty, in the final years of the reign of Emperor Hui Zong An (1101–1125), a group of outlaws banded together to create a stronghold on a mountain surrounded by marshes in Shandong province. The story of these hundred men and women who lead an army of thousands against a corrupt and oppressive government is immortalized in the famous historical novel *Outlaws of the Marsh*. Historians confirm that the story is derived from fact, and over time it evolved into the folk legends that form the basis for the book. The stratagems employed by the bandits have been cited again and again by martial artists and military historians to illustrate essential principles of strategy. Mao Zedong enjoined his commanders to study the tactics of China's mountain and marsh bandits, including those found in the fictional *Outlaws of the Marsh*, so that they could be used against Japanese and Guomintang forces that possessed superior numbers and firepower.[39]

The outlaws know the terrain. They often draw the enemy onto constricted or watery ground, using feigned retreats and other ruses to entice and manipulate the enemy. Because they are always outnumbered, the outlaws set up ambushes, luring the government troops onto disadvantageous ground that hampers mobility and disrupts the cohesion of their forces, preventing them from acting in a unified manner. By dividing the enemy forces, they can destroy them.

> Innovative tactics, subterfuge, and maneuver are all required once the encounters shift to circumstances in which heroic violence and simple carnage cannot prevail. Always outnumbered, the bandits must eschew direct, set piece, force on force confrontations for harassing campaigns, multiple prongs and sallies, and a variety of unremitting but never predictable measures to disorder and confuse the enemy. Nighttime raiders and internally mounted incendiary strikes terrorize the enemy and deny important resources; incessant noise and random missiles prevent rest; attacking shipments and seizing provisions impoverishes them while augmenting the army's own reserves just as Sun-tzu advocated.[40]

In one confrontation, Xu Ning teaches the outlaw troops the use of the barbed lance in order to counter the government's heavy linked cavalry, whose armored horses are linked together in tandem, presenting an irresistible shock-force in the attack. The bandits come out to meet the cavalry waving banners and with different units appearing from different directions. They use cannon fire to further harass the government troops, who split their own forces to deal with what seem to be multiple threats. The outlaws retreat as though fleeing and draw the linked cavalry into the marshy reeds, where their abilities cannot be used, and then attack from hiding with hooked poles, pulling down both horses and riders.[41]

Similar ruses and stratagems appear also in stories about Yue Fei, the famous general of the Song Dynasty. Yue Fei was also a great martial artist who purportedly created both Eagle Claw boxing and Xing Yi Quan. Yue Fei and his loyal commanders battled in vain against the Jin Tartars, steppe nomads from what is today Manchuria, who repeatedly invaded the Southern Song. The story of the barbed lances, this time used against the Jin linked cavalry, is repeated in relationship to Yue Fei. When he instructs his troops in this tactic, Yue Fei references his knowledge of the exploits of Xu Ning and the marsh bandits.[42]

The bandits' intimate knowledge of the marshy terrain in which they operate is exploited to the fullest in their stratagems, just as the Finnish army made the most of their frozen forests in the Winter War between Russia and Finland in 1939–1940. All great generals make use of the terrain and many battles have been lost because an army was forced to fight on unfamiliar ground not of their own choosing. In Ba Gua it is also understood that the tactics must conform both to the terrain and the circumstances of weather and light. Sun Lutang's earlier quote bears repeating: "In expanding and contracting, coming and going, distinguish the terrain: the distances and defiles, whether it is broad and narrow, whether it contains dead or alive things."[43] The importance of the terrain is also stressed in Ba Gua's rhymed mnemonics. On icy or snow-covered ground, one is advised to take small steps, to turn the front foot sideways (*kou bu*—hook step), to avoid straightening the body, and to strike high in order to avoid slipping.[44] When fighting at night ("when the palm is extended without seeing the hand") one is advised to "squeeze the eyelids and stare attentively" with the palm in the lower position. Lowering the body position is also advised, as it makes it easier to see an opponent in the dark.[45] In general, Ba Gua's mud-treading step allows one to adjust to uneven or obstacle-ridden ground before one's weight is committed.

Maneuver

The *Sunzi* uses elemental imagery to express its principles. Similarly, in Ba Gua, songs, rhymes, and metaphors are used as mnemonics to inculcate correct practice methods. These songs also elucidate key tactical and strategic principles in dealing with different situations and different opponents. In the *Sunzi* we are told that:

> War is based upon deception. Move when it is advantageous and create changes in the situation by dispersal and concentration of forces. When campaigning, be swift as the wind; in leisurely march, majestic as a forest; in raiding and plundering, like fire; in standing, firm as the mountains. As unfathomable as the clouds, move like a thunderbolt.[46]

In the practice of Ba Gua, similar imagery is used to convey ideas that are not easily put into words. Composite images of walking like a dragon, changing postures like an eagle, turning swiftly as a hawk, moving and turning like a lion rolling a ball, withdrawing as swiftly as a monkey seizing fruit, or crouching like a tiger convey the idea of changing, literally trans-forming, with the changing circumstances. Also similar to the *Sunzi*, the Ba Gua texts advise us to "move like the wind and stand as if nailed in place." The Thirty-Six Songs and Forty-Eight Methods of Ba Gua Zhang further emphasize conforming one's actions to the changing circumstances:

Observation Method (Xiang Fa)

Observe first in encountering a group of enemies,

It is natural to retreat before advancing.

In retreating inspect the situation and understand the changes,

To wait leisurely for a fatigued enemy, to lead them effortlessly.

Or adapting one's tactics to fit the situation:

Application Method (Yong Fa)

The high, strike low, the low strike high,

No need to hesitate, strike the fat obliquely.

In meeting the thin and tall, just pull and lead,

In meeting the old and unskilled just look at him up and down.[47]

Li Zi Ming summarizes the strategy of the Ba Gua:

The creator of Eight Diagram Palm understood the effectiveness of strik-ing to the heart when attacking opponents. Therefore, when the enemy attacks, it is important to protect our center (heart) as well, by turning the body. Strategically, the goal is to evade the real attack of the opponent while seeking a vulnerable spot to counter-attack. For these reasons, Eight Diagram Palm skills have been developed with walking and turning as its basic form. Tactically, there are multiple reasons for this walking and turning. The walking itself protects you and meanwhile allows you to observe the enemy. By walking you avoid a head-on confrontation with the enemy by flanking the lateral side or the back of the enemy in order to attack him. By walking, we can moderate the attack of the enemy by restricting him to fewer offensive options and wearing him down, while we wait to move from stillness, wait at our ease for an exhausted oppo-nent. There is a saying "Hundreds of exercises are not as good as simply walking, walking is the master of hundreds of exercises."[48]

Liddell Hart also describes this idea:

Thus a move round the enemy's front against his rear has the aim not
only of avoiding resistance on its way but in its issue. In the profoundest
sense, it takes the line of least resistance. The equivalent in the psychological sphere is the line of least expectation. They are two faces of
the same coin, and to appreciate this is to widen our understanding of
strategy. For if we merely take what obviously appears the line of least
resistance, its obviousness will appeal to the opponent also; and this line
may no longer be that of least resistance.[49]

The Chinese refer to Hart's idea of taking the line of least resistance as
"luring the tiger out of the mountain." In a military context, a "tiger in the
mountain" symbolizes a strong enemy who enjoys the protection of a walled
city, fortified camp, strategic mountain pass, or wide rushing water. One
should lure the tiger out of its impregnable position before engaging it in
battle. This allows you to fight the enemy on your terms and on favorable
ground. The Mongols were masters of this kind of stratagem, using baited
retreats to encourage pursuit, drawing the enemy out, and then, through
maneuver, unpredictable counterattacks, and envelopments, they would
destroy the enemy. In Ba Gua this kind of strategy is known as "dodge the
body and dissolve the shadow: when the enemy does not come I force him
to come, when he comes I dissolve his attack."[50] When the enemy won't
attack, the Ba Gua practitioner is advised to entice him to attack. When he
attacks, the attack is dissolved by combining defensive hand movements
with retreat and evasive footwork. When the attack falters, or when the
enemy is overextended, one should then pursue and defeat the enemy. Li
Zi Ming disciple Zhang Hua Sen liked to demonstrate this principle as a hit-
and-run maneuver against two attackers. Piercing directly at the first attack-
er's eyes to forestall his advance, Zhang would quickly change direction to
hit the second opponent high and low simultaneously. This movement then
immediately transformed into another attack at the first opponent just as he
began to regain his forward momentum.

The use of the tactical retreat, pinning the enemy forces, and envelopment from the flanks and rear is not unique to the Mongols or Ba Gua
Zhang. One of the stratagems the Chinese employed against the Jin Tartar

cavalry in the Song Dynasty was to battle and then feign defeat and retreat, enticing the enemy to pursue.

> After retreating for some distance, one stops and turns to challenge the enemy again, then feigns defeat and retreats. Eagerly seeking a decision, the enemy follows in hot pursuit, with no time to take a rest. On the other hand, one has planned the retreats beforehand and is able to use the intervals to rest and feed the troops. At nightfall, the enemy has become tired and hungry. Feigning defeat for the last time, one scatters cooked beans on the ground. When the enemy cavalry arrives, the horses are attracted by the fragrant beans and stop to feed.[51]

At that moment one can attack and achieve victory.

Contact with the horse people of the Eastern steppes, particularly the Huns, influenced Byzantine cavalry tactics. This tactical innovation emphasized mobility and flexibility over attrition-style warfare and was perhaps first employed by Byzantine military commanders like Belisarius in North Africa, against the Goths in Italy.[52] One of the tactics adopted from the steppe horseman was to ride in a curved arc when attacking a strong, static defensive formation. This allowed the Byzantine horse archers to shoot all along the arc of the attack, ensuring that the enemy would receive arrows from multiple directions, some of them striking against their unshielded side. This also allowed for the famous Parthian Shot, in which the rider turns backward to release a final missile as his horse is moving away from the opponent (the final arrow on the left in figure 1-1 on the next page).[53]

Tactics stressing mobility and the use of arcs to find and exploit weaknesses in the opponent's position are characteristic of Ba Gua Zhang's reliance on circle walking and the curved step as the foundation of its martial tactics. Gao Ji-wu specifically mentions this in his recent book, *The Attacking Hands of Ba Gua Zhang:*

> Ba Gua Zhang is a martial art characterized by walking the circle and rotating the body. The attacking and defending techniques are also based upon circle walking, and upon the palms. Striking the spot by surrounding it and striking from the side (at an angle) in order to avoid head-on conflict or striking the front from the side. Changes in circle walking and

rotation of the body are seen everywhere in the attacking techniques of Ba Gua Zhang.[54]

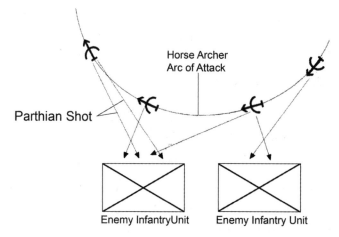

Figure 1.1. Cavalry tactics of mounted archers

These kinds of tactics, combining attacks that come from multiple angles while walking in arcs, are particularly visible in the Ba Gua Saber.

In the Second Punic War, after his famous crossing of the Alps into Italy, the Carthaginian general Hannibal Barca used maneuver tactics against a superior Roman force at Cannae in 216 BC. Hannibal deliberately placed his weakest troops, the lightly armored Gauls and Spaniards, in the center of his battle formation. Offset to the side and slightly back were the more reliable and more heavily armored African infantry. As Hannibal expected, the strong Roman center pushed his own center backward. Hannibal's center held, but folded around the blunt V shape formed by the Roman army. Meanwhile, Hannibal's heavy cavalry on the Carthaginian left flank attacked and broke through the opposing Roman cavalry. They then raced around the back of the Roman army to the right flank, where the rest of the Roman cavalry were pinned by the hit-and-run tactics of Hannibal's Numidian horsemen. Under this combined attack, the Roman cavalry fled the field. The Carthaginian cavalry then turned and attacked the rear of the Roman center, which was now trapped and unable to maneuver. Simultaneously, the African infantry turned inward and rolled them up from the side. The Roman army was massacred. With fifty thousand men against the Romans' estimated eighty-six thousand, Hannibal inflicted fifty thousand casualties, his own troops losing eight thousand men.

In the nineteenth century, the great warrior and leader of the Zulu nation, Shaka, reorganized the Zulu military system, creating a military force that defeated the disparate clans to form the Zulu nation. His basic battle formation relied heavily on maneuver, timing, and envelopment. The army was divided into four basic units: the chest (or center), which made contact with the enemy, pinning them in place; the horns, which rapidly moved out to envelop the flanks; and the loins, a reserve force that could be sent wherever it was needed.[55] In a battle with the Butelezi clan, he combined this tactical disposition with deception. Even though they outnumbered the Butelezi, he bunched his warriors at the beginning of the fight, having them hold their shields sideways, edge out, so that they seemed few. Then when the horns spread outward on the flanks they turned their shields to face outward, so that his army miraculously appeared to double in size in an instant. The enemy forces quickly collapsed under the physical and psychological shock of the attack.[56] Some Ba Gua practitioners like Gao Ji-wu use a variation of this type of tactic, throwing arced punches combined with a slight withdrawal and a hidden kick to pin the opponent in place. The hooking punches, like the Zulu horns, draw the opponent's attention to his flank, leaving him open for a rapid attack down the middle.

In schools of the internal martial arts, body movements must contain oppositional forces: extending/retracting, opening/closing, rising and falling, etc. In advancing there is also retreating. Within an inward holding, hooking, and wrapping force there is an outward, stretching, resisting force.[57] These oppositional forces must be in harmony. When they are harmonious, each spontaneously generates the other and there is potential for movement in any direction; the body can move naturally—advancing and retreating, moving inside and outside, up and down, front and back—all unfolding according to circumstances. If the opponent presses against the left side of the body, the left side becomes insubstantial and he is struck by the right side, like a door closing and opening, as though the body is hinged. Ba Gua and Xing Yi practitioners like to use the example of a snake to illustrate this dynamic. The snake's body is flexible, seemingly jointed everywhere. Grab the head and the tail attacks, grab the tail and the head attacks. Grab the middle and both head and tail attack.

In military strategy, the distribution of forces can also be used in this way, folding the center so the wings can envelop, or retreating one end of the line so the other end can extend, overlap, and turn the enemy's flank, like a door turning on its hinge. At Leuctra in 371 BC, Thebes defeated Sparta—the beginning of the end for Spartan supremacy in Greece. The Thebans under Epaminodas massed their phalanx fifty ranks deep on their left wing. Usually the mass of heavily armored infantry making up a phalanx was eight to twelve ranks deep. The men moved together to keep the line unbroken all along the front, and the mass of men provided enormous momentum that could break the enemy's line. The shields of the soldiers in the phalanx overlapped, each man's shield protecting the man on his left. This often produced a rightward drift, because each man would unconsciously move to his right to hide behind his comrade's shield.[58] For this reason the most experienced troops were placed on the right wing. Epaminodas arranged his battle line on the oblique, so that his weak right flank was pushed back and withdrew, thereby extending the Spartan left, while his massive left wing pushed forward, crushing the Spartan right and destroying their line so that they could be rolled up from the side.

The Schlieffen Plan employed in 1914 during World War I was the German army's overall strategic plan for the Western front. The plan called for weak German forces on the German left, where Germany bordered France. The main weight of the German army on the right would then sweep through Belgium and down to Paris, outflanking the French left flank and enveloping them from the rear. For various reasons the plan failed, but in conception it was a large-scale version of Epaminodas's strategy at Leuctra.

Boyd points out that part of the problem with the execution of the Schlieffen Plan was the *top-down command and control structure,* which restricted imagination and initiative in the lower echelons. This, and the obsession with attempting to achieve concentration of force, led to stagnation of movement and attrition through direct attacks against hardened resistance. Although the lethality of weapons had increased dramatically, battlefield tactics had not changed accordingly.[59] The German army learned from its mistakes, and during the invasion of France in 1940, with a somewhat similar general plan, but a very different command structure, organization, and strategy, they were successful.

Deployment

Ba Gua attempts to eliminate the problem of a top-down, structured chain of command through rigorous training aimed at unifying the entire body. There is no definite plan of attack or defense, only movements and changes that are designed to create and exploit opportunities, based on a deep understanding of instinctive human reactions. Rather than predetermined plans, Ba Gua seeks to find stillness within movement, so that the opponent's movements and intentions can be clearly apprehended, allowing one to seize the initiative at the appropriate moment. Often in learning Ba Gua, the student encounters seemingly obscure statements like:

> First seek stillness in the middle of movement, then seek movement in the middle of stillness.[60]
>
> Change postures like moving clouds.[61]
>
> You must change randomly. It is mysterious and unfathomable.[62]

Eliminating preset plans and a top-down command structure does not mean that the body is not connected. Although every part of the body is moving in arcs and circles, and circles within circles, the body is integrated at all levels, united by one qi. Hence, the emphasis on the Six Harmonies in internal boxing:

> Harmony between hand and foot
>
> Harmony between elbow and knee
>
> Harmony between shoulder and hip
>
> Harmony between heart *(Xin)* and mind/intention *(Yi)*
>
> Harmony between mind/intention and qi
>
> Harmony between qi and strength/force *(Li)*

This allows spirit, intention, and force to combine into one.

In Ba Gua, it is said that "intention is like a waving command flag, also like a lighted lamp."[63] In ancient China, troops were trained to change battle formations and to advance and retreat guided by waving a command flag. At night, lighted lamps were used instead to command the troops. In practicing Ba Gua, the movements must be guided by the intention and not performed carelessly or casually.

During the Taiping Rebellion in 1850, a large Qing Dynasty imperial force established a base close to the Taiping stronghold at Jintian. The Taiping forces took up defensive positions spread in a wide arc between the Qing forces and Jintian. Their defensive strategy employed sophisticated communications between their positions: "Each major Taiping encampment had its own signal flag, depending on its strategic location: red for the South, black for the North, blue for the East, and white for the West. The center had a yellow banner as well as a duplicate of the other four banners. With these large banners as the main signals, backed by smaller triangular flags to request troop reinforcements, complex instructions could be conveyed in the heat of battle, and at considerable distance."[64] For example, if the enemy is active in the east, the eastern section would hoist a small triangular white flag next to their main banner. The middle station would transmit the message to the west and the troops from the west would be dispatched to reinforce the east.[65] When the fighting began, the Qing commander attempted to force his larger army through the center of the Taiping line. The Taiping forces, in a coordinated attack, curved around the flanks of the imperial forces, routing them.[66]

The battle formation used by the Taiping rebels was an ancient battle array known as the Five Phase Formation. Students of Chinese philosophy know that the color and position of the banners correspond to the Five Phases or Five Elements. Other classical Chinese battle formations were the Four Animal Formation, corresponding with the four heraldic animals (azure dragon, red bird, white tiger, and black snake-tortoise); the Six Flowers Formation[67]; and the Eight Diagram Battle Formation. The Eight Diagram formation is attributed to Zhuge Liang, who employed it against the Wei army in the Three Kingdoms.[68] Zhuge Liang's arrangement is said to have had four sides and eight directions. Whichever part was struck, the two adjoining sections could come to aid it. Also, in this formation the front could quickly become the rear and vice-versa.

Ba Gua employs this same idea when walking on the circle or threading through the nine palaces. The nine palace diagram below and the eight trigrams below it are essentially Zhuge Liang's Eight Diagram formation. In

Ba Gua Zhang, the practice of nine palace walking, weaving between nine posts set in the ground (as illustrated below), teaches principles of combat and movement in relation to multiple opponents as well as how to manipulate and penetrate the Eight Diagram formation.

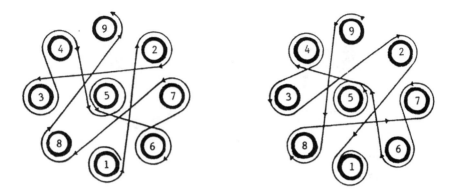

Figure 1.2. Nine Palace Arrangement in Ba Gua Zhang

Many Ba Gua practitioners relate the hand formations and postures of Ba Gua to the trigrams and hexagrams in the *Yijing (Classic of Change)*. These diagrams are composed of yin (broken) lines and yang (unbroken) lines. As with Zhuge Liang's formation, the lines and their positions are not fixed. A broken line can join to become unbroken and an unbroken line can stretch and separate to become broken. The diagrams, which can represent different troop formations or fighting postures, can change form moment to moment. Both in military strategy and in Ba Gua, one uses form to become formless, able to respond appropriately to the situation at hand. Ancient strategists advise: "First manifest form and cause the enemy to follow it. The pinnacle of military deployment approaches formlessness."[69]

The ancient Roman legions also employed a flexible and unique battle formation, which was organized in *maniples* ("handfuls"). Although no one is really sure how the Roman manipular legion fought, it is clear that it used a triple battle line with a screen of skirmishers to the front. Generally, a legion consisted of about 4,200 men. A swarm of the more lightly armored *velites* used javelins to disrupt and skirmish with the enemy, but could also close to fight hand-to-hand. Behind them came the more heavily armored

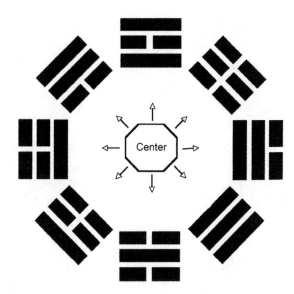

Figure 1.3. Nine Palace Arrangement of Yi Jing Trigrams

hastati, and then *principes* divided into ten groups each—the aforementioned maniples. Both groups had swords and *pilia,* heavy throwing javelins. Lastly, there were ranks of *triarii,* who carried long thrusting spears. Gaps between the maniples allowed maneuver and tactical flexibility—units could support one another while at the same time each maniple had an internal cohesion that allowed for some measure of independent operation. The gaps in the line may also have allowed troops to retreat through the lines with the triarii as a reserve to plug the gaps, if they were exploited by the enemy. Because the Romans fought a variety of opponents, in many lands and in many situations, such flexible tactics served them well in adapting to the situation at hand.[70]

Methods of hand-to-hand combat often emphasize stances, and a variety of ready positions are sometimes taught at the basic training level. In Chinese martial arts, stances such as *ma bu* ("horse stance") use the word *bu* ("step"), denoting movement or progress, as in *jin bu* ("advancing step" or "forward step"). Alternatively, postures are referred to as *shi,* which translates as "pattern." In Xing Yi Quan and Ba Gua Zhang, *san ti shi* denotes a posture or "body pattern" of mental and physical readiness that allows movement in all directions. *San ti shi* loads the body so that it can move in any direction with root and power. As a mental attitude, it conveys a readiness to act according to the changing circumstances. In Ba Gua and Xing Yi, combat techniques are merely an extension of standing and walking. Ba Gua in particular bases its strategy on walking, and walking itself stems from standing. Hence the importance of stake-standing or standing-post exercises (*zhan zhuang*) and fixed pattern/posture walking and turning (*ding shi*) in Ba Gua training. By creating offensive and defensive actions that arise from the most primal movements—standing, walking, breathing, pulling inward, and pushing outward—one can adjust flexibly and naturally to the situation at hand while maintaining body cohesion.

Flexibility and Adaptability

Liddell Hart observes that great military commanders always operate by having multiple objectives in mind. He points out that if the opponent knows your objective and methods, it is easy for him to protect himself and foil your aims. By implementing a strategy that threatens (or embraces) alternative objectives, you not only distract and confuse the enemy, you also leave your own options open. This is economical, as you keep your own forces flexible while pinning down the opponent's resources.[71] Napoleon Bonaparte called this *faire son theme en deux facons* ("present your theme in two ways"). Hart goes on to point out that seventy years later William Tecumseh Sherman relearned this lesson, which he called *putting the enemy on the horns of a dilemma*, during his march through Georgia toward the end of the American Civil War.[72]

Napoleon exploited to the fullest the new developments in weaponry, organization, and training that his predecessors had brought to the French army. The introduction of the independent divisional structure and the ability of troops to forage or "live off the land" increased tactical flexibility and removed the need for supply routes that were susceptible to attack. This, combined with the increase in light troops and mobile field guns, as well as abandonment of the traditional marching step in favor of the quick step, afforded Napoleon the ability to outmaneuver and outmarch his opponents and, more important, to react more quickly to the changing circumstances. In his 1805 campaign in Austria, Napoleon outmaneuvered the Austrian army at Ulm by feigning one line of march, to pin the enemy while marching around to their rear, cutting them off from their Russian allies and forcing a surrender. Later, at Austerlitz, Napoleon met the combined Russo-Austrian army. He tricked the allies, giving them the impression that his army was weak and that he desired to negotiate peace. He deliberately abandoned his strong central position and left his right flank weak. He counted on the allies to heavily attack the weakened right, thereby leaving their own center vulnerable. These tactics, combined with reinforcements secretly force-marching from Vienna, surprised the allies, resulting in a significant victory for the French.

Napoleon felt that rather than making definite plans, one must bend with the changing circumstance: "A battle is my plan of campaign and success is my whole policy."[73] Napoleon's strategy often involved isolating an opponent, either through diplomatic or military means. Militarily, he aimed at the destruction of the enemy's field army rather the occupation of terrain, therefore his strategic preparations often involved long and rapid advances that penetrated into enemy territory, but were not directed at a specific objective or location. This bold advance, by posing a threat that could not be ignored, drew the enemy out, forcing them to react and commit their forces.[74] This allowed Napoleon to know his opponents' intentions and to respond flexibly and appropriately, using terrain to restrict the opponent's movements while simultaneously employing maneuver, flanking, and envelopment tactics or operations on the enemy's interior lines, thereby splitting and dividing their forces. Similarly, Ba Gua employs the piercing palm, combined with deceptive footwork, to create a deep, penetrating attack that cannot be ignored, while blending and adapting the footwork and handwork with the opponent's response.

In his early campaigns, Napoleon adhered to this idea, creatively combining ambiguity, surprise, deception, and rapid maneuver to divide and defeat superior forces piecemeal. Napoleon employed highly mobile skirmishers, sharpshooters armed with rifles, to harass and confuse the enemy. These skirmishers were combined with screens of cavalry whose job was to mask the movements of the main body of French troops and search out weak points in the enemy's disposition. Meanwhile, his mobile horse artillery created confusion and weakened these chinks in the enemy's positions.

This allowed the infantry columns to move up, ready to exploit any weak point that presented. Cavalry and infantry screens could also cloud and distort strategic maneuvers that would open up flanking attacks, or allow Napoleon to split the enemy forces. All of these factors allowed Napoleon to seize and keep the initiative.

Using the same zheng and qi dynamic as Chinese strategists, Napoleon also employed forces that pinned the enemy in place so that he could maneuver to flank, divide, and envelop the enemy forces.[75] Similarly, Ba Gua uses the hands to screen the actions of the feet, and the hands and feet to cloak the movements of the body. If the enemy attacks fiercely and with great strength, the hands, combined with body alignment, create a structure that make them think and feel that the defender is still in front of them, while the defender's feet have already begun to transfer their body to the side. This allows one to end up standing next to the enemy with hands and feet poised to strike them in the flank or rear. When caught in the center between two opponents, the principle is the same. By using an arcing step that can change direction at any moment, one is able to initially meet both opponents' attacks, fixing them in place momentarily, while the footwork has already changed so that we can empty the central position and move around the flank of one of the opponents. This is one of the uses of the so-called Yin-Yang Boring Arcing Step. All of these tactics require cohesion or "internal connection" of the entire body in the same way that the various units of an army must maintain cohesion in order to be effective. This means linking the hands and the feet and driving the step from the *dantien* (the center of gravity located one to three inches below the navel), while the arms and body unite to split through the opponents like a wedge. This use of the body is described in one of the Ba Gua songs:

> *Pile the rear elbow, protect the heart with the elbow,*
> *Turn and drop the hand and extend it forward.*
> *Follow to the front elbow to create embracing power,*
> *The front and rear hand join together to gather spirit.*[76]

In later campaigns, Napoleon departed from the flexible thinking described above and relied increasingly on dense infantry columns, massed artillery fire, and cavalry charges that often ended up attacking directly into the enemy's strength.[77] Even when victorious, his armies suffered crippling attrition.

Blitz and Counter-Blitz

Sherman's concept of "putting the enemy on the horns of a dilemma" was exemplified by the German blitzkrieg ("lightning warfare") tactics as employed on the Western front in 1940 by imaginative commanders such as Erich von Manstein, Erwin Rommel, and Heinz Guderian. Surprising the French by quickly crossing the Meuse river, the Germans created multiple breakthroughs and threatened multiple objectives by employing fast-moving armored units combined with air support. Avoiding battles and their resulting attrition and stagnation of momentum and initiative, and exploiting developing opportunities, the Germans kept the larger French forces physically and psychologically off balance. The French counter-movements simply could not keep pace with the changing situation. They were confused by an enemy who did not appear to proceed according to a fixed plan. The German forces were trained to operate independently, constantly seeking and creating opportunities to penetrate and exploit gaps in the French dispositions, thereby controlling the timing and rhythm of the action. The French inability to adapt led to paralysis, loss of the initiative, and defeat.

Israel skillfully employed blitzkrieg tactics in the 1967 Six Day War against Egypt. Fluidly combining air power with armor, paratroops, artillery, and combat engineers, they grounded and destroyed the Egyptian air force. Simultaneously, they launched a series of lightning strikes by ground forces that avoided direct confrontation and, having bypassed the Egyptian units, were able to seize key routes of communication and effectively surround them. The entire action lasted four days.

A number of authors have commented on the time-rhythm component of the blitzkrieg as an important disrupting factor. Colonel John R. Boyd described the blitzkrieg principle as "presenting many (fast-breaking) simultaneous and sequential happenings to generate confusion and disorder thereby stretching-out time for the adversary to respond in a directed fashion. [This] multiplies opportunities to uncover, create, and penetrate gaps, exposed flanks, and vulnerable rears."[78] This has the result of creating shock, panic, and disorder, ultimately destroying the adversary's cohesion, bringing about paralysis and collapse.[79] To put it another way, being able to infiltrate, penetrate, or otherwise get inside the adversary's system generates many moral-mental-physical noncooperative centers of gravity.[80]

Li Zi Ming's description of attacking in Ba Gua is almost identical to Colonel Boyd's analysis above: "Twisting and coiling, turning and circling, each movement conceals many strikes. Therefore one would be able to change at any time according to the actual situation in combat. Attaining this level of performance is an extraordinary experience, calm in the mind and comfortable in the body and smooth in the hundreds of meridians so that the heart can feel at ease throughout. This results in the enemy becoming puzzled in mind, deranged in spirit, and thereby defeated in battle."[81]

Boyd also describes the blitzkrieg as employing "multiple thrusts, bundles of multiple thrusts, or bundles of thrusts inside bundles of thrusts."[82] In Ba Gua, the principle of the penetrating palm is to continuously pierce and thrust, moving into the enemy as one shifts right or left, inside and outside. This opens gaps in the enemy's defense, restricting their options and confusing them. Ba Gua practitioners repeatedly practice sequences of three penetrating strikes or "piercing palms" that come one on top of the other, screening the body, which changes its orientation with each strike. This type of attack is very difficult for the opponent to stop, hence the saying "Even the most marvelous under heaven fear the three penetrations."[83]

In Chinese military strategy this idea of having a flexible plan with multiple objectives in mind is often referred to as "attacking the east to attack the west, or making noise in the east to attack the west." The noise refers to an attack. The attack to the west does not necessarily imply that the west was the true objective. In the Chinese martial arts there is a saying, "True but not true, false but not false." Either attack could be the true attack or a false attack. If the enemy defends tenaciously, the true attack becomes a false attack, as one of the other objectives now becomes the true one. If the enemy does not defend, or if the defense is weak, then the initial attack was the true objective.

Wong Shi-tong, a disciple of Guo Gu-min (one of the great practitioners of Ba Gua in Beijing), explained and demonstrated these ideas in concrete terms. When Wong attacks to the face, it is both a feint and a real attack at the same time. If the opponent reacts by raising his hands to protect the face, the attack is already en route to another objective, such as the groin. If the opponent fails to react, or does not protect well enough, the original attack goes through to the face, because it was, from the beginning, true but not true. Similarly, Wong demonstrated the principle *straight but not straight, bent but not bent.* An attack that appears to follow a straight path can curve around the defense to attack an alternative target, or the same target from a different angle. On the other hand, a curving, indirect attack can suddenly become straight in order to make a direct attack. This principle is further exemplified in Ba Gua's unique use of curved steps that allow a defensive, evasive maneuver to suddenly become a direct attack, all within a single step.

A remarkably similar approach was proposed by President Lincoln during the American Civil War. Lincoln's difficulty was that the Confederate troops, though less numerous, were often superior on the battlefield. The Union had more troops, but at the "point of collision" troop concentrations often ended up being fairly equal. In a letter to two of his generals, Lincoln proposed gaining the advantage by "menacing him [the enemy] with superior forces at different points, at the same time; so that we can safely attack, one, or both if he makes no change; and if he weakens one to strengthen the other, forbear to attack the strengthened one, but seize and hold the weakened one, gaining so much."[84]

In Chinese military strategy, there is the phrase *besiege Wei to rescue Zhao.* To rescue an ally, it is better to invade the invader's territory and besiege the enemy's base, rather than attacking the enemy besiegers directly in a heroic rescue operation. Either the enemy abandons his attack on your ally, or he loses his base and his line of communication and supply is cut. The Roman general Scipio Africanus used this strategy to draw Hannibal out of Italy after years of futile attempts to defeat him there. Scipio landed in Africa and attacked and devastated the land around Carthage, while subverting the allies of the Carthaginians and disrupting communications and seizing vital supplies. This forced Hannibal's return, making him come to Scipio seeking battle. Scipio could now control the time and the place of their encounter. He drew Hannibal out into unfamiliar terrain, and by initially refusing battle, forced Hannibal to camp in an area not supplied with water. Hannibal could not retreat, as Scipio now had a large body of Numidian cavalry who could easily pursue and harass his army; nor could he simply hold position without water. Consequently, he was forced to do battle at Zama and was defeated.[85]

Li Zi Ming describes the Ba Gua version of these tactics as follows:

Like the tactics of "relieving the Zhao State by besieging the Wei State," or the method of "making a feint to the East while attacking the West," when I am under attack from all directions I must be calm in the mind and behave like nothing is happening around me. If enemies are attacking from all sides, my gestures cannot be sluggish or empty, but rather crisp and sudden so that I can confuse the enemies with a movement as difficult to track as a butterfly fluttering among the flowers. With the enemies puzzled and confused, I can deal with front as well as the back. I can advance and retreat as I like. I can also evade the real method to conquer the enemy by mixing the real and the false according to individual situation and circumstance.[86]

Li Zi Ming's remarks give insight into strategies for countering the blitzkrieg, or "blitz-attack" as it is sometimes called in hand-to-hand combat. In Ba Gua, when strikes with fists and feet are coming rapidly from all directions, one should follow the dictum: *The quicker you are, the slower I am.* To move slowly means to be harmonious and still within movement, changing postures freely, observing the opponent and waiting to strike his weak point with the power of the whole body.[87] The practice of Ba Gua trains the mind to be calm and the breathing to be relaxed and natural. This allows the vision to be clear and the reactions quick even in the heat of battle.

The principles of the "counter-blitz," according to Boyd, are similar and yet more specific. He advises using obstacles and delaying actions, along with hit-and-run tactics and/or baited retreats, in order to disrupt and disorient the enemy. Disrupt the rhythm of his attacks, attempt to stretch his actions out in time and make his maneuvers pile up, thereby breaking the opponent's momentum. Simultaneously and/or alternatively, break up the enemy's cohesion by channeling and redirecting his momentum and then counterattacking. Hit the enemy unexpectedly through gaps in his flank or rear, or blindside to make a decisive stroke.[88] Ba Gua also employs this idea of redirection by turning the body: "In fighting, if I cannot use my hand and foot, because the opponent is close to me (adheres to me), it is advisable to adopt the chest-withdrawing and waist-turning method. Only in this way can the danger be avoided, and the unfavorable situation be reversed."[89]

Guerrilla Warfare and Counterinsurgency

Ba Gua practitioners often liken their art to guerrilla warfare. Guerrilla warfare subverts the normal clashing (of fighters and/or armies), which often heavily relies on power, numbers, and strength of the defensive posture. It does this by being dynamic, continuously changing, transforming, and moving. "Static defense has no part in guerrilla action, and fixed defense no place, except in the momentary way involved in laying an ambush."[90] Guerrilla actions seek to avoid battle, evading direct engagements in which damage and attrition might be suffered. In Ba Gua this is achieved through hit-and-run tactics that employ timing, footwork, turning, and evasion, combined with the use of "hidden kicks and ambushing hands." Beijing Ba Gua exponent Gao Ji-wu is a master of the hidden kick. He screens his kicks by combining them with evasive footwork and deceptive arcing hand strikes. The opponent only sees his hands attacking; the kick, concealed within the footwork, comes in undetected from below.

T. E. Lawrence realized the potential of guerrilla warfare during the Arab Revolt against the Turks in 1918. A keen student of military history, Lawrence noted early on that the more mobile but weak Arab forces could only win by avoiding contact. "Most wars were wars of contact, both forces striving into touch to avoid tactical surprise. Ours should be a war of detachment. We were to contain the enemy by the silent threat of the vast unknown desert, not disclosing ourselves till we attacked."[91] Lawrence used hit-and-run tactics that took place over a wide area and prevented the Turks from concentrating their forces against his own. The Arabs could not afford to lose men, so rather than attacking the Turkish troops, the Arabs focused on attacking the enemy's empty spaces: destroying sections of track and trains, cutting telegraph wires and harrying small outposts, thereby severing lines of reinforcement, communication, and supply. Appearing suddenly out of the desert, only to disappear again, through this war of a thousand pinpricks Lawrence's men wore down the enemy, sapped his morale, and hampered his mobility and initiative.

Similarly, in the Peninsular War (1808–1814) Spanish guerrillas prevented the French from concentrating their forces against the Duke of Wellington's much smaller army. They cut off convoys, seized dispatches, severed communications, and harried reinforcements. At one point, the French were losing an average of a hundred men a day to guerrilla attacks![92] A more recent example of the effectiveness of guerrilla tactics was in Vietnam, where the United States had difficulty fighting an enemy that was everywhere and nowhere, "hard to isolate from the civilian population and therefore difficult to target and track, whose shoestring logistics were hard to interdict, and whose political elite were far more disciplined than our own."[93]

Guerrilla warfare "inverts one of the main principles of orthodox war, the principle of 'concentration.' Dispersion is an essential component of survival and success on the guerrilla side, which must never present a target and thus can only operate in minute particles, though these may momentarily coagulate like globules of quicksilver to overwhelm some weakly guarded objective. For guerrillas, the principle of 'concentration' has to be replaced by that of 'fluidity of force.'"[94] In Ba Gua, dispersion and fluidity are manifest in the ability to literally melt away from the incoming attack, redirecting it into "dead" space. This is known as *escape and hide the shadow* or *dodge the body* and *dissolve the shadow without a trace.* In order to employ this type of tactic, the footwork must be fluid. The famous Ba Gua practitioner Zhang Rong-jiao said that the mud-wading step *(tang ni bu)* should be "stable, but light and fast like flowing water." [95] This type of walking *(zou)* is related to the concept of "leaking." When the opponent stops you or attempts to lock you out, you step or flow around him like water leaking through a crack or seeping into a hidden chink or gap.

Mao Zedong described guerrilla warfare as "constant activity and movement."[96] Guerrilla units are composed of small groups acting independently. These groups focus on movement rather than positional defense. Thus they have no "rear." Instead, they operate at the enemy's rear. Similarly, Ba Gua's turning movements effectively allow the rear and the front, right and left, and up and down to interchange from moment to moment. At the same time, the goal is to get to the side or rear of the opponent. Ba Gua's arcing step allows one to get to the enemy's side or rear in a single step. With the same single step, all eight directions can be covered and the front can become the rear.

About guerrilla warfare, Che Guevara said: "The blows should be continuous. The enemy soldier in a zone of operations ought not to be allowed to sleep; his outposts ought to be attacked and liquidated systematically. At every moment the impression ought to be that he is surrounded by a complete circle."[97] Che describes the war of mobility as a minuet, a dance. The guerrilla bands encircle an enemy position, with five or six men at each of the four points of the compass. They must be far enough away to avoid being encircled themselves. When the engagement starts, it can begin at any one of these points. As the enemy moves toward that point, the guerrilla band retreats, always maintaining visual contact while an attack is initiated from another point. This can be repeated indefinitely, immobilizing the enemy and forcing him to expend large amounts of ammunition.[98]

Ba Gua has also been likened to a dance in which one moves next to and revolves around one's opponent, leading him to the left and right, front and back, up and down. In the "eight contraries," differences between fighting strategies in Ba Gua and those in other styles of Chinese boxing are delineated: "Everyone advances forward with a straight step, but we advance on an angle with a twisted step. Everyone likes to turn the whole body around to face the rear, but in a single step we can move to deal with the eight directions."[99] By using the footwork to move next to the opponent, one is able to moderate the enemy's attack, thereby restricting his options and finding his weak points. Mao also advocated finding the enemy's weak points at his flanks and rear and advises that one attack and annihilate him there.

For Mao, the guerrilla's ability to seize the initiative is dependent upon dispersion, concentration, and the alert shifting of forces.[100] Guerrillas can disperse to harass a stronger or entrenched enemy, or one deficient in supplies, limited by the terrain, encircled, or out-positioned. Similarly, they can concentrate their forces when the enemy is demoralized, when his forces are isolated or trapped, or when he can be destroyed without excessive losses. There is never total concentration. In taking the offensive or in counter-offensives, there must be concentration of force ("pit ten against one"[101]), but even when falling on the enemy and destroying him, all one's forces are not committed. Elsewhere, other units are carrying out other operations.

Reserving some of one's forces is akin to the power-storing method of Ba Gua Zhang. "The power should not all be released at once. It is necessary to always reserve some power. If every bit of power is released like shooting an arrow that doesn't return, it is very easy to be at risk."[102]

Ba Gua masters say: "If the method is not proper, don't use it. If the first attack misses attack again."[103] Mao's advice is the essentially the same. When confronted by the enemy, the guerrilla shifts his forces in a way appropriate to the situation. If they cannot fight here, they shift, attacking somewhere else. "Their tactics must deceive, tempt, and confuse the enemy. They must lead the enemy to believe they will attack him from the east and the north and they must then strike him from the west and the south. They must strike, then rapidly disperse."[104] The CCP army and other Chinese guerrilla forces employed these tactics in 1940 against Japanese forces in northern China, carrying out a campaign of disruption, harassment, and sabotage.

In Ba Gua, it is through the footwork that the power of the body is stored and released. When storing power, there is an appearance of softness and gentleness, even weakness. When releasing power, the whole body is firm and powerful. When evading and redirecting, soft, winding dispersing power is applied at the pivotal point or moment. When striking, power accumulates and concentrates to hit with effect. In releasing power, some power is always retained, already beginning the next action. "The power must be firm and gentle too, difficult to achieve skill if firmness or gentleness is overemphasized. It is true that too hard will surely break, too soft is equivalent to nothing."[105] Therefore, gentleness and firmness must be in harmony, each promoting the other, like a constantly turning wheel. Too much emphasis on either is incorrect. Just as with the guerrilla tactics of concentration and dispersion, the use of gentleness and firmness must be appropriate to the situation. Hence the statement: "It is the correct method when he is firm, I must be gentle. It is also a good method when I am firm, he is gentle."[106]

The views of the English naval strategist Julian Stafford Corbett regarding the concentration and dispersal of forces are remarkably similar to those of Mao. Corbett felt that the massing of forces in order to deliver a decisive blow restricted mobility, rendering an army rigid and inflexible. On the other hand, careful contemplation of dispersal as a method of strategic deployment is characterized by flexibility and freedom of movement.

Dispersal conceals one's intention from the enemy, while at the same time allowing adaptation to any plan of operations he may adopt.[107] "Without division, no strategical combinations are possible."[108] For Corbett, dispersal implies the maintenance of an elastic cohesion that allows the diverse segments of one's disposition to condense and gather around a strategic center. In naval warfare, if the enemy concentrates his forces in one place, he leaves his ports and lines of communications open everywhere else.

> The object of holding back from forming the mass is to deny the enemy knowledge of our actual distribution or its intention at any given moment, and at the same time to ensure that it will be adjusted to meet any dangerous movement that is open to him. Further than this our aim should be not merely to prevent any part being overpowered by a superior force, but to regard every detached squadron as a trap to lure the enemy to destruction. The ideal concentration, in short, is an appearance of weakness that covers a reality of strength.[109]

In Ba Gua Zhang, through footwork and turning the body, one attempts to lure the opponent into committing his full strength in the attack. Once he is committed, positioning, footwork, and body movement can be used to redirect his force, making his strength fall into emptiness, thereby leaving him open to counterattack. By letting the opponent initiate an attack, by letting him momentarily take control and gather his power, one can follow, conforming one's footwork and body position to his movements. Ba Gua's unique stepping (mud-wading step) induces the opponent to commit their step first so that one's own foot placement and weight shift occur just after theirs, allowing one to lead and guide the other's movements, while concealing one's own. The nature of the stepping in Ba Gua is that the feet are moving while the hands are still. When this is combined with the rotation of the body, the opponent feels as though you are still in front of him (i.e., still at the point of engagement), while your feet have already carried your body past the point of engagement. The hands are like scouts screening the movements of the main force (the body), which has already changed its position, so that the power of the opponent's attack enters the space you are already leaving and dissipates into emptiness, even as your own attack is coalescing.

During the Winter War between Russia and Finland in 1939–1940, one million Russian troops invaded Finland, opposed by a Finnish Army consisting of 175,000 men. The Finnish infantry operating in the harsh climate of their northern forests used *motti* or "logging" tactics against their more numerous but predictable opponents. The large road-bound Russian columns were psychologically, tactically, and logistically unprepared for a style of warfare in which their columns were divided and cut into smaller units like firewood. "Individual and small-unit initiative, expert camouflage, rapid movement on skis, quick concentration and quick dispersal, the technique of large-scale as well as small-unit ambushes—all of these skills were honed to a fine edge in the Finnish army."[110] In the Suomussalmi campaign, Finnish troops on snowshoes and skis repeatedly outmaneuvered the slow-moving Russian columns, dividing them into small pockets that were then isolated and destroyed. One drawback of these motti tactics was that they could not destroy larger units that, although isolated, became concentrated pockets of resistance that could not be drawn out.[111] The Finns simply lacked the necessary concentration of force, in terms of men and firepower, to finish the job. Because the Russians often refused to leave their island of safety even to rescue wounded comrades, the Finnish forces were willing, but sometimes unable, to follow the advice of Chinese strategists:

> Since the enemy is entrenched in a stronghold, confrontation with him calls for trying to make him jittery, where he is situated. Attack the place where he feels he must rush to the rescue and thus compel him to leave his entrenched position. Find out the intention of his movements, lay a trap and prepare troops for ambush and reinforcement. Attack the enemy when he is in movement.[112]

Any discussion of counterinsurgency and anti-guerrilla tactics leads to a larger discussion of grand strategy, organizational and political will. Strategy in this context goes beyond military victory and connects with the greater scope of human endeavor. These issues are an important component of Chapter II of this book. Guerrilla warfare involves these larger issues, and because Ba Gua Zhang is a martial art linked to a unique philosophical system, any discussion of Ba Gua must address these larger issues as well. To put it simply, a street fight might just be just a street fight, limited in scope and consequences, or it may have larger, more global ramifications.

Sunzi said:

> Victory is the main object in war. If this is long delayed, weapons are blunted and morale depressed. When troops attack cities, their strength will be exhausted. When the army engages in protracted campaigns, the resources of the state will not suffice. When your weapons are dulled and your ardor damped, your strength exhausted and your treasure spent, neighboring rulers will take advantage of your distress to act. And even though you have wise counselors, none will be able to lay good plans for the future. For there has never been a protracted war from which a country has benefited.[113]

As Brian Steed points out in *Armed Conflict,* these ideas neatly summarize the current philosophy of the United States government. Steed writes that while there is no benefit to protracted war for a wealthy industrialized nation like the United States, for poorer, more disadvantaged nations with a large disenfranchised population, a prolonged war against a stronger, more modern power works to their advantage.[114] Steed goes on to say that America's past, present, and perhaps future adversaries have based their strategies on this idea. Vietnam was a prime example. "According to Truong Chin, the preeminent North Vietnamese theoretician, 'the guiding principle of the strategy of our whole resistance must be to prolong the war.' This would lower enemy morale, unite the Vietnamese people, increase outside support, and encourage the antiwar movement to tie the enemy's hands. 'To achieve all these results, the war must be prolonged, and we must have time. Time works for us.'"[115]

More than one military analyst has pointed out that America has forgotten its own war of revolution, in which George Washington, after losing several more conventional battles, realized that just by keeping his army intact and in a position to constantly harass and threaten British forces, he could wear the enemy down. Washington did not need to control cities or territory, he merely had to force the British to disperse their forces and their efforts in order to cover and control large areas of colonial America. The British Army never had more than about 35,000 men to cover the large area of the thirteen colonies.[116] They could merely hold key ports and make occasional forays into the countryside, where they encountered a combination of regular continental troops and irregular militias led by men like Francis Marion (dubbed the "Swamp Fox" by the British), who had learned irregular tactics during the French and Indian War, fighting the Cherokee. The unconventional tactics of the militia troops caused a British general to remark in 1776 that "the Americans would be less dangerous if they had a regular army."[117]

This "war of the flea" against a ubiquitous, relentless adversary that is too small and too diffuse to come to grips with eventually leads to exhaustion of one's political will and resources.[118] Antiguerrilla tactics therefore involve a broad scope of strategic and tactical countermeasures aimed at denying the enemy freedom of time and space, and isolating them physically, politically, and morally:[119]

- Infiltration of the guerrilla's command and control structure to gain intelligence and foreknowledge of their plans and movements.
- Fluidity of action, the ability to adjust to the guerrilla's changes and to adapt unconventional approaches.
- The use of infiltration tactics, surprise, and shock to upset their plans and break their cohesion.
- Upsetting their cohesion means destroying their legitimacy and bolstering your own.
- This means bringing justice, equality, and prosperity to the areas in which the guerrilla operates, thereby weakening their political and social argument.
- To do this, security and stability must be brought to areas in which the guerrilla operates.
- This helps to destroy their base, the sea of people through which the guerrilla moves unseen, thereby bringing their movements out in the open.
- This in turn hampers their mobility, upon which their war of movement relies.
- Having the will to outlast them, the patience to continue and build slow, cumulative gains against the guerrilla until they are destroyed or no longer supported.
- Military operations must be relentless and coordinated with political and economic factors.

Successful operations by modern industrial powers against guerrilla armies or insurgent populations are not numerous. The Spanish ruled much of the Philippines from 1570–1898, however they were never able to suppress the Moro rebels and pirates who raided their outposts. Particularly in the Southern Philippines, the Moros kept the Spanish largely confined to their forts. Although they sent out expeditions to destroy Moro strongholds, they could not consolidate their gains. The Spanish tried employing privateers to attack Moro settlements and ships, but the depredations of these groups, little more than pirates themselves, merely stiffened resistance and undermined the legitimacy of Spanish rule. The Spaniards were unable to make the Moros pay tribute as they had with native peoples in other parts of the Philippines and in the New World. Instead, through a kind of rebate system, the Moros got the Spanish to pay them for returning escaped slaves. Spain even paid certain sultans a kind of protection fee by subsidizing their harems. All of these factors contributed to a loss of prestige and respect for Spanish rule.[120]

When the Philippine archipelago was ceded to the United States in 1898, the Moros in Mindanao and Sulu resisted American rule in an open insurrection. Leaving aside the moral question of some of America's actions in the Northern Philippines, the American forces gradually learned to conduct an effective campaign against the Moro forces. They created a civil government supplemented by military aid. Unlike the Spaniards, who had remained trapped in their forts and unable to penetrate into the Moro areas, thereby allowing the Moros to operate with impunity, the American troops made frequent reconnaissance missions to enforce the new laws and reduce slave trading and piracy. This gave them legitimacy with the rest of the local population. In campaigns in Mindanao, they mapped the trackless country so that they could locate and destroy Moro strongholds and bring order to remote areas. Some commanders, like Brigadier General Funston, set up effective spy networks that helped target insurgents while leaving the local population untouched.[121] Amnesty was also offered to local villagers who had been forced to help the guerrillas. The Americans discovered that resistance would have to be reduced section by section, gradually denying the enemy a base of operations and simultaneously installing and supporting the rule of law in each area. This required going out among the

Filipino people and taking the fight to the enemy. In part the ability to do this depended upon having capable field officers who earned the respect of their adversaries.[122]

An important, often overlooked aspect of success was that the Americans also did not interfere with the Islamic religion of Moros, as the Spanish had done with forced conversions and baptisms. Further, they did not allow themselves to buy up large tracts of land. "They avoided schemes like opium monopolies. They redistributed land to peasants from wealthy church estates, and built roads, railways, ports, dams, and irrigation facilities. American expenditures on health and education led to a doubling of the Filipino population between 1900 and 1920, and a rise in literacy from twenty to fifty percent within a generation."[123] However, despite these successes, American special forces units are involved to this day in aiding the ground forces of the Philippine government to suppress and contain Muslim insurgents in the southern Philippines.

Other examples of counterinsurgency campaigns that had a measure of success are the Boer War and the British operations in Malaysia against the Malayan Peoples Anti-British Army. In both cases the strategy was to fight the guerrilla forces on their own terms, while simultaneously separating them from the support of the local population. In the Boer War this was done through blocking communications and movement in the open veldt, and instituting constant patrols that could interdict the Boer's plans and movements. The population was also removed from support by the questionable expedient of removing them from their farms by force and interning them.[124] In Malaysia, similar results were effected through the British policy of signaling their own intention to pull out of their former colony while simultaneously guiding the Malaysians toward independence. Resettlement into "New Villages" that housed villagers and Chinese workers separated the population from the insurgents. These villages, surrounded by fences and barbed wire, offered their occupants property rights, giving the Chinese population an investment in land ownership. Food control measures prevented the guerrilla forces from living off the food of the local people, thereby cutting off their supplies, while small patrols trained in jungle warfare and supplemented by local troops took the fight to the enemy.

Gradually the army learned that "shoulder-to-shoulder" sweeps were not productive but actually counterproductive; instead of massing troops, the army developed small patrols that used the skills of native trackers and intelligence provided by surrendered enemy personal and Special Branch infiltrators. Use of heavy firepower was minimized. "We concluded that given accurate information as to a target then there would be merit in considering bombing as a means for attacking it. But to use bombing on a random basis would really be far too costly. And could well perhaps do more harm than good."[125]

British counterinsurgency methods against the IRA over a period of thirty years were also effective, despite many false starts. Martin Van Creveld's dispassionate analysis in *The Changing Face of War* gives great insight into dealing with crisis situations effectively. In Ireland, the British used time to wear down the opposition and prevented themselves from being provoked (for the most part) into indiscriminate firing on crowds or collective punishment of large portions of the population. In this way they did not completely alienate the public. Creveld attributes the ability of the British soldiers to maintain self-control and morale to their superb training, discipline, and leadership.[126]

In Ba Gua Zhang, which itself employs guerrilla tactics, an adversary who uses hit and run tactics is countered by Ba Gua's circular stepping. By walking and rotating, transformation from attack to defense, from dispersion of force to concentration of force, can take place instantaneously. The cohesion of the body and its direct link with the intention is maintained by Ba Gua's unique practice of circle walking. Walking simultaneously affords protection from attack and the ability to observe the opponent. Walking involves movement, progress, and the ability to change and transform in accordance with the opponent's changes, so that one is appropriate at every moment. Walking allows one to take the fight to the enemy while at the same time protecting one's own vital areas. Through walking it is possible to avoid direct confrontation, restrict the opponent's options, limit his use of the terrain, and discover his weak points.

Ba Gua Zhang uses the walking the circle form to control a very large space. To reach, restrict, and strike the enemy is its objective. Ba Gua

Zhang walking the circle form uses walking as the shortest road to cover the largest area, thus it gains time, also economizes body strength, creating a fighting victory over the enemy. Ba Gua Zhang uses the method of walking the circle, changing position and direction, and makes use of the principles of a lever and changing strong points to strike the enemy.[127]

Innovation

Innovation is an important aspect of both the martial arts and military endeavors. Innovation can be technological, the development of new technologies and weapons systems that radically change the face of warfare; or tactical, in the sense of applying weapons in a creative and effective way. Innovation can also be a change in the overall strategic situation. In 1945 this happened with the dropping of the first atomic bombs.

Innovations are not just in the form of new weapons, but also new technologies. The Chinese wheelbarrow was, by all accounts, created by Zhuge Liang as a solution to the problem of supplying his army with grain. Zhuge Liang referred to these devices as wooden oxen and gliding horses because they allowed his men to easily move supplies without tiring and without the need to feed and water horses. The wooden ox was a small barrow with shafts projecting forward resembling ox horns.[128] This innovation allowed him to outwit the Wei army, who had counted on Zhuge Liang's troops being destroyed by a food shortage.[129]

Technological innovations in warfare have often changed the formation of armies and initially given one side or another the advantage for a time. The development of the crossbow in China, and the stirrup in the fourth century, both had profound effects on the nature of warfare and on strategy and tactics, but as with Zhuge Liang's transportation devices, within a short time the other side acquired the same technology. German knights in Lithuania and Estonia also encountered this problem. Initially their armor, superior missile weapons and siege engine technology, gave them a huge advantage over the local population. This of course eventually had the effect of spreading the technology to those they sought to conquer.[130]

In Ba Gua Zhang, new weapons like the Mandarin Duck Knives or the Rooster Claw Yin Yang Knives, with their multipointed surfaces and the ability to hook and control the enemy's weapon, may have initially confused opponents bearing swords and spears, but for the most part the technology was on par with what an opponent might have. In most cases, martial arts weaponry has lagged behind military weapons. For example, practicing with swords, spears, and various exotic multi-edged weapons is useful for developing *shen fa* or "body skills," but these weapons are impractical for modern warfare, police tactics, or for today's self-defense needs. Yet, some innovation and adaptation has occurred. In the past, spear tactics were adopted to the bayonet. Some Ba Gua styles substituted the gentleman's cane for the traditional walking stick when practitioners moved from the countryside to the city. Others developed concealed weapons and knife fighting techniques for more urban settings, and improvised weapons for use in situations where carrying weapons was illegal. Another example of innovation and adaptation is John Painter, who learned the use of the Mauser C96 machine pistol from his Ba Gua teacher Li Long-dao and went on to apply Ba Gua principles to the use of other modern firearms, and defenses against firearms.[131]

Hand-to-hand combat has not changed in its basic skills, but the outlook, approach, and application of traditional martial arts constantly change and innovate as time goes on. The creation of Ba Gua Zhang was in and of itself a tactical innovation, with its stress on walking or mobility as the primary tactic. This has not changed, but different practitioners have added technical and tactical refinements and adjustments. Cheng Ting-hua is noted for combining Ba Gua with *shuai jiao* wrestling and throwing techniques. Yin Fu combined Ba Gua with Lohan or Arhat Boxing, and other practitioners have incorporated sophisticated seizing and locking *(chin na)* methods. Another notable modification is the creation of the Sixty-Four Hands, attributed to Liu De Kuan, a famous Xing Yi practitioner and an expert with the spear. It is thought that Gao Yi-sheng, a student of Cheng Ting-hua, created the sixty-four linear (post-heaven) forms of Gao-style Ba Gua by combining Ba Gua with Da Hong Quan (Big Red Boxing). Another refinement is the crane step of Song-style Ba Gua, which helps develop sophisticated kicking skills.

In ancient warfare there were many tactical innovations that changed the balance of warfare. The phalanx, as wielded by the Spartans, was the undisputed tactical formation of the Hellenistic world. Philip of Macedon had been a hostage in Thebes when the Thebans, under the leadership of

Epaminodas, destroyed Sparta's vaunted phalanx at the battle of Leuctra in 371 BC. Taking a clue from the Thebans, who greatly deepened the battle line, Philip created a Macedonian phalanx sixteen ranks deep, giving it greater shock force than the Spartan formation. The Macedonian phalanx employed longer spears called *sarissas,* which were seventeen to twenty feet in length and were held with two hands, so that shields had to be strapped to the body for protection. The spears of the first eight ranks extended forward, while the rear ranks held their spears at an upward, oblique angle in order to block missile weapons. The points of at least four or five spears then extended out in front of each man in the front rank, making the formation like a porcupine. Professor Garret Fagan graphically describes this formation of ten to twelve thousand men as follows: "coming on in unison, maintaining a steady pace, the sarissa points poking and jabbing in undulating waves, the onset of the Macedonian phalanx must have been a terrifying and awe-inspiring sight."[132] Philip also integrated the phalanx with heavy cavalry, who were used to deliver rapid, shocking assaults to the enemy, as well as support infantry and missile troops and siege engineers and sappers. This created an adaptable professional military machine that the levies of the Greek city-states could not stand against.

Philip's son, Alexander the Great, further developed the Macedonian military machine through intensive training. The Macedonian phalanx was able to rapidly change from thirty-two to sixteen to eight ranks in depth, an ability that Alexander exploited at the battle of Issus against the Persian army of Darius III in 333 BC.[133] At Gaugamela in 331 BC, Alexander employed the Macedonian order of battle to devastating effect against a much larger Persian army led by Darius. His elite heavy cavalry on the right wing shifted to the right, thereby extending his line to the right. This opened a gap between the Persian left wing and center. Alexander's cavalry wedged open this gap, while the Macedonian phalanx in the center first pinned and then wreaked havoc on the Persian center. Caught between the "hammer and anvil" of the phalanx and cavalry,[134] the Persian forces were split and routed, despite having created their own breakthrough on Alexander's left.

There are many reasons the Roman's military machine was superior to the varied enemies they encountered over the centuries. As mentioned earlier, the manipular legion was one tactical innovation that worked well for the Romans for a variety of reasons. The arrangement of units in maniples or handfuls allowed for flexibility, in effect creating a group of smaller units operating in concentrated actions under local command.[135] The manipular formation relied on the strict discipline inimical to the Roman war machine, and allowed the Romans to take advantage of their prowess as swordsmen in single combat. At the battle of Pydna in 168 BC, when the ranks of Macedonian phalanxes became uneven the Romans were able to wedge their way into the ranks of the enemy and separate them, leaving their front and rear vulnerable. The phalanx then broke and ran and was quickly destroyed.[136] Much later, the Roman armies came to rely less on infantry tactics and more and more on heavily armored horsemen known as *cataphracts,* their name derived from the word *kataphraktoi* or "covered over." In the Eastern Roman Empire, these troops combined the shock power of heavy cavalry with the mobility and missile power of mounted archers. Cataphract cavalry came to form the nucleus of the army of Belisarius in his battles against the Goths.

The phalanx did not disappear with the ancient Greeks. Massed pike formations remained on the battlefield for centuries. One adaptation of the phalanx was employed to devastating effect by the Swiss pikemen of the confederacy of cantons during the fourteenth and fifteenth centuries. They arrayed themselves in deep columns of pikemen wielding eighteen-foot ashen spears. Like the Macedonian phalanx, the bristling wall of spears presented a formidable obstacle for infantry and heavy cavalry. The Swiss did not wear much armor, which allowed for rapidity of movement both on the march and in battle. "In the face of such a foe it was hard for the slowly moving feudal or mercenary armies of the fifteenth century to maneuver— whether strategically in the general campaign, or tactically on the actual battlefield. When once the Confederates were in motion, the enemy was usually forced to fight, not how or where he chose, but according to the desire of his more mobile opponents."[137]

Perhaps the ultimate development of the Swiss order of battle were the Spanish *tercios* of the sixteenth century. Developed by the Great Captain Gonzalo de Cordoba, the tercio formation was composed of pikemen forty ranks deep, flanked by arquebusiers who protected the formation from cavalry attacks. Relentless and almost unstoppable, the tercio dominated the battlefields of Europe for almost a century.[138]

Gustavus Adolphus became King of Sweden in 1611. He later reorganized the Swedish military, instituting a reformed conscription. Like most armies during the Thirty Years War, the Swedish army was composed largely of mercenaries. Adolphus made the core of the army Swedish, and mercenary troops trained under Swedish officers. He also introduced new tactics that required rigorous training to perfect. Adolphus thinned the ranks in the battle formation, improving flexibility and firing capability. He attached musketeers to the cavalry and the pikemen.[139] By coordinating their actions, the cavalry and pike men could move through the ranks of the musketeers after they fired. The musketeers were trained to fire simultaneously in order to blast open gaps in the enemy line, into which the cavalry or pike men could charge while the musketeers reloaded. Gustavus also equipped his infantry with mobile field cannons. Lenart Torstennson, the great commander of the Swedish artillery, had redesigned the gun carriages of the twelve-pound cannons to improve mobility. He also employed cartridged ammunition, wiring the cannon ball to the charge, which increased the rate of fire.[140] At Breitenfeld in 1631, the Swedes used musketry and artillery to halt the attack of Tilly's forces while their cavalry routed the imperial cavalry and then turned in to attack the imperialist center, which collapsed under the combination of concentrated firepower and cavalry assault.

Napoleon took the innovations of Gustavus Adolphus further. One of the many changes that influenced his strategy was the *levée en masse*, which created almost universal conscription and allowed an enormous increase in the number of soldiers in the French army. By 1800, Napoleon had fought campaigns with more than 200,000 men and the army of France had over a million men.

The army itself was reorganized into divisions, which were self-sufficient and able to operate independently, but also to combine and coordinate to achieve a common goal. This allowed for greater flexibility and the ability to achieve multiple objectives and create multiple threats. Troops could now be employed the moment contact occurred, rather than waiting for the entire army to arrive. Further, independent divisions traveling by separate routes could forage for supplies, living off the land. This allowed Napoleon's armies to travel light and not be tied to fixed supply routes.

The mobility of the army was further enhanced by abandonment of the traditional marching step in favor of the quickstep. The quickstep increased the marching pace to 120 paces a minute, allowing the army to cover twenty to thirty kilometers a day. Different army corps marching on separate routes made for a faster, more efficient movement, which could not be attained by keeping the army together and marching along a single route. This appearance of being not united could be used to confuse the enemy and keep options open, while in fact each separate army corps converged on a line of operations toward an operational objective. The deployment of the army could then "shrink and expand in order to tackle natural obstacles or confuse the enemy."[141]

At the battle of Jena in 1806, Napoleon's strategy relied heavily on the speed and surprise these innovations afforded his army. He had to bring his forces to bear against the Prussians before their Russian allies could reach the front. Through quick maneuver, the French caught one Prussian division at Saalfield and destroyed it. Then they advanced quickly behind a screen of cavalry. The main body was split into three columns, each taking a different route, but remaining close enough to support one another. The fast-moving columns allowed for a flexible battle plan, as they could maneuver to attack in any direction or combine and concentrate strength at the enemy's weak points. The fast advance and unpredictable line of attack kept the Prussian army off-balance and outmaneuvered throughout the battle, so that they were destroyed piecemeal before they could concentrate their forces.

Napoleon took full advantage of improvements in artillery, modifications of gun carriages, and shorter barrels allowing for greater mobility.[142] Standardized parts and packed rounds also improved efficiency. Artillery could now be brought to bear close to the front and used to shock and shatter, creating gaps in the enemy dispositions.

Another change in tactics was the use of mobile skirmishers armed with rifles, who were detached from the main force in order to harass and confuse the enemy. They could screen or mask the movements of the main body of French troops by making the enemy think he had encountered a unit attached to a larger force. Cavalry were also employed to screen troop movement, gather information, and deliver shocking charges when the enemy's line had been damaged by artillery fire.

Finally, Napoleon employed dense attacking columns, rather than then a thin defensive firing line. This emphasized shock power, which he could employ to good effect when properly coordinated with the skirmishers and cavalry, to screen and confuse, and concentrate artillery fire.

Napoleon's influence extended even into the Civil War, when innovations in technology made Napoleonic tactics dangerous. The transition from the smoothbore musket to the rifle increased the range and effectiveness of infantry fire. The enormous casualties inflicted in Civil War battles were in part due to the fact that officers tried to duplicate Napoleon's use of massed formations and the tactical offensive that they had studied at West Point. They were slow to see that something had changed.

> Time and again generals on both sides ordered close-order assaults in the traditional formation. With an effective range of three or four hundred yards, defenders firing rifles decimated these attacks. The old-fashioned cavalry charge against infantry, already obsolescent, became obsolete in the face of rifles that could knock down horses long before their riders got within saber or pistol range.[143]

World War I saw huge changes in the industrialization of war. European observers on American Civil War battlefields had seen how the industrialization of the North, combined with mass conscription and the ability of railroads to move troops quickly to the front lines, had overwhelmed the South by increasing the North's ability to concentrate force quickly and massively. In addition, the Civil War illustrated to both American commanders and their European counterparts that industry is part of the organizational process of war, and that destruction of the opponent's industry and his means to make war was a key element to victory on modern battlefields.[144]

These innovations, when applied in World War I, led to the vast slugging match on the Western Front. Both sides could mobilize huge masses of men to a front in which there was no room to maneuver and no flank to turn.[145] To some degree this was dictated by being tied to railheads for supplies and reinforcements, and to some degree by the increased power of the developing weapons systems. As the British attackers found out at the battle of the Somme, the increased range and accuracy of rifles and machine guns—combined with artillery barrages and, at close quarters, flamethrowers—wreaked havoc on direct assaults that attempted to break the deadlock. The tank and airplane also began to play important roles as tactics adapted to fit these developing technologies.

Toward the end of the war, commanders like General Erich von Ludendorff began to use innovative tactics that took advantage of newly developed weapons systems and situations. The Germans in particular "selected and trained infantry troops as elite Sturmtruppen, storm troopers, soldiers who specialized in infiltration and conducting fast, hard-hitting attacks before moving on to their next target. They would mount a surprise assault after a short 'hurricane' bombardment and then move on as fast as possible into the opponent's territory."[146] The brief, intense bombardment included gas and smoke shells that disrupted defense and obscured the assault. *Stosstruppen*, small teams equipped with light machine guns, flame throwers, and other weapons, moved in behind the barrage, which rolled toward the enemy. They were instructed to seep into any gaps or weaknesses they could find, to penetrate the enemy's defenses, maintain momentum, and exploit openings that would widen the penetration and consolidate gains. Small battle groups known as *Kampfgruppen*, consisting of infantry, mortar teams, artillery observers, and machine gunners, would follow up to mop up centers of resistance or cave in exposed flanks.[147]

By necessity, these teams had to operate independently and take advantage of opportunities as they presented themselves. Boyd describes the effectiveness of such tactics: "Taken together, the captured attention, the obscured view, and the indistinct character of moving dispersed/irregular swarms deny the adversary the opportunity to picture what is taking place. Infiltration teams appear to suddenly loom up out of nowhere to blow through, around, and behind disoriented defenders."[148] These ideas were not new. In the Three Kingdoms period in China, many commanders, such as Cao Cao, employed specially trained "dare-to-die" shock troops to break through the enemy's defenses.[149] What was different were the specific tactical problems that needed to be overcome and their interaction with a weapons technology that was rapidly changing.

Although infiltration tactics were a mixed success—able to create gaps and drive the enemy back, but not in such a way as to lead to overall strategic success—these experiences helped lead to the development of the fabled blitzkrieg tactics employed on the Western Front in World War II. The German army surprised the world with the speed of their success, using the innovations of modern warfare in an unanticipated and innovative way.

> The next step was to think about synchronizing tank action with the infantry, artillery, and the air force—a development made possible by the introduction of the radio. The Germans understood that it was the tank units that were the ones to be supported and for this to be possible the other arms had to move at the same speed. So were born the Panzer Grenadiers (armored infantry) and the other arms, artillery, and so forth, were also equipped to move in direct support of tanks.[150]

Blitzkrieg warfare effectively combined dive bomber aircraft, tanks, mobile infantry, and engineer divisions with parachute units to confuse and disrupt communications and to subject the unprepared enemy to unrelenting and furious fast assault, exploiting new weapons, tactics, and strategy to the fullest. Rommel used the combined arms tactics of the blitzkrieg against the British armies in North Africa with great success. "The Desert Fox and his clear-thinking companions were skilled and well trained in combined-arms tactics. Since their panzers were in no way superior to some of the British tanks, they worked their tanks, anti-tank guns, artillery, and infantry in harness, so that none was without protection from the others."[151] The British, on the other hand, relied on modified World War I tank doctrines that were outdated.

The German officers in the Second World War were better able to embrace the new technology and the mindset necessary to apply it than were their contemporaries in other countries, who still envisioned set piece battles or relied on fortress strategies. Between World Wars I and II, the German army was transformed into a professional conscript army. Great stress was placed on the rigorous training and selection of officers and NCOs. The training was long, arduous and merit-based; candidates had to display initiative, decisiveness, a talent for improvisation, and a willingness to work hard and shoulder responsibility.[152] Training informed doctrine and vice-versa in an endless cycle. Attention was given to field exercises in all forms of modern warfare, which were carefully observed and analyzed. General staff candidates rotated between field commands and headquarters staff positions, keeping them from becoming too complacent and theoretical. This kind of training, conducted at all levels, from headquarters staff officers to non-commissioned officers, created a shared doctrine and experience that inspired creativity, problem solving, and flexibility. A British officer observed that the German officers were "far quicker to adapt themselves to the changed conditions of war and to the emergencies of the situation" than their British, French, or Russian counterparts.[153]

Napoleon's revolution in warfare was unique for its time and perhaps for all time. The innovations that took place in the French army tactics and larger strategic approach were, to a large extent, born out of the French Revolution, the Napoleonic code, and Napoleon's personal genius. His ability to command, inspire troops, and control the battlefield, combined with the abilities of the French army, could not readily be duplicated by other nations or commanders. Even his nemesis, the Duke of Wellington, acknowledged that "Napoleon's presence on the battlefield was worth 40,000 men."[154]

If the Grande Armee and Napoleonic warfare were a unique entity born out of the French revolution and the genius of Napoleon, one could say that Greek *hoplite* warfare was a product of the Greek city-state and an ethos that pervaded Greek life, culture, and politics.[155] Greek hoplite battles were struggles between small landholders who by mutual consent sought to limit warfare (and hence killing) to a single, brief nightmarish occasion.[156] The terrifying clash of phalanxes on an open plain—composed of men locked into tightly packed formations—with its shared risk and its dependence on group cohesion also provided an ultimate, almost Homeric, test of individual courage.

The legendary English longbow made famous at the battles of Crecy and Agincourt was a weapon unique to the English foot soldier. Previously the crossbow had been the auxiliary weapon of knights and foot soldiers. Richard Coeur de Lion wading through the surf, leading the attack to relieve the siege of Jaffa with a crossbow on his shoulder, is an enduring image of this earlier period. The longbow seems to have developed among the South Welsh. It had an advantage over the crossbow in its astonishing rate of fire, and it rivaled, if not surpassed it, in penetrating power: "A knight of William de Braose received an arrow, which first went through the skirts of his mail shirt, then through his mail breeches, then through his thigh, then through the wood of his saddle, and finally penetrated far into his horse's flank."[157] Although in use earlier, the longbow came to the fore in the thirteenth century during the Welsh wars of Edward I. Edward had discovered the effectiveness of combined arms, using cavalry and infantry armed with missile weapons. At Agincourt, archers made up five-sixths of the English army.[158] The English knights dismounted and the archers wreaked havoc among the French knights.

The use of the longbow was not an easily acquired skill. It seems to have been peculiar to certain groups from the English countryside, and the high level of skill necessary to use such a weapon required that the archer literally grow up hunting with his bow. This is not dissimilar to the abilities of the horse peoples from the Eastern steppes, such as the Huns and the Mongols. Their abilities as horse archers and their unique method of warfare could no more be duplicated by the English bowman than they could duplicate his. Innovation is one thing; being able to employ it and capitalize on it is another. These abilities are to some degree a product of one's orientation, which Boyd defines as "an interactive process of many-sided implicit cross-referencing, projections, empathies, correlations, and rejections that is shaped by and shapes the interplay of genetic heritage, cultural tradition, previous experiences, and unfolding circumstances."[159]

Similarly in the internal martial arts, each person's ability to use and employ any learned set of principles is shaped by their orientation as described by Boyd. In Ba Gua Zhang, different teachers emphasize, innovate, and teach things differently, based on their background in other martial arts, their size and body type, temperament, strengths and weaknesses, their cultural heritage, the environment they grew up in, and their unique life experiences. No two people will do things the same way, or look exactly the same in their performance and application. Larger people will do things differently than smaller people, and tactics and overall strategy will, to some degree, be dictated by what has worked in the past and what has not—and to take it a step further, what has worked against whom, and in what particular circumstance. One person's strengths cannot necessarily be duplicated by another, but they can be overcome by judicious application of other tactics and other skills, by the limitations and advantages of terrain and weather, by the ability to adapt and change with the changing circumstances. Therefore, it is necessary to go beyond the external form and beyond the assimilation of specific skills. Attempting to assimilate too many skills can be debilitating, as it creates a difficulty in integration of skills at the unconscious level.

Martin van Creveld points out a version of this problem vis-à-vis the Germans in the Second World War:

> It has been argued that almost every weapons system deployed from 1945 to 1991, including in particular, certain kinds of submarines and many kinds of missiles, was already on the German drawing boards in 1944–45. However in some ways, this very inventiveness worked against them. It resulted in a very large number of different types, models, and versions of weapons, which in turn led to frequent changes, disrupted production schedules, and endless maintenance problems; at the end of 1941, Army Group Center, fighting in front of Moscow, needed a million different spare parts.[160]

In Vietnam, the American forces had the stronger force, more firepower, greater strength. Yet despite this advantage and the use of the most modern weaponry available, they could not overpower the Vietnamese. Numbers, firepower, technology, and industrial power do not necessarily equate to the capacity of a military force to use them effectively.

> There is no absolute measure of the strength or power of a force. First, because even with advanced technology, it is ultimately human: real people operate all the platforms, systems, and weapons and real people direct them. A force is therefore an organic unit with a body, a mind, and a will. You can count soldiers, weapons, and equipment, but that will give you only an idea of the potential power of a force, not of its true capability.[161]

Part of America's lack of capability in applying force in Vietnam was its inability to interactively shape its tactics and its political, military, and national strategies in relation to those of the North Vietnamese. Throughout the conflict, the United States essentially fought a high-tech, conventional war against an opponent who refused to play the game. To make an analogy with martial arts, different styles of martial arts promise different results and skill sets, yet they are only as good as the person using them. Additionally, even if one is skilled, if one's abilities cannot be employed effectively in relation to the opponent, who has his own unique skills and perspective, then greater power and speed or superior technique will not necessarily guarantee victory. It is not uncommon for an untrained fighter with good instincts to upset the trained fighter's game, particularly if he refuses to "play by the rules." Chinese strategists state this succinctly: "If you use the same battle formation every time, you will not win victory. Only when you use different battle formations in different circumstances will you be able to defeat the enemy."[162]

Similar problems have occurred in Iraq. The Iraq War of 2003 was an easy initial victory for the American forces. The Iraqi weapons were outdated and their forces no match for the better trained and better equipped American forces in open battle. The Iraqis made the mistake of directly engaging the United States in a high-tech, conventional war. Although the U.S. forces were initially "victorious," soon insurgents armed with light weapons were attacking, with everything from assault rifles to mortars, rocket launchers, and homemade bombs. In this type of warfare the heavy weapons of the Americans (i.e., tanks, armored personnel carriers, helicopter gunships, aircraft, and radio-controlled drones) were not so effective. American reliance on technology often leaves troops vulnerable to an opponent whose dispositions are not subject to being identified and targeted. In an interesting turnabout, technology has also been used against its creators. Taking a page from Che Guevara, who advocated that the guerrilla use the same ammunition as the enemy in order to let them provide him with ammunition, the Iraqis and other insurgents have learned to use American ordinance against American troops. "Associated with every bombardment is unexploded ordinance. Those bombs and shells can easily be booby trapped or otherwise returned to sender. Over the years, America's adversaries have never suffered from a shortage of explosives."[163]

During the Iraq War, American military officials noticed that the increase in equipment and the heavy body armor, which limit movement, took a toll on combat troops. Increasingly they were being sidelined by injuries such as stress fractures or overuse injuries of the back, legs, and feet. Additionally, the more lightly equipped enemy was more maneuverable and able to evade the overloaded American troops.[164] This kind of problem has led some experts to call for a change in tactics and equipment—returning to the use of light infantry as a component in American ground forces. The role of light infantry has not substantially changed since Napoleonic times. Even today, they are needed to effect surprise attacks, screen maneuvers of tanks and artillery, and engage in the attack and ambush techniques which are a part of infiltration tactics.[165]

New technologies can often be creatively adapted to more traditional tactics with great success. Soviet tactics in Afghanistan had begun to be successful when the focus changed to the use of air power combined with mobile helicopter–supported operations aimed at interdicting the supply routes and support structure of the Mujahedeen. The Afghan rebels liked to bait traps in narrow valleys for Soviet aircraft. As the Russian planes swooped in, they received plunging anti-aircraft or heavy machine-gun fire from both sides of the gorge.[166] The effectiveness of these kinds of ambushes greatly increased in 1986, when the Afghanis were supplied with Stinger surface-to-air missiles produced by the United States. By 1987 the Soviet forces were losing one and a half aircraft a day, greatly reducing the effectiveness of their operations, which had become centered around the use of helicopters.[167] Stinger missiles also forced Soviet combat aircraft to fly much higher, interfering with their ground support role to the extent that ground troops derisively referred to the pilots as "cosmonauts."[168] The end result was that the Soviet army could no longer use the tactics that had been effective, nor could they resupply outposts that had been cut off from ground reinforcement. This meant they began to lose control of sections of the country that had previously been denied to the rebels.

Similarly, tactical innovation can be created out of the need to adapt to unique circumstances or unexpected obstacles. American troops in Normandy during World War II encountered hedgerows planted by Celtic farmers that could be as much as ten feet thick. This *bocage* country created a dangerous series of deathtraps for American troops. Tanks could not penetrate them, and if they tried to ride over them, they exposed their vulnerable underbellies to anti-tank weapons. The Germans fortified the hedgerows, the farmhouses, and the narrow lanes that connected them. Under machine-gun fire, American troops were forced to take cover behind hedgerows, hiding places that had been previously targeted for German artillery and mortar attacks. Eventually the Americans devised a kind of infiltration strategy reminiscent of World War I trench warfare. By using "hedgedozers," tanks that had been outfitted with bulldozer blades, the American troops found they could create holes in the hedgerows. Combat engineers would also widen the gap or create new gaps with explosives that tanks could enter, supported by infantry. This combination of infantry and armor would drive back the German machine-gun and anti-tank units into positions that could be hit with mortar fire.

Innovation in warfare inevitably leads to countermeasures. The more successful the innovation, the more the enemy will develop countermeasures against it. In the late fifteenth century, when the French battered down medieval Italian fortresses using siege cannon, they ushered in a new era of fortress building. Italian engineers responded by developing new kinds of fortresses, which were modified in subsequent centuries.[169] During the reign of Louis XIV in the sixteenth and seventeenth centuries, these new fortifications reached what was perhaps their peak of development with Sebastian Le Prestre de Vauban, whose impressive fortresses can still be seen in France today. The main enclosure of the fortress became a polygon with star-shaped projecting bastions that subjected attackers to a crossfire. Ditches and a *glacis* (an outer, downward-sloping rampart) were added. Each part of the main enclosure was protected by flanking strong points, which were within musket range of each other, so that each part was protected by another part, with the whole structure adapted to the surrounding terrain. This created a "defense in depth."[170] With these improvements in defense also came innovations in siege-craft. Vauban used temporary fortifications, parallel interlocking trench systems, and earthworks to protect advancing troops as they patiently dug and tunneled under the walls, while bringing up siege guns and other equipment within close range of the fortifications.

Martial arts have undergone similar adaptation, innovation, and counter-innovation. Military arts become modified and are employed for self-development and self-protection in times of peace. Grappling methods are used to counter striking methods and vice versa. Weapons and defenses against weapons change according to the time, place, and culture. Traditional schools of martial arts in Japan taught methods specific to fighting armored opponents with swords, while in the Philippines many of the knife defenses taught by Eskrima practitioners in Cebu in the 1980s were designed specifically to counter the types of street attacks that were common at that time.

Information operations are part of the growing technology of warfare. These operations can range from computer hacking to computer viruses that jam or destroy enemy information systems. Using information technology, one can gain an advantage by exploiting information more quickly and simultaneously denying the enemy access to information. As with any technology, overreliance creates its own problems. Its very strength can also be its weakness, as information can also be disrupted or corrupted by enemy computers. "It has been suggested that the increase in information combined with the paralyzing effect of 'information overload' may actually increase the 'fog of war' rather than clarify combat decision making."[171]

In martial arts there exists a similar problem. Too many technologies—techniques, methods, styles—are difficult to integrate into the body's automatic responses. On the other hand, overreliance on one set of skills impairs one's ability to adapt and allows the opponent to develop specific and effective countermeasures. In the following passage, the famous Xing Yi boxer Guo Yun-shen sums up the problems of overreliance on one technology or one sphere of ability and knowledge:

> It is necessary not to be stubborn in training the boxing skills. If strength is sought on purpose, it can be restricted by strength. If qi is sought on purpose, it can be restricted by qi. If heavy ability is sought on purpose, it can be restricted by heavy ability. If light and floating ability is sought on purpose, it can be dispersed by light and floating ability. Therefore, in those with smooth training forms, strength can take place naturally. In those with harmony in the interior, qi can generate itself and the spiritual intention can return to the Dantian area and the body can be as heavy as Mt. Taishan. In those who could transform the spirit into voidness, their body can be as light as a piece of feather naturally. Conclusively, it is necessary not to seek it on purpose. If something can be obtained in seeking them, it seems to exist but not exist and seem to be true, but is false. It is necessary to obtain them by unhurried and steady steps, without forgetting and assisting them, without thinking and over-management of them.[172]

Belisarius: A Study in Strategy

The campaigns of Belisarius, a commander in the Byzantine army under the Emperor Justinian, who reconquered Africa, Southern Spain, and Italy, provide some of the greatest examples of the tactics described above. The success of these campaigns was achieved through the tactical and strategic genius of Belisarius. In the words of Liddell Hart:

> That achievement, associated mainly with the name of Belisarius, is the more remarkable because of two features—first, the extraordinarily slender resources with which Belisarius undertook these far-reaching campaigns; second, his consistent use of the tactical defensive. There is no parallel in history for such a series of conquests by abstention from attack.[173]

In one of his early campaigns, Belisarius defended Daras, an important frontier fortress, against a Persian army double the size of his own. To prevent the siege from taking place, Belisarius placed his army outside the walls of the fortress. The center, composed of his weaker infantry, was drawn back or "refused" with a small ditch in front of them, while the cavalry wings were placed forward. Hunnish cavalry guarded the flanks of the infantry, and Belisarius and his personal bodyguards of cavalry were behind them. Finally, a small body of cavalry hid behind a hill that anchored the left flank. The Persians encountered the wings first and drove back the Roman left wing, only to have the hidden cavalry fall on their rear while the Hunnish cavalry charged their flank. On the Roman right, the Persians, led by the crack shock troops known as the "Immortals," drove the Roman cavalry back to the walls of the city. This initial victory separated the Persians from their center, allowing Belisarius to insert his reserve of Hunnish cavalry into the gap. These were followed by the Huns from the left flank, and finally by Belisarius and his bodyguard unit. This broke the Persian left and allowed Belisarius's troops to converge on the Persian center, which collapsed and was decimated.[174]

In AD 535, after the fall of the Roman Empire in the West, Justinian attempted the re-conquest of Italy, which was then held by the Goths. Belisarius entered Italy after having subdued the Vandals in Northern Africa. As the Goths were busy fighting the Franks, they left Rome lightly defended, allowing Belisarius to easily recapture it. By the time the Goths returned with an army exceeding one hundred thousand men, Belisarius's much smaller army of ten thousand had greatly improved the city's defenses and laid in large stores of food. Early on in the siege, the Goths conducted a general attack on the fortifications. Their siege towers were rendered useless when Belisarius ordered his men to shoot at the oxen pulling them. After that, the battle raged throughout the day as the Goths attacked the city at several points. At the end of the day, the Goths, repulsed on all sides, had lost thirty thousand men. "Amidst tumult and dismay, the whole plan of attack and defense was distinctly present to his [Belisarius's] mind; he observed the changes of each instant, observed every possible advantage, transported his person to the scenes of danger, and communicated his spirit in calm and decisive orders."[175]

Following these initial assaults, the siege settled into a blockade, and Belisarius conducted an active defense, using his highly mobile cavalry units to harass the Gothic troops, leading them into blind attacks that cost them many casualties. This, combined with disease, gradually reduced the numbers of the besiegers. Belisarius then initiated far-ranging cavalry raids that cut the Goths' supply lines and disrupted their communications, a tactic so effective that eventually they were forced to abandon the siege.

Even as his opponents abandoned the siege, Belisarius took advantage of the situation to strike a final blow. He waited until half of the Gothic army had crossed over the Tiber via the Milvian Bridge. Then his troops sallied out and attacked their rear.

> As Belisarius expected, the passage of the Milvian bridge soon became encumbered by the runaways from one bank, and the reinforcements from the other, and great numbers were precipitated into the Tiber, whence the weight of their armor prevented them from rising. Thus the troops on the opposite shore could yield but little assistance to their comrades. The victory of Belisarius was complete; a large share of the Gothic rear was cut to pieces.[176]

Belisarius was a master of deception, using a variety of tactics to confuse and dishearten enemy commanders. In campaigning against the Persians, who were attempting to capture Jerusalem with an army of two hundred thousand, Belisarius, rather than directly blocking their advance, chose a more indirect strategy. He led a small force of hand-picked troops into a town left behind by the Persians during their march, effectively blocking their return to Persia and interrupting the Persian line of communications. This caused Nushirvan, the Persian commander, to have misgivings about Belisarius's true strength and intentions. He stopped the Persian advance and sent an envoy to Belisarius's camp, ostensibly on a diplomatic mission, but actually to spy on Belisarius's numbers and dispositions. In a strategy reminiscent of Zhuge Liang's Empty City Ploy (see Appendix III: The Thirty-Six Stratagems: number 32), Belisarius advanced a large part of his army a distance from his camp. They pretended to be a small detachment that was ranging ahead of the main force. The Persian envoy closely observed this body of the largest and fiercest-looking warriors relaxing, engaged in hunting, their weapons laid aside and their attention focused only on the chase. Meanwhile, Belisarius kept his other troops in constant movement in the distance, spreading them out to create an appearance of large numbers. The lighthearted attitude of Belisarius and his "detachment," combined with the sight of squadrons of cavalry of unknown numbers conducting maneuvers in the distance, convinced the envoy that he had encountered only the outermost forces of a vast army.[177] Upon receiving the envoy's report, the Persian commander ordered his forces to retreat back into Mesopotamia.

In other campaigns Belisarius had his men light a far-reaching chain of campfires at night, to give the enemy the impression that they had encountered a large force. During the day, he achieved the same effect by producing artificial clouds of dust, convincing them that a large force was on the move. In Chinese military strategy this is known as *the cicada sloughs its skin* (also the name of a movement in the Ba Gua). From a distance the newly sloughed skin of the cicada looks exactly like the cicada itself, deceiving the enemy as to the actual position and disposition of the cicada.[178]

During his second foray against the Goths in Italy, Belisarius used pretend deserters, who joined the Goths so they could report on their dispositions. When the Gothic commander Totila blocked the Tiber by constructing a massive bridge and fortress manned by crack troops, these false deserters reported the exact position and measurements of the bulwarks. Belisarius then lashed two large boats together and constructed a tower higher than the ramparts of Totila's fortress, which was adequately protected from missile fire and could fire combustibles onto the wooden ramparts.[179] In his recapture of Rome, he sent in another false deserter to convince the genuine deserters who had joined Totila's garrison to rebel and deliver the city to Belisarius. This led to a very costly siege attempt by the Goths after Belisarius had once again repaired the ruined walls and gates. In the final engagement, the Gothic troops were routed and forced to retreat to Tivoli.

Without fighting a single major engagement, with an army of less than ten thousand men, Belisarius, through maneuver, negotiation, ruses, and strategic vision, took city after city and broke the power of the Goths in Italy. Keeping his forces on the move, he retook many cities from the Goths. Far-ranging units of his army threatened multiple objectives while cutting communications and supplies. In this way he could press the Goths closely, while simultaneously baffling their stratagems. He took Naples by having a small body of men enter the city through an aqueduct, while the main force attacked the walls. He besieged Ravenna, eventually taking it by allowing the Goths to believe he would ally with them against Justinian. When his army finally entered the city, the much more numerous Goths could not believe that they had been defeated by such a small force.

When asked by contemporaries about his successes against much more numerous opponents, Belisarius said "in the first small skirmishes with the Goths I was always on the lookout to discover what were the strong and weak points in their tactics, in order to accommodate my own to them, so as best to make up for my numerical inferiority."[180] He found that the Gothic heavy cavalry was only effective in close combat and was thus vulnerable to missile fire. The Byzantine heavy cavalry, the *cataphractoi,* could match the shock power of the Gothic horseman, but in addition were skilled archers who could keep out of reach and rain arrows upon the Goths. The Gothic foot archers, in turn, could not risk being caught in the open by the Byzantine cavalry, and so tended to be cautious. "The effect is that the Gothic cavalry were always trying to get to close quarters, and could be easily galled into an ill-timed charge, whereas the infantry tended to hang back when the shielding cavalry got far ahead—so that the combination broke down, while a gap was created into which flank counterstrokes could be driven."[181]

This weakness in the Gothic forces was repeatedly exploited by Belisarius. When the city and harbor of Portus on the Tiber was captured by the Goths, it was much harder for Belisarius to get supplies from the sea to Rome. He had his cavalry attack the Gothic camp at Portus, instructing them to maintain distance and fire arrows until all their arrows had been discharged, and then retreat. As expected, after suffering many losses the Goths charged after the retreating Romans, who drew the Goths within missile range of their fortifications. Many Goths were killed in this manner. Belisarius was able to use similar maneuvers several times, which weakened both the enemy's forces and their morale.[182]

In campaign after campaign, Belisarius triumphed against much larger forces by understanding the enemy's tactics, his strengths and weaknesses, as well as his psychology. Belisarius's only defeat occurred early in his career, against the Persians in Syria, when his troops talked him into directly attacking a retreating enemy he had already successfully outmaneuvered. The Persians retreated toward home, shadowed by Belisarius, who camped each night in the area occupied by the Persians the night before. The Roman troops and officers under Belisarius, eager for glory, urged him to attack the Persians directly. His response:

> The most complete and most happy victory is to baffle the force of an enemy without impairing our own, and in this favorable situation we are already placed.... Deprived of refuge in case of defeat, the Persians will fight with all the courage of despair, whilst we, enfeebled by a rigorous fast, wearied with rapid marches, and having by our speed outstripped several of our slower battalions, must enter the field with diminished strength and unequal chances of success.[183]

In the end, he agreed to the demands of his troops. The Roman attack caused the Persians to fight tenaciously, defeating Belisarius's forces. Chinese strategists also realized that closing in on a weakened enemy who has nothing to lose stiffens his resistance. They echo Belisarius when they advise generals to *leave at large, the better to capture:* "Close in upon the almost defeated enemy and it will strike back. Let it go and its position will weaken. Follow it closely, but do not press it too hard. Fritter away its strength and sap its will. After it has scattered, subdue it without staining the swords with blood."[184]

In subsequent campaigns, Belisarius consistently employed Ba Gua–like methods. Rather than engaging the enemy directly, he used flexible tactics with multiple objectives that were adaptable to the changing circumstances, in order to dislocate the enemy's ability to concentrate his larger forces against him. Once the enemy's forces were disrupted and overextended, Belisarius could then strike him at his weakest point. "Belisarius demonstrated that numbers don't count as much as resolve, toughness, and vision. His battlefield heroics demonstrate to the student of war that tactical durability is the sine qua non of small force theory. Small, well-trained, highly mobile units, confident in their equipment, are the components of fighting outnumbered and winning."[185]

Even as an old man Belisarius was a formidable commander. In 559 AD, against the invading Bulgarians, he was brought out of retirement to meet a force of seven thousand with a few hundred men and a mass of untried peasants armed with stakes. He concealed his veteran cavalry in the woods nearby, on either side of a narrow defile through which the Bulgarians would have to pass in order to attack what appeared to be his main force, the mass of peasants who brandished the stakes as though they were weapons. When the Bulgarians attacked, the concealed troops fell on their flank and rear, routing them without the loss of a single life.[186]

Belisarius is the most famous of a number of very skilled military commanders of the Eastern Roman Empire. His successor, Narses, also defeated the Goths in Italy, where Belisarius had in the end failed—although Narses was better supplied and had the Emperor Justinian's favor. George Dennis, in his translation of *Maurice's Strategikon,* a Byzantine book on strategy attributed to the Emperor Maurice in the late sixth century, points out that the Byzantine generals were professionals who made a serious study of the art of war, who knew their enemy's tactics and methods, and who were expected to succeed through intelligence, foresight, and planning rather than force of arms alone. The *Strategikon* echoes the *Sunzi* in the advice it offers Byzantine commanders: "A good general is one who utilizes his own skills to fit the opportunities he gets and the quality of the enemy."[187] And, "The best leader is one who does not willingly engage in a hazardous and highly uncertain battle, and refrains from emulating those who carry out operations recklessly and are admired for their brilliant success, but one who, while keeping the enemy on the move, remains secure and always in circumstances of his own choosing."[188]

The Analogy of Water

It is useful to understand that the ideal of military strategy in China, and by extension the tactics of Ba Gua Zhang, is to be like water. Water cannot be grasped, yet it is powerful; it has no form, yet can take the shape of a container. Water is flexible, adaptable, always changing and flowing. When one attempts to block it, it flows around the obstacle, never confronting it head-on. Water does not move in straight lines but rushes, spirals, and eddies unpredictably. It is substantial, yet when one attempts to grasp it, it slips away. Water is soft and yielding, yet it is powerful, like a pounding wave containing a heavy mass of water that can exert tremendous force.

Water shapes its current
from the lie of the land.
The warrior shapes his victory
from the dynamic of the enemy.

Water has no
Constant dynamic;
Water has no
Constant Form

Supreme military skill lies
In deriving victory
From the changing circumstances
Of the enemy.[189]

François Jullien writes:

> True strength is definitely characterized by the fact that it is not forced. Chinese thought never tires of this theme: it is the nature of water to flow downward; and the reason why it can even carry stones along with it is that it is content to follow the slope offered it. "The conformation of troops must resemble water. Just as it is in the conformation of water to

avoid what is high and incline toward that which is low, similarly, the conformation of troops must be to avoid the points at which the enemy is strong and attack it where it is weak." The strong points are where the enemy is full and may act as a barrage [dam]; the weak points are where the enemy is empty—deficient or unprepared. The general, like water, steers clear of obstacles and insinuates himself wherever the way before him is free; like water, he always sticks closely to the line of least resistance and at every moment seeks out where it is easiest to proceed.[190]

CHAPTER II

Strategy and the Eight Dispositions

Several general points about the making of strategy bear repeating. The first is that those involved, whether statesman or military leaders, live in a world of incomplete information. They do not know, in most cases, the strategic intentions and purposes of other powers, except in the most general sense, and their knowledge of their own side is often deficient. Second, circumstances often force them to work under the most intense pressures. When a crisis occurs, they have little time for reflection. As a result, they often focus on narrow issues without looking at large long-term choices; in other words, they will see some of the trees but miss the forest. Few can express their ideas in a logical or thorough fashion, either on paper or face to face. Most merely react to events, rather than mold them to their purpose. Like politics, strategy is the art of the possible; but few can discern what is possible. And neither history nor, consequently, strategy has ended with the end of the Cold War. Great storms bring not calm, but rather new struggles between rulers, states, alliances, peoples, and cultures.[191]

—On Strategy, in *The Making of Strategy*, Williamson Murry, et. al

Strategy and Grand Strategy

Strategy is not just tactics on the battlefield or even the movements of multiple army groups over large areas. To think more broadly about strategy, it is necessary to understand both strategy and grand strategy. Grand strategy is much broader than military strategy. In grand strategy, military action is just part of the larger picture, which includes economic, political, diplomatic, and social factors, as well as the overriding vision of the state or group involved. Carl Von Clausewitz is generally acknowledged as the greatest military thinker in the West. In his book *On War (Vom Kriege)*, Clausewitz said that "war is the continuation of policy by other means."[192] Military action is not an isolated act, but an expression and extension of the political purpose, and as such is a means to achieve political goals. In this sense it is utilitarian.[193] War is a political action, stemming from political motives, and has at its root a political object.[194]

Clausewitz and Sunzi are two of the most influential theorists on strategy, yet they present opposing paradigms. For Sunzi, war and strategy encompass a wide scope of perspectives and considerations, many of which are not military—diplomatic (alliances), economic, psychological, and political. Although Clausewitz sees war as an extension of political activity, he largely addresses strategy from a military viewpoint. Sunzi favors extensive use of deception and psychology to attack the opponent's center of gravity—his systems of alliances and his will to fight. If you disrupt the enemy's center of gravity, his ability to resist will collapse. For Clausewitz the opponent's center of gravity is his army and, like Napoleon, he advocates direct concentration of force to destroy the opponent's field army. Once the enemy's army is destroyed, collapse of the enemy's will follows.[195]

Julian Stafford Corbett, writing on naval strategy at the end of the nineteenth century, expanded on the ideas of Clausewitz. He felt that even after the enemy's army is destroyed, forcing the peace is still a difficult and separate task. The country of the enemy must feel the burdens of war with such weight that the desire for peace prevails.[196] Corbett states that even the great commander Napoleon Bonaparte often failed to grasp this point. Some of Corbett's ideas show remarkable congruence with the ideas of Sunzi. For example, Corbett felt that the key point in obtaining command of the sea, and by extension the battlefield, is to command the enemy's communications. By controlling communications and points of distribution, pressure can be exerted on the citizens and their *collective life*.[197]

More than one author has pointed out that the object of war (or conflict) is to attain a better peace. This new state of peace is hopefully better than that which existed before the conflict. Devising a strategy to achieve this aim often involves compromise and adaptation. No perfect strategy or plan exists that can fulfill this aim. The enemy or the competition are simultaneously doing their best to fulfill their aims and implement their strategy, so following a fixed, goal-oriented plan is not desirable. Rather than a plan, strategy is an expression of the aim, and linked to the overall purpose and context of the situation. This also means that strategy is linked to limitations that emanate from the various economic, political, social, and organizational structures.

Liddell Hart wisely points out that although some consider conflict and war to be contrary to reason, they do provide a means of deciding issues, by applying force when other methods fail. However, if one is going to engage in conflict, it must be controlled, particularly if one hopes to fulfill the object (a better peace) of engaging in the conflict in the first place. Hart lists five important strategic principles to be considered when engaging in conflict:

1. Fighting is a physical act, but one that is directed by the mind and will. The better the strategy, the less it will cost, as it will be easier to gain the upper hand.
2. The more strength one wastes, the greater the chance that things will turn against you. In that case, even if one is victorious, there will be less benefit from the peace that follows. This could be understood as reduced ability to capitalize on the opportunities that victory presents.
3. The more brutal one's methods, the more resistance one will encounter, and the more that resistance will harden, thereby strengthening the resolve of the opponent, and aligning and uniting the adversary's troops, people, and leadership in their opposition.
4. The more you try to impose a peace or resolution of your own making by force, the more resistance there will be.
5. If you achieve your aim, the more you demand of the defeated or outmaneuvered adversary, the more he will desire to reverse your success.[198]

Hart's five points seem simple, but their implication is profound. Strategy does not end with victory or defeat—they are in themselves nothing but another set of changing circumstances. Edward Luttwak's discussion of "culmination and reversal" echoes these ideas. Victory and defeat can reach the extreme and reverse. The "victorious" army, in extending itself into the enemy's territory, can overreach, creating a situation that weakens them, while prolonging the conflict and thereby paradoxically strengthening the "defeated."[199] Napoleon's invasion of Russia is an example of this phenomenon (see also Appendix III: Strategy 30—Reverse Positions of the Host and Guest). As the attacking army moves forward, it moves farther away from its line of supply, making it more difficult to protect communications, and leaving it more exposed to unknown terrain and weather for which it may be unprepared. The enemy's will to resist becomes stronger as the invading army penetrates farther into their homeland. The enemy may gather allies, or may bargain to buy time as they rebuild their forces.

One of the central concerns of Chinese strategists is that success itself often sows the seeds for the reversal of one's fortunes. For Clausewitz, the point of culmination and reversal are directly connected to the question of when to terminate the conflict.[200] "The superiority one has or gains in war is only the means and not the end; it must be risked for the sake of the end. But one must know the point to which it can be carried in order not to overshoot the target."[201] Michael Handel rightly observes that the "point of culmination" fluctuates, and is therefore difficult to identify with precision. The winner may think that his victory is a permanent condition, rather than something that needs to be constantly reevaluated.

> Suffering from what the Japanese call "the victory disease," the victor is typically intoxicated by his recent success. Those who have enjoyed military success, particularly in a war's early phases, are seldom in a frame of mind to entertain the notion that they could suffer a serious setback. By the time they realize the actual long-range direction of the relative power trends, they will already be in a weaker bargaining position.[202]

Both Clausewitz and Sunzi understood that a successful strategy looks beyond victory. Sunzi advocated taking the enemy state intact, so that its resources and military forces could augment one's own. "Treat prisoners of war kindly, and care for them. Use victory over the enemy to enhance your own strength."[203] In the Three Kingdoms period, both Cao Cao and Zhuge Liang punished troops who trampled the crops of the enemy's citizens or stole food from them, because they hoped to win the enemy populace and troops over to their side.

Clausewitz sees war as a rational decision aimed at attaining political goals. "Since war is not an act of senseless passion, but is controlled by its political object, the value of this object must determine the sacrifices to be made for it in magnitude and also in duration. Once the expenditure of effort exceeds the value of the political object, the object must be renounced and peace must follow."[204] For Clausewitz, there are many ways of achieving success: destroying the enemy's forces; taking over his territory; temporary invasion and/or occupation; achieving various immediate political objectives; or defense in the form of repelling enemy attacks. "Any one of these may be used to overcome the enemy's will: the choice depends on the circumstances."[205]

Wars can also be more minimal, for example threatening the enemy to facilitate negotiations.[206] Although the ancient Romans are often thought of as ruthless conquerors, the Roman Empire frequently employed the potential application of military force as a means of effecting political control. The conversion of both potential and former enemies into client states who protected the Empire's borders was effected through the threat of the Roman legions, and the promise of benefits and rewards. This freed Rome from having to station troops everywhere in the Empire.[207]

Professor Garrett Fagan reminds us that "the power of war to attract the discontented, destitute, and disenfranchised should not be underestimated."[208] The Greek historian of Rome, Polybius, wrote that Alexander the Great attacked Persians on the pretext of revenging Persian wrongs inflicted in earlier wars, but that the real cause was that Persians were weak and ripe for invasion.[209] The mere perception of weakness often invites attack, particularly if a state is rich. There will always be those who will attempt to take what they want, and success will create its own legitimacy and even approval. There is deterrence in the perception of strength, but it must be backed up by the willingness to act decisively.

> War, its objectives, and their attainment can be difficult things to assess. Perhaps this is why Sunzi starts *The Art of War* by saying: "War is a grave affair of the state; it is a place of life and death, a road to survival or extinction, a matter to be pondered carefully."[210]

Strategic Planning

To formulate a strategy, there must be information and intelligence covering all phases of its conception and implementation. This information must be subjected to some kind of analysis in order to create and implement plans. Thus, the decision-making process, and the structure and organization that surrounds this process, is critical to successfully implementing any strategy on any level. Strategic planning, however, has a wide context. Aside from political, diplomatic, economic, and military resources and objectives, other key factors must be considered. Geography, cultural factors and ideology, historical experience and conditioning, as well as organizational culture and structure all play important roles in the formulation of strategy. "Strategic thinking does not occur in a vacuum, or deal in perfect solutions; politics, ideology, and geography shape peculiar national strategic cultures. Those cultures in turn make it difficult for a state to evolve sensible and realistic approaches to the strategic problems that confront it."[211]

Israel's strategy has been dictated to a large degree by its borders with hostile nations and a lack of territorial depth with which to absorb attack and invasion. This has led to the development of a preemptive attack strategy, so that the conflict can be conducted outside of Israel's borders. At the same time, Israel's much smaller population in relation to the surrounding Arab states has led it to favor unconventional tactics that promise quick victories and avoid attrition.[212] In contrast, Russia's strategy during the Napoleonic Wars and in World War II largely relied on its ability to absorb attacks within its huge geographic area, and on the willingness to employ its large population in a war of attrition against invading armies.

Psychological and social factors also play an important role in the evolution of a strategy. The struggle for survival that the Jewish people have endured for centuries has generated an isolated self-reliance born of insecurity and a mistrust of both alliances and the peace process.[213] To some degree, the Israeli strategy has been based on the goal of simply existing, as a state surrounded by hostile powers. For this reason, shorter-term military objectives, often limited in scope, have often taken precedence over long-term strategic planning.

A different example can be gleaned from the chroniclers of the Norman knights of the eleventh and twelfth centuries, who ascribe Norman success in the conquest to a set of innate psychological characteristics, rather than advanced technology or strength.[214] The Normans, to some degree, deliberately cultivated an image of irrational brutality in order to foster terror and submission in their opponents. This, combined with their rugged mindset and prowess at arms, enabled them to achieve their immediate aims: gaining land, wealth, and title, in lands as far-flung as Sicily, Ireland, and, for a time, the Holy Lands of the Middle East. The Byzantine Emperor Alex I Comnenus and his subjects disliked the coarseness of the Normans, but also feared their unpredictable ruthless audacity. They quickly found that diplomacy and reason would not work in dealing with the marauding Normans. Anna Comnena, the daughter of the emperor, described the Norman Bohemond, Prince of Oranto, as having "a wit that was manifold and crafty and able to find a way of escape in every emergency. For in the whole of his body the entire man showed implacable and savage both in his size and glance, or so I believe, and even his laughter sounded like roaring. He was so made in mind and body that courage and passion reared their crests within him and both inclined to war."[215]

Although the Normans may have worn their *terribilita* like a garment,[216] they cannot compare with the ruthlessness of ancient Rome. Alvin Bernstein cites Rome as a successful example of how violence can acquire its own legitimacy as a strategy: "Only in the most unusual circumstances, did Rome *not* go to war."[217] The men that made foreign policy lived in a competitive warrior state where political advancement and public support came from success on the field of battle, thus it's no surprise that war was often the default setting in foreign policy. "Roman strategy provides the most vivid illustration of an instinct for the jugular. The Romans' unerring sense of the prerogatives of power stemmed from a pragmatic ruthlessness unencumbered by competing imperatives."[218]

Edward Luttwak suggests that this aspect of Roman strategic policy was calculated. Rome depended on its "client states" to help protect its borders. Client states, like Judea under Herod the Great, received various rewards and benefits for their services in protecting and helping rule the Empire. This allowed some of the legions to be stationed closer to home, able to provide a visible military presence that could cope with domestic unrest and serve as a reserve, to be sent where needed. The client states also helped to field the auxiliary troops (cavalry, engineers, skirmishers, and missile troops) that supported the heavy infantry of the Roman legions. The "armed suasion" represented by the *potential threat* of attack by the formidable Roman legions assuaged the need for Roman troops to be stationed all along the Empire's borders, and depended to some extent on a willingness to do battle and a demonstrated ruthlessness.[219]

Luttwak cites the siege of Masada in 70–73 AD as an example of such a policy of deterrence. He points out that the fortress, containing a few hundred Jewish rebels, was of no strategic importance and that the Romans could have starved the rebels out or stormed the fortress. Instead they chose to engage in a three-year siege involving costly and time-consuming works of engineering to build a ramp up the mountain. This sent a message to others that might consider rebellion: the Romans would not use half-measures to suppress insurrection.[220]

National pride, personal and societal prejudices, greed, misperception, fear, wishful thinking, and a hundred other human foibles are bound up in the implementation of strategy. The more clearly they can be observed and understood, the more clearly an effective strategy can be employed. Sunzi put it simply: "Know your enemy and know yourself and you can fight a hundred battles without peril."[221] The defensive strategy of Athens, advocated by Pericles during the Peloponnesian War, did not fully take into account the psychological impact it would have on the Athenian people. The standard method of resolving conflict among the Greek city states was a clash of phalanxes on the open plain. Because the Spartans were more likely to win this kind of encounter, Pericles advocated that the Athenians wait behind their long walls while their fleet, which was much stronger than that of the Spartans and their allies, raided the Peloponnesus. This meant that the Athenian people would have to endure insults without going forth to do battle, thereby violating the Greek ideals of heroism and bravery. Further, they would have to endure their homes, temples, and fields being ravaged by the invading Spartan armies. Pericles's strategy did not fully take into account the psychology of the Spartans, who perceived the Athenian strategy as a sign of weakness, and who were therefore not sufficiently deterred by raids along their coasts to end the war.[222]

Analysts of modern military and business culture are familiar with many of the problems inherent in organizational culture: its ability to kill new and innovative ideas, and its difficulty in responding appropriately in times of crisis. Organizations often produce a consistent pattern of thinking about goals, tasks, and human interactions. These institutional patterns of thought and logic in turn play an important role in whether change is embraced or rejected. "Changes that conflict with the dominant group's ideas on preferred roles and missions—the essence of the organization—will not be adopted. Leaders of the organization, conditioned by the culture they have absorbed through years of service in that organization, will prevent changes in the core mission or roles."[223] How an organization remembers the past—both past successes and failures, or even the perception itself that they were defeats or failures—will often define how the organization adapts to change. If the organization can only learn from the last past event, then it can never adapt to or anticipate change, and its intentions, predictions, plans will be ineffective. Nassim N. Taleb, author of *The Black Swan*, uses the analogy of a turkey. The turkey is well fed every day. Each feeding confirms its belief that the next day will be the same, and that humans are beneficent creatures. But then, on the day before Thanksgiving, suddenly, the unexpected happens.[224]

To escape the limitations of one's strategic culture is not easy; one must look at the larger pattern of events and the forces shaping them, and realize that they cannot be controlled by rigid plans and schemes. The unexpected will occur, and intentions, plans, and goals will then, to some degree, be shaped by events. Events that surround even what seems to be a single direct operation must be taken as a whole. According to General Rupert Smith, this requires information, intelligence, and an organizational framework that can make use of their potential. Information and context are essential, for without them there is a tendency to see each event as separate from the whole "and in so doing fail to realize that tactical success is leading to operational failure."[225]

Strategy operates on many levels at the same time: from technological measures and countermeasures, to tactical deployment and engagement on the battlefield, to operations involving multiple engagements, etc.—right up to the level of grand strategy, with its political economic and social dimensions. Edward Luttwak describes strategy as having five levels and two dimensions. Technological measures and countermeasures at the first level; move upward to engage with the tactical level of maneuver and counter-maneuver, the stratagems of the engagement, and of the battlefield. The operational and theater levels encompass an increasingly larger strategic scope that connects with grand strategy and its economic, social, and political considerations.[226] These five levels can be diagrammed as follows:

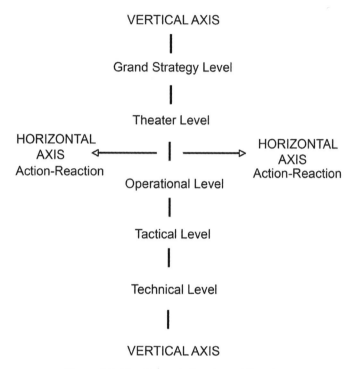

Figure 2.1. Five Strategic Levels and Two Axes

These different levels interact with one another, and on each level there is a dynamic logic of action and reaction unfolding. Action and reaction can also move between levels, as in a tactical response to an operational action. The levels themselves are "in agitated motion, sometimes to the point of breaking through into another level, just as in the dynamic reality of war the interactions of the vertical levels themselves combine and collide with the horizontal dimensions of strategy."[227] Grand strategy in Luttwak's analysis does not just occupy a place at the top of the hierarchy. It affects and is affected by what happens on all the other levels, as action and counteraction flow dynamically on and between each level. In a nation-state, grand strategy encompasses the political, economic, and diplomatic spheres and their interactions.

General Rupert Smith employs a similar hierarchical scheme, with four levels: political, strategic, theater, and tactical. Ideally, power and decision flow from the political level, so that the strategic level and political decisions are closely intertwined—the strategic level being defined as "an expression of the aim and its links to the overall purpose and the context of the conflict, together with the limitations on action that flow from that political purpose in the circumstances."[228] For Smith, the theater level is the link between the tactical level and the strategic and therefore the political level.[229] Smith, like Luttwack, recognizes that these levels interpenetrate and mutually influence one another. Even at the tactical level, success or failure can have consequences politically and diplomatically.

Smith implies that coherence among these levels allows the best chance of obtaining one's aims. At the same time, he recognizes that there can be no perfect strategy, particularly because the opponent is seeking to undermine this coherence. Luttwack rightly states that strategy, by its nature, is burdened with many difficulties that must be overcome in order to obtain positive outcomes. There will always be large uncertainties, unknowns, and unquantifiables in devising strategy and grand strategy. Success itself can be a problem, because it can allow errors to become systemized, allowing the small errors that initially did not prevent a positive outcome to become larger ones that do.[230]

Strategy and grand strategy are not just employed by states or opposing armies. In China it is said that "life is strategy." One might argue that in many of our daily interactions, we consciously or unconsciously engage in and employ strategy on all five levels. A potential street fight can begin with diplomatic overtures, bargaining, or leaving an opponent a face-saving exit, and throughout may employ deceptions. One can mask their strength, or project strength that may or may not exist. The "fight" itself, if and when it unfolds, may employ theater or operational strategies, such as planning coordinated attacks, or attempting to divide the opponent's strength or attention, and, at a tactical level, feints, withdrawals, advances, and attacks, or fleeing the field altogether to preserve oneself. At a technical level, different techniques are employed, and these may be adjusted in response to the opponent's techniques. At each of these levels, strategy moves horizontally as well. Each participant is gathering intelligence, using his senses to observe and analyze the opponent's capabilities, strengths, and weaknesses. This takes place on both conscious and unconscious levels. One must be aware of the environment, possible allies, potential allies of the opponent, the terrain, potential escape routes, etc. These kinds of considerations are not unique to warfare and hand-to hand combat—they are also employed daily in the marketplace by business entities of all types.

In talking about self-defense and survival on the street, Marc "Animal" MacYoung stresses awareness. Part of awareness is what in the military parlance would be called *information and intelligence.* For MacYoung, awareness means understanding the operating systems that shape people's behavior and intentions.

> Violence occurs for many reasons. In the scope of things, what is considered by most people as a "fight" is actually a very small portion of the violence that actually occurs. There is much more going on beneath the surface, that most people have no real concept about. What I've written about here is an overview of various operating systems that normally lead to violence. Learning about these other operating systems will keep you from being blindsided by them. If you learn how to read the different operating systems and how they affect people's behavior, you will be much safer.[231]

For MacYoung, an operating system is the accepted values by which a group governs itself. These values flow from cultural and ethnic background, family values, and personal values shaped by one's experiences. Each operating system has its own rules, some that are "deep surface," unwritten and unspoken, and some that are "surface," written and understood. Survival and effective application of strategy rely on being able to read, understand, and even mimic both the deep surface and surface rules.[232] This comes back to observation and awareness, which are as important on the street as they are in the conflicts of nations.

Luttwak finds that strategies that are successful, in general, harmoniously engage with both the vertical and horizontal dimensions of strategy. He gives numerous examples of disharmony and harmony in strategic engagement, which look beyond the immediate conflict to the larger long-term outcome.[233] One such example of strategic disharmony is Israel, whose initial military weakness and later military strength led it to focus on military consider-ations and solutions at the expense of political and diplomatic ones. Israeli success in military operations made the reliance on military solutions even more pronounced. Yet as Michael Handel points out, one could argue that the Egyptian–American initiative, which created a treaty between Israel and Egypt, helped Israel more than its previous victories had.[234]

In the same way, winning a street fight, if it leads to manslaughter or murder charges, may not be strategically sound, particularly if other solu-tions were possible. Although one can argue that being in jail is better than being dead (*Better to be judged by twelve than carried by six*, as the saying goes), focusing only on fighting ability and winning at all costs may prevent one from connecting with strategy on both the vertical and horizontal dimen-sions (diplomacy, escape, limited engagement, etc.), which might prevent the physical violence from occurring at all and lead to a better overall out-come. Sergeant Rory Miller, who teaches courses in police defensive tactics and confrontational simulations, sums this up neatly:

> Goals differ in different situations. Real violence is a very broad subject and no two encounters are the same. What is a "win" in one situation may not be in the next. The goal is how you define the win in that particular encounter. If the goal changes so does everything else. If you have only trained for one goal, you will be hampered when the goal is different.[235]

Systemization of strategy based upon prior success or institutional ori-entation has, in the past, often led to the inability to jettison ineffective strategic approaches. According to John Nagel, this was part of the problem for the United States in Vietnam. Even when the U.S. military attempted to evaluate its strategies for achieving its goals in Vietnam, the institutional culture prevented original and innovative thinking from taking place. *The "can do" attitude of the professional American military stifled prospective dissent and precluded more theoretical thinking.* This, combined with the fact that those doing the analysis were the same people who formulated the strategy, made it unlikely that that analysis would be free of prior assumptions. General Westmoreland was insulated from bad news by the institutional culture, thereby curtailing learning at the top levels of command.[236]

Similar institutional failures have plagued the planning and execution of the 2003 War in Iraq and its aftermath. America failed to learn from the mistakes made by the British occupation of Iraq in 1917–1920. The same insular command structure and refusal to change the paradigm that occurred in Vietnam also operated in Iraq. The Bush administration and the architects of the war and occupation often ignored events and information that did not fit in with their analysis of the situation. Military officers and others that disagreed with the administration or warned of difficulties were ignored, discredited, or dismissed. By not correctly assessing the actual situation, as opposed to the perceived situation, by not understanding the nature of the people and culture they were interacting with, and by not correctly and continuously matching and shaping strategy and tactics to the actual rather than the perceived situation, both the Americans and the British set themselves up for failure in Iraq:

- The British saw themselves as liberators when they arrived in Iraq, but in a few years had a major revolt on their hands. American forces expected to be welcomed by the Iraqi people, and to some degree they were, but it did not take long for resistance to their occupation to begin.
- The Iraqis doubted the stated intention of the British, to implement self-rule. The Americans have had similar problems. Courting local leaders who were seen as puppets was a problem for both.
- Like the British, the Americans opted to use air power and heavy weaponry, which caused many civilian casualties and collateral damage, thereby hardening resistance.
- Iraq's large population, containing many men with military training, made it difficult to identify insurgents; and its extensive borders made the country very difficult to control and police.
- British troops were isolated, with communications cut off and conveys attacked, just as the American troops had been isolated and confined to the Green Zone.
- Military officers and others that disagreed with the administration or warned of difficulties were ignored, discredited, or dismissed.
- Britain eventually quelled the rebellion, but British troops remained in Iraq until 1952.

Vietnam and Iraq are examples of a weaker force either defeating or confounding a stronger force. Power and force matter. In a conflict in which there is a vast disparity of power between the two sides, one would expect the stronger side to win. However, in analyzing conflicts occurring from 1816 to the present, Ivan Arreguin-Toft has noticed that not only does the weaker side win more often than it should, but the stronger side has been losing *more and more* over time.[237] Arreguin-Toft argues that although power matters, as do the nature of the strong and weak players themselves, it is the interaction of the strategies the players use that predicts the outcome:

> If we think of strategies as complex but discrete plans of action which include assumptions about the values of objectives, as well as tactical and leadership principles and rules of engagement, different interactions should yield systematically different outcomes independent of the relative power of the actors involved. . . . [F]or purposes of theory building, the universe of real actor strategies—blitzkrieg, attrition, defense in depth, guerrilla warfare, terrorism, and so on—can be reduced to two ideal type approaches: direct and indirect. My central thesis is that when actors employ similar strategic approaches (direct-direct or indirect-indirect) relative power explains the outcome: strong actors will win quickly and decisively. When actors employ opposite strategic approaches (direct-indirect or indirect-direct) weak actors are much more likely to win, even when everything we think we know about power says they shouldn't.[238]

These strategic approaches are similar to the ideas of qi and zheng, taking place at all levels, from technological measures and countermeasures up to political and diplomatic levels of interaction. Chinese strategists therefore advocate a similar approach when strong and weak actors come into conflict. When confronted by a much stronger enemy, Sunzi advises one to retreat, thereby eluding the enemy. Sun Bin echoes this advice: "Avoid contact so as to make the enemy swollen-headed, entice the enemy so that he gets tired out and then attack him unexpectedly, catching him unprepared. Hence, it is necessary here to fight a protracted battle."[239] Mao Zedong described this as seizing the initiative through appropriate dispersion and concentration of forces, so that the enemy's weak points can be found and exploited (see Chapter I). Sunzi clearly understood that this kind of strategic planning and action must take place at many levels. He advocates attacking the enemy's plans rather than his armies, thereby disrupting his ability to use his power to his advantage: "Thus the best policy in war is to thwart the enemy's strategy. The second best is to disrupt his alliances through diplomatic means. The third best is to attack his army in the field. The worst policy of all is to attack walled cities (i.e.: his strong points]."[240]

In Malcom Gladwell's fascinating article on basketball, underdogs, and strategy, he describes the strategy of Rick Pitino, who has coached numerous college teams to basketball championships. Pitino employs an unrelenting full-court press against teams with better players and wins. Rather than retreating to set up a defense around the basket that allows the more skilled players on the other team to use their skill in shooting, dribbling, and play-making, Pitino's team denies them the use of their skills through a disruptive strategy that focuses on stealing the ball and upsetting their rhythm of play. The other teams, steeped in conventional tactics, cannot adapt, and in losing their tempo of play make even more mistakes. Pitino has shown that a stronger team with better players will often lose to a team who uses the opposite strategy and refuses to interact in the conventional way. Although the stronger team could also in theory play the unconventional game, the reality is that they are neither psychologically nor physically prepared to do so. Instead, they fall back on the more conventional game.[241] This is not only true on the basketball court. The conditioning and training of modern conventional military forces makes them susceptible to insurgent forces who refuse to pit strength against strength. Such conventional forces do not have an impressive record in defeating insurgents who are determined. Recent "small wars" around the world have shown that conventional military supremacy has limited utility against unconventional threats.[242]

Retired soldiers and military theorists Williamson Murray and Mark Grimsley neatly summarize the difficulties involved in strategic planning: "Strategy is a process, a constant adaptation to shifting conditions and circumstances in a world where chance, uncertainty, and ambiguity dominate. Moreover, it is a world where actions, intentions, and purposes of other participants remain shadowy and indistinct, taxing the wisdom and intuition of the canniest policymaker."[243]

Strategic Plans Disrupted: Friction

Perhaps part of the fascination with military history is the uncertainty of any military enterprise. Most of our analysis of battles and strategy is in hindsight. Hindsight allows us to impose a rational cause and effect structure to past events. Yet the fog of war is vast, and the number of elements involved in even a fairly limited conflict are too many to easily categorize. The best-laid plans often go awry on the battlefield.

After the defeat of the Army of the Potomac at Gaines Mill, George McClellan, the commander of the federal forces, pulled his troops back toward James River. Robert E. Lee had good intelligence as to Union troop movements and hoped to hit the Union troops from different directions while they were pulling back. He created a complex plan in which seven Confederate divisions would converge along six different routes near the village of Glendale. The first, Huger's division, quickly became stuck in the woods through which they had been instructed to advance and wasted time cutting a road through the dense brush. Holmes, marching along the unobstructed River Road, encountered federal troops who, warned of his advance by the clouds of dust raised by his troops, subjected his men to fierce artillery bombardment, thereby stopping their advance. Magruder was ill, which perhaps affected his judgment, but his march also took longer than planned because of the lack of guides. This, combined with confused orders, exhausted both Magruder and his men. Meanwhile, Jackson was bogged down in White Oak Swamp, attempting to rebuild a destroyed bridge, while ignoring subordinates' suggestions that he ford the river. As a result, only Longstreet and A. P. Hill were able to get their divisions into action, fighting a fierce battle that gained them little advantage.[244]

The famous Western military theorist Carl von Clausewitz referred to this tendency for ideal plans to fail as "friction." "Everything is very simple in War, but the simplest thing is difficult."[245] For Clausewitz it is friction, the occurrence of small, but significant, yet unexpected or uncontrollable events, that distinguishes real war from war on paper. He gives as an example the unpredictability of weather. "Here fog prevents the enemy from being discovered in time, a battery from firing at the right moment, a report from reaching the General; there the rain prevents a battalion from arriving at the right time, because instead of for three, it had to march perhaps eight hours; the cavalry from charging effectively because it is stuck fast in heavy ground."[246] The well-known proverb "For Want of a Nail" describes friction in a nutshell:

> *For want of a nail the shoe was lost.*
> *For want of a shoe the horse was lost.*
> *For want of a horse the rider was lost.*
> *For want of a rider the battle was lost.*
> *For want of a battle the kingdom was lost.*
> *And all for the want of a horseshoe nail.*

How does one prepare for the unexpected, which is always inevitable? General Rupert Smith points out that "the profession of arms, as the pursuit of soldiering and the command is rightly called, is practiced by few men on few occasions. Most of the time soldiers, sailors, and airmen of whatever rank are preparing for the event; they are in and out of the profession, but not in practice or action. The result of this lack of practice is that commanders must learn from the past by studying previous campaigns and the decisions of the commanders at the time."[247] Although this is standard practice among military academies the world over, it is but a part of the picture. No matter how many battles one studies, no matter how many potential situations the martial artist trains for, no matter how expert one becomes, there is always the possibility of being caught in a situation for which one is not prepared. MacGregor Knox reminds us that ultimately individuals make and implement strategy and thus strategy is subject to their individual *ambitions, vanities, and quirks.* Even simple strategic decisions are subject to personal or organizational intrigues, conflicts, and ideologies.[248]

Mao Zedong viewed the uncertainty of war as being relative rather than absolute, "a factor that can be controlled and even exploited to one's advantage through meticulous planning."[249] The information we have about the enemy, the signs we see and trends that can be read in their behavior can form the basis for relatively objective planning or a general calculation. Mao acknowledged that plans will change, but felt it essential to have a long-term plan that is flexible as opposed to planning only one step at a time. Part of effective planning is the willingness to change plans frequently in accordance with circumstances.[250] "Planning must change with the movement (flow or change) of the war and vary in degree according to the scale of the war."[251] Nassim Nicholas Taleb adds that the problem with plans or models is that it is easy to view the world from inside the model. Unexpected developments lie outside the model and are therefore not accounted for. In fact, we don't know where to look for them, because events have a way of blindsiding even the best forecasters. "We cannot truly plan, because we do not understand the future—but that is not necessarily bad news. We could plan while bearing in mind such limitations. It just takes guts."[252]

In 2000, the United States Joint Forces Command ran an extensive war game that employed highly realistic simulations involving hundreds of military experts and analysts. United States forces ("Blue Team") were pitted against a "rogue state" ("Red Team"). Blue Team had highly sophisticated satellite intelligence, sensors and computers that allowed them to control the flow of information, disrupt Red Team's communications, shut down their power grids, and even politically influence Red Team's imaginary state. Red Team, deprived of modern technology, resorted to more primitive courier-based communications and used light signals to guide aircraft rather than sophisticated electronic tracking systems that could be monitored and rendered inoperable. Blue Team assumed that their technological advantage would make Red Team's strategic planning transparent and impossible to implement, giving them the ability to initiate and control the action. However, the reverse occurred. Employing a loose chain of command, Red Team made decisions on the ground. Red Team employed more "primitive" technologies that could not be easily monitored, or interdicted electronically, thereby negating Blue Team's advantage, and instead, disrupting *their* plans and expectations. Rather than lifting the "fog of war," Blue Team's advanced technologies made them susceptible to surprise attacks and preemptive strikes. They did not know what the enemy was thinking or where he would strike next.[253]

The Chinese Way of Strategy and the Ba Gua

Sunzi passed on the following maxim: "A victorious army will not engage the enemy unless it is assured of the necessary conditions for victory, whereas an army destined for defeat rushes into battle in the hope that it will win by luck. The skilled warrior seeks victory by cultivating the Way and strengthens the rules and regulations and in so doing gains the initiative over his enemy."[254] Chinese strategists like Sunzi focus on two key concepts: *xing,* the situation or configuration, and *shi,* the potential implied by and emanating from that configuration.[255] The aim is to seek a strategic advantage that arises from one's ability to conform with the propensity inherent in a given situation. This propensity and the ability to move with it creates such an advantage that the battle itself is merely a continuation of an ongoing policy of taking advantage of developing events and circumstances, a policy that results in dislocation and disruption of the opponent's intentions and internal cohesion. Thus, the battle is not won by luck, but is decided before it begins.

> In consequence, Chinese military strategy is not affected by the theory-practice relationship. By the same token it also avoids the inevitable inferiority ascribed to practice as opposed to theory, which has hitherto crippled Western theory, that of Clausewitz included. In short, it does not have to cope with "friction," since, whereas friction is a threat to any plans drawn up in advance, adventitious circumstances are themselves precisely what make it possible for the implied potential to come about and deploy itself.[256]

Looked at in this way, strategy avoids the pitfalls of systemization and is much more than making plans. Plans and goal-setting are specific ways of getting from point A to point B. Rather than defining strategy, they stem from it. Strategy is then linked to intention and observation. Colonel John Boyd defines strategy as "a mental tapestry of changing intentions for harmonizing and focusing our efforts as a basis for realizing some aim or purpose in an unfolding and often unforeseen world of many bewildering events and changing intentions and many contending interests."[257] On the level of grand strategy, Boyd sees grand strategy as a vision so attractive and so imbued with a clarity of consciousness that the opposition is undermined while others are attracted, thereby strengthening the scope and strength of the vision; so that "it acts as a catalyst or beacon around which to evolve those qualities that permit a collective entity or organic whole to improve its stature in the scheme of things."[258]

This much larger view of grand strategy can be applied to anything: to military actions, to social conflict, to business, or to one's own life. What are the elements of this "tapestry of intentions" and how can they be applied in order to focus our efforts and realize our aims? Chinese strategists would agree with Boyd's ideas, but they lay greater stress on a key element: following the principle of the natural order of things (the Dao or Way) allows one to shift back and forth between things as they come into being, and the propensity they simultaneously emanate for the next coming into being.[259]

In the yin and yang polarity implied in the concepts of xing and shi there is constant shift or oscillation, back and forth between two complementary, but opposite, poles, creating endless alternations of change. These patterns of change are a key focus in Chinese philosophy, as exemplified in The Book of Changes or *Yijing*. The *Yijing* employs eight archetypes, the eight diagrams or trigrams *(ba gua)*, as a way of understanding the manifold phenomena of existence and their intertransformation and interpenetration. These diagrams are composed of broken (yin) lines and solid (yang) lines. Each force or principle is given a symbolic name, which has various connotations:

QIAN DIAGRAM
Name: The Creative
Image: Heaven
Nature: Creativity; Strength; Vigor
Trigram: Qian is Three Links (Qian San Lian)

KUN DIAGRAM
Name: The Receptive
Image: Earth
Nature: Yielding; Receptivity
Trigram: Kun is Separated into Six Sections (Kun Liu Duan)

ZHEN DIAGRAM
Name: The Arousing
Image: Thunder
Nature: Exciting; Arousing; Emerging; Renewal
Trigram: Zhen is an Upturned Jar (Zhen Yang Yu)

GEN DIAGRAM
Name: Keeping Still
Image: Mountain
Nature: Immovable; Stillness
Trigram: Gen is a Toppled Bowl (Gen Fu Wan)

LI DIAGRAM
Name: The Clinging
Image: Fire
Nature: Attachment; Cohesion
Trigram: Li is Empty in the Middle (Li Zhong Xu)

KAN DIAGRAM
Name: The Abysmal
Image: Water
Nature: Enveloping; Adaptable
Trigram: Kan is Full in the Middle (Kan Zhong Man)

DUI DIAGRAM
Name: The Joyous
Image: Lake
Nature: Joy; Pleasure
Trigram: Dui Lacks in the Top (Dui Shang Que)

XUN DIAGRAM
Name: The Gentle
Image: Wind; Wood
Nature: Penetrating; Pliable
Trigram: Xun is Broken in the Bottom (Xun Xia Duan)

Interactions of the Eight Trigrams

Fu Xi, one of the great sages of the Chinese people, who is also credited
with having invented ideographic writing, is said to have seen the pattern
of the Ba Gua (eight trigrams) on the back of a turtle, and then organized it
in a way that was beneficial to mankind. The Ba Gua of Fu Xi shows eight
fundamental or primal forces that govern life. Each of these fundamental
forces reveal the polar (yin-yang) nature of the universe. The highest principle was identified with light, the force of Heaven, the creative principle

of the universe associated with the heavens. It pairs with Earth, which is associated with darkness, receptivity, and form. Therefore, the primary vertical axis is composed of these positive and negative poles:

- Qian-Heaven–Pure Yang gives things a sovereign.
- Kun-Earth–Pure Yin harbors/holds them.

  "The nature of Qian is vigor, like the ever changing scenes of the firmament. Its time is the passing of autumn into winter. Qian also represents heaven."[260]

  "The nature of Kun is submission. It is like the earth supporting the firmament. Its time is the passing of summer into autumn. Kun also represents earth."[261]

Heaven
(Qian)

Earth
(Kun)

Figure 2.2. Heaven and Earth (Qian and Kun)

The first two trigrams express the polarity of yin and yang. Qian—The Creative (Heaven) is the first trigram, composed of three solid lines. Kun—The Receptive (Earth) is the second trigram, composed of three broken lines. Heaven 天 *(tian)* in Chinese culture refers to a natural operating system, an overarching organic system that governs everything and is all-encompassing. Hence it has a capacity for creativity and action. Earth is receptive, it responds to the creative force of Heaven, bringing to completion Heaven's initiating force.

The second axis expresses the principles of Qian and Kun on the horizontal terrestrial plane:

- Rain-Kan-Water moistens things.
- Fire-Li dries them.

> "The nature of Kan is sinking, like creatures going into hibernation in winter. Kan also represents water."[262]

> "The nature of Li is attachment. It is like fire which can only consume in the presence of substance. Its time is summer. Li also represents fire."[263]

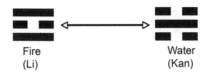

Fire
(Li)

Water
(Kan)

Figure 2.3. Fire and Water (Li and Kan)

Fire is a bright and moving, burning substance that is able to produce light. It is associated with the sun. Water is dark, cold, and heavy, but able to absorb light and warmth. It is associated with the moon. Fire burns upward toward the heavens, water flows downward towards the lowest point on the earth. The yin lines on the outside of the Water trigram indicate formlessness and pliability, with strength within. The yang lines on the outside of the Fire trigram show power on the outside, while the yin line in the center represents pliability and softness within, the quality that allows fire to cling to what it burns.

The fundamental principles described on these two planes give rise to other observable forces, which require their own symbols to be understood.

- Zhen-Thunder causes things to move.
- Xun-Wind disperses them.

> "The nature of Zhen is movement. It is like thunderbolts in spring, and the stirrings of life in spring. Zhen also represents thunder."[264]

> "The nature of Xun is going into [penetrating]. It is like the wind carrying a kite into the sky. It depicts life thriving and its time is the passing of spring into summer. Xun also represents wind."[265]

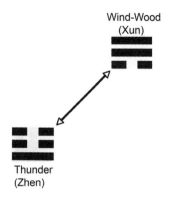

Figure 2.4. Thunder and Wind-Wood (Zhen and Xun)

Thunder represents the arousal and sudden release of powerful invisible energies. The energy of the first yang line is released and moves unobstructed through the yin lines. Lightning and thunder are representative of this sudden release, but Zhen can also refer to the life forces that animate living things, released at the moment of creation, or the creative spark of an idea. This is Heaven-related movement. Wind shows powerful movement that is Earth-related. Wind penetrates in the sense that Wind touches everything on the Earth. Wind's broken first line reflects the idea that wind can be felt, but not seen. It fills the space, yet is immaterial.

Xun is also associated with Wood. Thunder and wind produce rain, which nourishes the plants and trees that come out of the Earth and grow. There is a dual association of Xun with Wind and Wood, because they are both Earth-related movements that push forward slowly, but continuously and powerfully. The tree with its spreading roots and branches grows steadily, just as wind spreads and penetrates. This slow but steady motion is in contrast to the sudden explosive movement of Thunder (Zhen).

The final axis is that of Dui (Lake) and Gen (Mountain):

- Gen-Mountain restrains/stops things.
- Dui-Lake-Joy makes them happy.

   "The nature of Dui is delight, like the ripening of things. Its time is autumn. Dui represents marsh [lake]."[266]

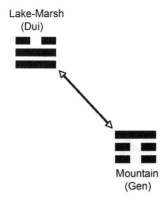

Figure 2.5. Lake and Mountain (Dui and Gen)

"The nature of Gen is stopping. Its time is the passing of winter into spring. Gen also represents mountain, which is immovable."[267]

The Mountain represents solidity, and the yin energy of Earth. The two broken lines of the trigram show Earth reaching its zenith or its limit at the heavens. The strong yang line at the top reflects the yang upward lifting energy of the mountains that is rooted in the earth, itself represented by the two broken lines. The Mountain also represents restraint, movement stopping at the top yang line. Lake represents transparency, reflection, lightness, and volatility. The lake can reflect both the Mountain and the light of Heaven. The broken line at the top of Dui represents the ability of the surface of the water to move or transform, for example to be blown by the wind, or to evaporate and transform into mist or clouds, which can cause rain to fall on the mountains. Mountain and lake can also represent human interaction. The Mountain is solitary, aloof, and restrained, while the Lake represents gathering together, the delight and joy of human interaction.[268]

In Wang Bi's commentary on the *Yijing*, written in the third century, he describes the numinous qualities of the trigrams as follows:

Of things that make the myriad things move, none is swifter than Thunder. Of things that make the myriad things bend, none is swifter than Wind. Of things that make the myriad things dry, none is a better drying agent than Fire. Of things that make the myriad things rejoice, none is more joy giving than the Lake. Of things that moisten the myriad things, none is more effective than Water. Of things that provide the myriad things with ends and beginnings, none is more resourceful than Restraint [Mountain]. That is why Water and Fire drive each other on, why Thunder and Wind do not work against each other, and why Mountain and Lake reciprocally circulate.[269]

From Wang Bi's description, it is clear that Fu Xi's diagram (below) is not a static state. The trigrams reflect forces, activities, or states of being that continuously interact and inter-transform. Change and movement in Fu Xi's diagram arise out of the tension between polar opposites.

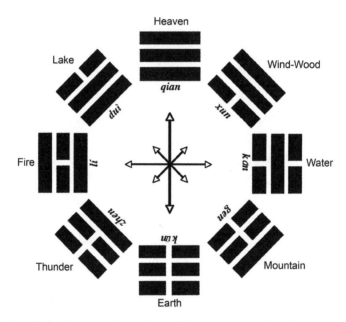

Figure 2.6. Eight Trigrams: Oppositional/Complimentary (Fu Xi) Arrangement

King Wen (1171–1122 BC) is credited with rearranging the trigrams to more clearly reflect the passage of time and human beings' temporal sense of the changes in heaven and earth. Here, rather than primordial opposing forces, the passage of time through the seasons and through one's lifetime is reflected. In King Wen's diagram, the top is represented by Li (Fire), which is associated with summer and the South, while the bottom is the North, associated with winter and the Kan trigram (Water). Zhen (Thunder) is in the East and is associated with spring thunderstorms and new growth. Wind in the Southeast represents the fullness of spring, while Earth in the Southwest is the early fall, when growing things reach their peak just before the harvest. Dui in the West is the gathering that takes place in the harvest, and Heaven in the North is associated with early winter and represents striving, the power of transition that drives all things. Mountain is the stillness and consolidation of the Earth's energies that takes place in late winter before the new spring.

- All things are said to come forth in Zhen-Thunder, which lies in the East where the sun rises.
- They are set in order in the Southeast in Xun-Wind, which arranges and is compliant.
- In Li-Fire they become manifest, they are visible. Li is in the South.
- In Kun-Earth all things are nourished and supported. Kun is in the Southwest.
- Dui-Lake is in the West in Autumn. Dui is associated with the harvest, when all things rejoice.

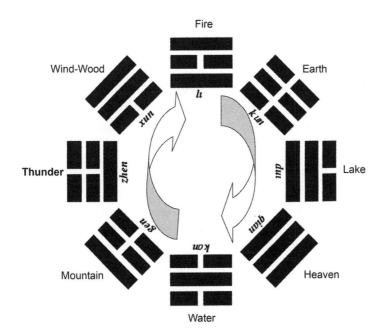

Figure 2.7. Eight Trigrams: Cyclical/Temporal (King Wen) Arrangement

- Striving is in the Northwest, associated with Qian-Heaven, in which things interact or exert pressure upon one another.
- Kan-Water is in the North. It is the trigram of toil and labor.
- Gen-Mountain is stopping and restraint. It is in the Northeast. All things find completion or ending here, but it is also the place of starting and beginning.[270]

The Eight Dispositions or Eight Intentions

The *Yijing* archetypes, their associated trigrams, and their role in symbolizing and embodying the dynamic of change and its potential, articulate eight intentions or dispositions that manifest effective strategy. In examining each of the Eight Intentions/Dispositions, it must be remembered that they are not separate entities, but operate (as in the diagrams above) as a dynamic system of change and potential that simultaneously oscillates back and forth and endlessly cycles.

Figure 2.8. Cyclical (Post Heaven) Ba Gua Yin Yang Diagram

1

Qian-Heaven

Disposition of Heaven (Qian)

- Three Strong Lines: Firmness and Strength
- Strong Force that Penetrates or Pushes Apart Anything in its Way
- Moving Forward and Upward
- Expanding Outward
- Intention
- Intention Leading to Formulation of Goals
- Progress/Advancing Force
- Creative Force
- The Yang/Dynamic Aspect of the Will
- Assertion

The attitude of Heaven represents the intention and strength of will to move forward and progress. The three strong lines irresistibly move forward and upward.

In Strategy: Heaven is the operating principle, the grand strategy, the active intention that forms the basis of the overall vision.

In Ba Gua Zhang: Heaven represents power that moves upward and outward. Heaven's movement is effortless and unceasing.

2

Kun-Earth

Disposition of Earth (Kun)

- Receptivity
- Repose
- Responding
- Devoted
- Yielding
- Sheltering
- Nourishing
- Drawing/Contracting Inward
- Receptive Response to the Ideas and Events as they Unfold
- The Yin-Receptive Aspect of the Will
- The Concrete Actualization of Heaven's Plan

Earth responds to heaven's pattern, yielding to and cultivating Heaven's will so that it can become manifest. The yin lines yield, absorbing and drawing inward.

In Strategy: Earth is the physical sustaining of Heaven's creative intention; the will to nourish, develop, and respond to the vision as it unfolds. Earth is the plan/intention made manifest. It is also the terrain (both geographic and conceptual) upon which the plan/intention will be carried out.

In Ba Gua Zhang: Earth absorbs and receives, drawing power inward and downward. Earth's power embraces and holds, in contrast to Heaven's expansive outward/upward movement.

3

Disposition of Thunder (Zhen)

Zhen-Thunder

- Arousing
- Instigating; Stimulating
- Shock
- Renewal
- Beginning; Emergence
- Newness
- Sudden Movement
- Movement in a New Direction (dual movement of Thunder up and down)
- New Ideas, Improvement, and Innovation
- New Thinking, New Methods
- Creativity Manifested; Creative Breakthroughs
- Yang; Exciting

Thunder is the beginning of new movement and/or taking new directions; the creative force manifest in movement and action. The single yang line is unobstructed, moving upward and outward, or even in multiple directions between the yin lines.

In Strategy: Thunder is movement and shock. The ability to meet and respond to challenges. Thunder is the initiation of movement. It is maneuver, mobility, and unpredictability, which can surprise and shock the opposition.

In Ba Gua Zhang: Thunder is characterized by shocking force manifesting suddenly and unexpectedly. Thunder represents shock power *(fa jin)*, which explodes and vibrates outward. Thunder can move in multiple directions. In Ba Gua Zhang this refers to the unpredictability of the movements and the forces employed.

4

Gen-Mountain

Disposition of Mountain (Gen)

- Stopping
- Stillness; Inner Stillness
- Withdrawal/Non-interaction
- Waiting
- Grounded
- Immovable
- Solid
- Restraint
- Control
- Reliable
- Humility
- Tolerance

The Mountain represents stillness and solidity, restrained movement waiting to resume, and the reining in of that which is going too far. The strong line at the top stops or restrains forward and upward movement.

In Strategy: Mountain represents positioning and knowledge of the terrain. Thunder initiates movement, and Mountain is the cessation or restraining of movement. Knowing when to advance and when to be still is critical. Holding position, grounded and immovable—waiting—is as important as movement. Each is the corollary of the other.

In Ba Gua Zhang: The Mountain represents stability, stillness, and rootedness. Within action there is internal stillness, within movement there is rootedness. The image of the Mountain conveys the ability to withstand attack and to wait for the right moment to move. The Mountain also tactically represents the idea of displacing the opponent's root and center with one's own.

5

Disposition of Wind/Wood (Xun)

Xun-Wind/Wood

- Persistent and Penetrating Softness: Though Soft and Invisible, Wind Can Create Effects that Endure.
- Wind Moves from High to Low Pressure: Allowing it to Permeate, Insinuate, and Penetrate Everywhere and in All Directions
- Penetrating Yet Soft (Wind Moves Through, but Does Not Harm the Rooted Grass)
- Compliance
- Pliability
- Sensing
- Intuition
- Penetration of Mind and Consciousness
- Wind's Penetration and Movement Drives Away Clouds
- Receptiveness of Faculty and Assimilation
- Too Much Penetration Creates Indecision: A Thousand Doubts and Considerations Can Arise

Wind spreads outward in all directions, penetrating and insinuating itself everywhere, touching everything, assimilating everything. It is soft and pliable, as is wood, which bends with the Wind. The bottom yin line is soft, representing force softened by compliance, receptivity, and pliability.

In Strategy: Wind represents far-seeing, anticipating based on information. Wind's penetrating quality reaches into things to understand their nature. The attitude of Wind represents the gathering knowledge and information and the use of spies. Controlling the flow of information, guarding it and disseminating it at the proper time, controls expectations and helps inform one's actions.

In Ba Gua Zhang: Wind is compliant and soft, but like water it penetrates into the smallest cracks. It can be gentle yet inexorable, moving softly yet continuously. Wind spirals and swirls constantly and is swift and unpredictable. Manifesting as wood, it is like bamboo, pliable and bending, yet strong and firm at the same time.

6

Dui-Lake

Disposition of Lake (Dui)

- Serenity of the Mirror-like Lake
- Reflects Light—Yet Depths are Dark-Mysterious
- Motion in Stillness: Water Sinking Downward, Yet Evaporating Upward
- Self-Reflection: Reflective Inner Knowledge
- Joyous and Attractive, but with Mysterious Depths
- Inner Strength
- Contentment
- Supple on Top and Strong Below

The Lake embodies the stillness and hidden depth of self-reflection and inner knowledge. Its attractiveness is a manifestation of inner joy. Its mirror-like surface is serene yet can reflect unseen forces moving across it, because the yin line is malleable and changeable. The yang lines move upward and interact gently with the outside via the yin line at the top.

In Strategy: Lake represents internal reflection on events and information and the sensitivity necessary for leadership. It also represents contentment and joy in one's intentions, dispositions, and interactions.

In Ba Gua Zhang: The Lake is placid and soft on the surface but strength and depth lie within. When Wind whips and agitates the surface of a lake, it can transform and change unpredictably, while strength and power are exerted from below.

7

Kan-Water

Disposition of Water (Kan)

- Water Moves Downward
- Fluidity of Movement
- Tumbling, Spiraling, Flowing Movement
- Adaptability
- Formless
- Seeks the Path of Least Resistance
- Moving Water: Rain, Storms, Streams, and Rivers
- Dark
- Deep
- Cold
- Dangerous: The Abyss
- Deceptive
- Outwardly Soft and Strong Within

Water moves following the path of least resistance, conforming to the ground it runs over and through; tumbling, spiraling and flowing around obstructions and seeping into gaps and fissures. It is formless, but takes on the shape of its container; it is deceptive and dangerous in its unpredictability and infinitely adaptable and malleable. The yin lines on the outside represent water's soft adaptability, while the central yang line indicates hidden force and strength.

In Strategy: Water represents adaptability; the ability to change plans, movements, and intentions according to changing circumstances. It seeks the path of least resistance. Water is flowing and unpredictable and therefore can be dangerous. Water also represents deception, the ability to take on form according to the situation.

In Ba Gua Zhang: Water, like wind, can enter any space, leaking around obstructions. It is soft and formless; it tumbles and spirals, while taking the path of least resistance. When concentrated, Water has the power and weight of a rushing river or a breaking wave.

8

Li-Fire

Disposition of Fire (Li)

- Light; Bright
- Warmth
- Depth of Feeling
- Clarity of Consciousness; Psychic Awareness
- Insight
- Revealing; Revelation
- Lightning
- Movement that can be Sudden and Unpredictable
- Lateral Thinking
- Clinging: Fire Clings to and Coils its Nourishment (Its Fuel)
- Attachment
- Cohesion
- Pliant Within and Resolute Without

Fire represents the warmth of the heart and the clarity of consciousness; the awareness and flash of insight that stems from the heart's perception. This is the cohesive force that draws us together as human beings, and attaches us to other living beings. Fire clings to and consumes what fuels it. It burns upward, shedding light that clears away darkness. It moves laterally and can burst upward, changing erratically.

In Strategy: Fire represents the ability of the heart to discern the truth and the connection of the heart and mind in insight and reasoning; the ability to see through the fog of confusion to perceive what is hidden. Wind's penetration clears away the clouds of confusion by gathering information and intelligence, but Fire is the discerning insight that can understand what is hidden. Fire also represents the quality of leadership, which draws people together like a guiding light.

In Ba Gua Zhang: Fire attaches and clings like a flame, adhering and coiling around the opponent. It can also burst or flare upward suddenly and with great force.

Another way to look at these eight dispositions is to divide them into four inner and four outer dispositions:

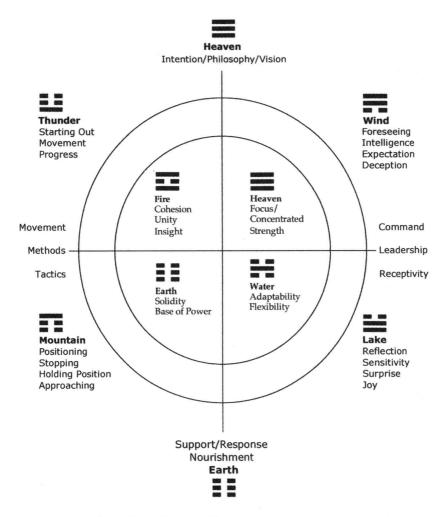

Figure 2.9. Eight Dispositions and Strategy: Inner and Outer Dispositions

Liddell Hart summarizes eight axioms that condense the fundamental essence of operational strategy and tactics into a brief and practical list.[271] It is easy to make a correspondence between this list and the Eight Dispositions:

1. Adjust Your End to the Means: **Lake**
2. Keep Your Object Always in Mind: **Heaven**
3. Choose the Line of Least Expectation: **Wind**
4. Exploit the Line of Least Resistance: **Water**
5. Take a Line of Operation Which Offers Multiple Objectives: **Thunder**
6. Assure That Both Plan and the Dispositions are Flexible—Adaptable to Circumstances: **Fire**
7. Do Not Throw Your Weight Into a Stroke Whilst Your Opponent is on Guard: **Earth**
8. Do not Renew an Attack along the Same Line (or in the Same Form) After it Has Once Failed: **Mountain**

Phillip Bobbitt asserts that the great powers of the twenty-first century will repeatedly face five questions regarding the use of force that cannot be characterized in the "zero-sum, conflictual way of strategic warfare."[272] Here again, correspondence with the Eight Dispositions can be useful in expanding one's understanding.

1. Whether to intervene? **Heaven** and **Mountain**
2. When to do so? **Thunder** and **Water**
3. With what allies? **Fire**
4. With what military and non-military tools? **Wind** and **Lake**
5. For what goals? **Heaven** and **Earth**

For General Rupert Smith, the questions regarding application of force in a confrontation are very similar. Drawing on his experiences in the first Gulf War, Bosnia, and Northern Ireland, Smith feels that the following factors are of critical importance.

1. The nature of the objective in question: **Heaven**
2. The strength of the opponent: **Wind**
3. The nature of the coalition forces and their cohesiveness with each other: **Fire**

4. The ability to sustain the fight materially and morally: **Earth, Heaven, and Fire**
5. The confrontational context of the fight: **Thunder**
6. The physical context of the fight: **Mountain, Earth**
7. The people among whom the fight will take place: **Water, Lake**[273]

Although application of the Eight Dispositions to the ideas of Hart, Bobbitt, and Smith is interesting, the focus is still largely limited to the operational strategic theater, and the questions and considerations are logical and linear. Many more interesting non-linear questions need to be asked when formulating and employing strategy. The Eight Dispositions serve as an ideal model for understanding, forming, and implementing strategy, because they form an organic, cognitive strategic whole that informs both implicitly and explicitly. Rather than acting as cogs or stages in a mechanistic linear process, each of the Eight Dispositions references and interacts continuously and simultaneously with all of the others on multiple levels. Another way to say this is that each is simultaneously informing and being informed by the others. The following section presents a sample of the kinds of practical strategic questions the Eight Dispositions can generate.

Strategic Questions

 Heaven

What is our overarching vision?

How does this vision manifest in intention?

What are the intentions from which our strategy will flow?

Can our visions and intentions coalesce into a strategic outlook and general plan?

How do we allow our visions and intentions to unfold in relationship to the visions, intentions, and dispositions of others (both competitors and opponents or allies and coworkers)?

How does our vision translate into plans and the ability to align oneself with circumstances?

How will our vision and intentions capitalize on the potential inherent in the configuration—the pattern of events and circumstances?

Earth

How will we manifest our vision, intention, and plans?

How will Heaven's vision—our strategic outlook—be nourished and supported?

What are the practical considerations and logistics involved?

What forces and support structures need to be mobilized, and how, and where?

What will be the response of others and how can we either aid (in the case of allies) or interfere with (in the case of opponents) their ability to manifest their intention, vision, and plans?

What is the terrain/environment on, or within which, our plan will unfold?

 Fire

How can we bring clarity and insight to our strategic outlook?

How can we clear away any uncertainty and doubt regarding our plans and their implementation?

Does our vision, and the intention and plans that flow from it, have a clarity of consciousness that attracts people, thereby strengthening the vision and broadening its scope?

How do our vision and intentions draw people together to undertake unified cohesive action?

How do our vision and intentions, and the plans that stem from them, simultaneously undermine the opposition's ability to strengthen and broaden the scope of their vision?

How do our vision, intentions, and plans interact or interfere with the cohesion and unity of the opposition?

Is our vision imbued with warmth and humanity toward both our supporters and our opponents?

 Water

Is our strategic outlook fluid, flexible, and adaptable?

Do our intentions and their resulting actions take the path of least resistance?

Do our strategy and plans coordinate with the Earth disposition's ability to support them, like water flowing through channels in the earth?

Can we limit the opponent's ability to change and shape his or her strategic plans in accordance with changing circumstances?

Thunder

How will our strategy and its support mechanisms translate into action?

How and where (Earth-Mountain) do we initiate action?

What direction or directions will this action take?

Are we prepared to shift to new directions or new ground if circumstances demand it?

Have we allowed and prepared for unexpected sudden breakthroughs or shifts to occur, and will we be able to take advantage of them?

Can we contain, limit, or disrupt the opposition's or competitor's ability to act?

Can we make the opposition waste effort while maximizing the effects of our own efforts?

 *Mountain*

Do we know how and where to wait for the next opportunity to appear?

When should we hold our position and wait for circumstances to change before moving again?

Can we employ restraint and tolerance when they are appropriate?

Can we act with humility?

While waiting, what can we do to prepare ourselves for action?

Can we use stillness to induce the opponent to move at the wrong time?

 Wind

Have we gathered sufficient information or intelligence to make and actualize our intentions and plans?

Have we carefully and accurately observed both our own situation and that of our allies and competitors?

Do we understand the orientation, mindset, and thinking of our allies and opponents?

What parts of our strategy should be made visible?

How can we control the flow of information to both our allies and our enemies?

Can we feed our opponents false information?

Are we receptive to new information and new ideas?

Is our thinking pliable?

Are there ways in which we can employ the unseen pressure and the soft
   pliability of wind, rather than direct action, to achieve our goals?

When can compliance be useful?

 Lake

Are we sensitive to the environment in which we are operating?

Are we sensitive to the needs and goals of our allies and coworkers, as well
   as those of our opponents?

How can we reflect on our plans and actions in a useful way?

As events unfold, can we reflect on and rethink our intentions, plans, and
   goals, and our means of achieving them?

Do we bring joy and enthusiasm to our undertakings, and invoke these
   feeling in those we are leading or collaborating with?

Can we follow as well as lead?

Hexagrams of the Eight Palaces

The Eight Dispositions can be applied in a wide variety of circumstances.
When two of the trigrams and their associated intentions or dispositions are
combined, a hexagram with six lines will be generated. The yang, solid lines
are considered to be like a gate opening, and the yin, broken lines like a gate
closing (the opening of the gates is called Qian the Creative, and the closing, Kun the Receptive). This gives one the image of movement constantly
occurring within the lines; an image of the door that was open becoming
closed and the door that was closed opening; yin and yang lines constantly
changing from one to the other. A dynamic tension between the lines of the
hexagram is implied. Another way to look at this tension is that yang lines
stretch, separating to become broken lines, and broken lines merge and join
to become solid yang lines.

Each line has a place in the hexagram as a whole, which can further
elucidate levels of meaning. The first line can represent the beginning of an
action or situation, or the entrance onto the field of action, and the last line,
the end or the departure from the field. This indicates a temporal sequence.
The six lines of the hexagrams are always in step with the movements of
time. The increments can be moments or years, depending on context and
situation. For example, a changing line in the third place (the third line) can

indicate that change will occur during the third time increment. It is implied that the preceding lines contain the factors that precipitate or "set up" the change. The arrangement of the lines can therefore describe how the earlier stages can modify or amplify the movement of succeeding stages of change. Events develop subtly in the beginning and later, as things develop and manifest, they are more obvious.

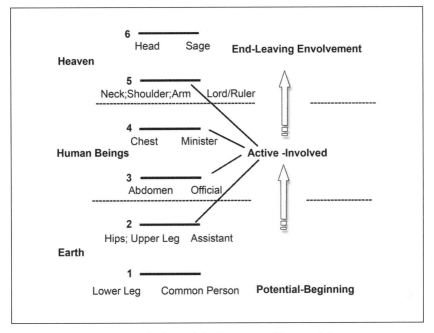

Figure 2.10. Symbolism of the Hexagram Lines and Structure

Each line in the hexagram reflects not only temporal change, but position on the field of action. These positions can change over time. The designation of a line as relating to a "common person," "minister," "ruler," etc. can be taken to be metaphors that represent the power dynamic between the participants involved in the situation, which is unfolding, changing, and transforming over time.

Lines can also be "correct" or "incorrect." The first, third, and fifth places are considered to be yang, so it is correct if they contain a yang line. The second, fourth, and six places are considered to be yin. If a yang line is in a yang place it is considered to be correct. If it is in a yin place it is incorrect. For yang lines, the fifth place, that of the ruler or king, is the most superior position in the hexagram. The third place is subordinate to that of the fifth, just as an official is subordinate to his ruler. However, for yin lines, the second place is superior to that of the fourth. The minister, although higher than the official, is closer to the ruler and therefore his place is more dangerous.[274] In hexagram 63 (After Completion/Fulfillment) the lines are in their proper places.

 After Completion/Fulfillment (Ji Ji)

While these ideas might on the surface seem arbitrary, arcane, or outdated, at their core they reflect a deeper wisdom. To move through life and actualize one's goals, plans, and intentions requires paying attention to position, timing, and opportunity. In life, on the battlefield or in hand-to-hand combat, position and timing, taking advantage of opportunity, changing with the changing circumstances—i.e., making the right move at the right time or being in the right place at the right time—spell the difference between victory and defeat.

The trigrams contained in each hexagram look at the lines in groups, to illustrate how the Eight Dispositions are applied in a variety of changing circumstances. Hexagrams can be analyzed and grouped according to the inner and outer trigrams. For example, in hexagram five, Waiting *(Xu)*, Water is above Heaven:

 Waiting (Xu)

The lower or *inner* trigram is Heaven and the upper or *outer* trigram is Water. The inner trigram reveals the inner, perhaps hidden, nature of the situation, while the upper trigram reveals its outer nature.

The eight trigrams, with Heaven as the bottom or inner trigram, are known as the Palace of Heaven. Each palace contains eight hexagrams that have a relationship based around the inner trigram. The following diagram shows the Eight Palace arrangement of the hexagrams. This is sometimes referred to as the Pre-Heaven or *Xian Tian* arrangement. The horizontal

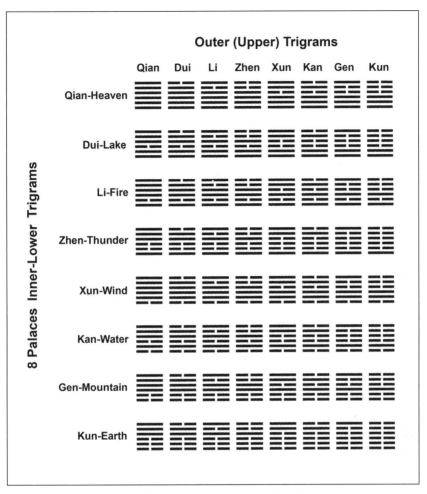

Figure 2.11. Eight Palace Arrangement of the Hexagrams

rows show the eight palaces, dictated by the inner trigram. The vertical rows show the relationship based on the outer (upper) trigrams. The hexagrams that are emblematic of each palace are composed of doubled trigrams that run like a thread on the diagonal, going from top left to bottom right. Heaven doubled lies in the first place in the first row; Lake doubled lies in the second place in the second row; Fire doubled lies in the third place in the third row; and so on, down to Earth doubled in the eighth place in the eighth row.

■ PALACE OF HEAVEN

The following eight hexagrams contain Heaven as the inner trigram. In each situation, the three strong lines move upward, directly and powerfully. The implication is that this kind of strength should be applied appropriately and precisely so that growth and advancement are in accord with the natural order—harmonious and balanced.

The Creative (Qian): Strong; dynamic. The doubling of Qian (Heaven) gives the image of powerful and constantly repeated movement that is strong, dynamic, and self-generating. The six lines emanate power. When yang moves, yin appears. Taking direct action and moving ahead to completion allows one to prevail.

Great Strength (Da Zhuang): Thunder above and Heaven below. Inside, Heaven is strong and powerful, and outside, Zhen (Thunder) initiates movement. Their union means great strength. Yang flourishes as yin retreats. Using great power with appropriate action and correct application of strength brings success. Power applied imprecisely or impulsively can be obstructed.

Waiting (Xu): Water above Heaven. Clouds in the heavens, rain will come when it is time, but it cannot be made to come, so one must wait. It also means that danger, the abyss, lies in front, so firm strength stops, stays away from danger, and waits. Strength in the face of danger bides its time, takes precautions, and is patient.

Great Accumulation (Da Xu): Heaven within Mountain. There is firmness and accumulation at the top. The mountain checks the strong yang movement, so that things accumulate and strength is stored. The top line of the Mountain trigram also represents the leader, who through calm firmness gathers and holds Heaven's strong, dynamic energy. On the other hand, inappropriate accumulation, too much strength gathered at the top, is unbalanced.

Peace (Tai): Earth (Kun), the Receptive, stands above Heaven. Earth wants to move downward and Heaven wants to move upward. They meet, intertwine, and are in harmony, so all things are in harmony and at peace. The weak lines are departing as the strong lines advance. This represents growth and advancement that is harmonious and tranquil.

Small Accumulation (Xiao Xu): The yang lines above and below respond to the weak line in the appropriate fourth position. It holds in place (tames) or temporarily checks the strong yang lines rising upward. The gentle flexibility of Wind softens Heaven's three strong lines, slowing them, allowing strength to accumulate as it moves so that the outcome can be successful. The image is of clouds condensing, but rain not coming. For rain to fall, strength must be accumulated little by little. The yin line in the fourth place is correct, a minister in the right place but not yet strong enough to succeed.

Great Holding (Da You): Fire and light above indicate clarity uniting with strength below. The weak fifth line holds and welcomes the five strong lines; there is power and strength, but it is tempered by civility and insight. Heaven's strength responds to Fire's clarity and truth. Firm strength acting with vision and insight will prevail by bringing things and people together in fellowship.

Resolution (Kuai): The strong lines take action to remove the weak and petty sixth line. The Lake has risen too high; water from the Lake rises to Heaven. There will be a breakthrough, as in a cloudburst, or erosion. One can forestall collapse and erosion by taking action, employing the judicious use of strength to push out the petty. If direct force is applied too strongly the weak and petty will be pushed out, but strength will also be dissipated and resistance can be engendered.

■ PALACE OF EARTH

The following eight hexagrams contain Earth as the inner trigram. In each situation, the receptivity and responding quality of Earth gathers strength, represented by three hollow yin lines adapting to change through their yielding, soft quality. This generates support by union, by a bringing together of like ideas and intentions—progress that is unforced and natural. In situations that are not favorable, Earth's yielding quality directs one to yield to circumstances or retire from action until the time is right.

Standstill/Obstruction (Pi): The three yang lines of Heaven move upward and away, while the Earth below sinks downward. Above and below are not communicating; there is no interaction; there is obstruction. Strength is decreasing and the inferior and narrow-minded are inside, increasing. In this situation, one should not be tempted by honors, rank, or wealth, but instead withdraw and rely on inner strength.

Enthusiasm/Contentment (Yu): The upper trigram (Thunder) represents movement, while the lower (Earth) is receptive and obedient. This is action stemming from compliance and obedience. Thunder bursts forth and the earth shakes. The yin lines respond to the strong moving line in the fourth position. Enthusiasm and contentment enable things to be accomplished with willing help.

Union/Holding Together (Bi): Water on the Earth connotes flowing rivers and oceans held by the Earth. The weak lines are gathered and held together by a strong line (the fifth line) holding the place of the ruler, so they come together. The ability to prevail depends on the cooperation and support of the group, which relates to the receptivity and openness represented by the Earth trigram.

Splitting Apart/Falling Away (Bo): Mountain over Earth. The weak, dark lines are moving upward and driving out the last firm, light line. The soft and weak are changing the strong. Circumstances cannot be restrained by using firmness and strength (direct confrontation); instead, stillness, restraint, and avoidance of action (represented by the Mountain) are indicated. Another way to look at this is that the Mountain is perched on a weak foundation. This threatens collapse. Wait. After things fall away, a new cycle will begin.

Receptive/Responding (Kun): Earth above Earth. This is Earth stretching to respond to Heaven, the Creative. The yin lines of Earth are hollow and receptive; they yield and respond to the yang lines of Heaven. Kun does not combat, but completes Heaven. Through accommodation, Earth can exercise its transformative power. Instead of taking the lead, respond to the ideas and leadership of others. Use sensitivity and quiescent, gentle strength to guide or move others. Proceed slowly and remain attentive.

Contemplation/View (Guan): Wind blows over the Earth, moving from high pressure to low pressure. The image is of a ruler traveling everywhere to inspect the people and the land. The leader views those he leads and in turn is viewed, setting a lofty example. Wind is unseen as it moves across the Earth, bending the grasses as it moves. In the same way, the power of the leader may not be understood, but it is felt. By deepening one's perspective and understanding, one can lead by example. This involves both outward perception (Wind) and inward self-perception (Earth).

Advance/Progress (Jin): Fire over Earth; the sun rising over the Earth. An advance toward fulfillment. The light above is followed by the obedient earth below. The yin lines of Earth are hollow and receive the light. A soft and yielding advance allows one to progress forward. Fire above symbolizes a clarity of vision that allows one to move forward with support from one's peers, subordinates, and superiors.

Gather Together (Cui): Lake over Earth in this hexagram is similar to the image of hexagram 8 (Union/Holding Together). Water in a Lake collects or gathers. The implication is that there is an innate tendency for like things to gather together. With Water this happens naturally in a Lake. This is joy over obedience and receptivity. This gathering of energies is positive, without coercion, with joy and compliance. Success requires gathering together while eliminating negative elements that lead to divisiveness and factionalism.

■ PALACE OF THUNDER

The following eight hexagrams contain Thunder as the inner trigram. In each situation, the strong line at the beginning (the bottom) moves upward and forward, representing movement stirring, excitation, and shock: the birth of something new, movement after stillness.

Thunder/Quake (Zhen): Thunder above and below. The strong yang line at the bottom moves up to join with the fourth yang line, which also moves upward. The yang lines below the weaker yin lines move upward forcefully, shocking and startling. This is movement stirring, bursting through, pushing and progressing forward and upward. This kind of shock carries an element of fear, the excitation making one alert and wary, ridding one of laziness and indolence. Shock and fear can lead to self-cultivation and self-examination. This is a way to advance smoothly and unobstructed.

Difficulty at the Beginning (Zhun): Water over Thunder symbolizes danger or difficulty at the beginning of an enterprise. The upward moving yang line is held down by yin Water. One can take action in the midst of danger, but everything is in motion, still unformed and even unclear, so things must be organized and sorted out to achieve success. The yang line at the bottom cannot rush ahead into danger, but must stabilize the situation before moving forward.

Nourishment (Yi): This is the harmony of movement and tranquility. Mountain *(Gen)* is stopping motion; Thunder *(Zhen)* is initiating movement. The strong yang line at the bottom initiates upward action. Its path is unobstructed but it is stopped before it can overreach itself, by the strong line at the top. The hexagram resembles an open mouth, signifying nourishment. Care and nourishment must be regulated properly, just as activity and inactivity must also be regulated and balanced. This means moving and stopping at the proper time. The proper interplay and rhythm of movement and stillness bring success.

Return (Fu): Thunder Under Earth. After the weak lines have pushed the strong lines out of the hexagram, a new strong line appears. After a movement in one direction reaches its extreme endpoint, an opportunity for movement in the other direction begins, arising naturally and spontaneously. The single yang line, although weak, has an unobstructed path. In the winter, life energy is under the Earth, hidden. After the winter solstice, it returns and slowly grows, a natural renewing. The single yang line gathers more strong lines (like-minded people or energies) before moving ahead with strength.

Increase (Yi): Wind above and Thunder below. Thunder and Wind strengthen and increase each other. When they support each other, their energy is doubled. Fierce winds come with earth-shattering thunder. Thunder symbolizes firm resolution within. Wind symbolizes penetrating outward action. As the lines in the top trigram push upward, they increase the movement in the lower trigram. Decrease above (outside) leads to increase below (inside). When initiating movement, Wood/Wind supports and enhances action, allowing one to pass over difficulties ("crossing the great river") by penetrating insight and correction of faults.

Bite Through (Shi He): The image is an open mouth with an obstruction between the teeth. One must bite through the obstacle for the teeth to meet. The yang lines on the top and bottom of the hexagram are lips, and the fourth line is an obstruction to be ground by the "teeth" of the other three yin lines. Fire and Thunder together create lightning. When their union is obstructed, the obstruction must be removed. It will not vanish of its own accord. Judgment (Li) and deliberate action (Zhen) are required to clear the way. Fire (Li) is yielding, but Thunder (Zhen) is hard. Together they command respect and can mete out judgment and justice in order to bring things and people together.

No Falsehood (Wu Wang): Zhen is dynamic and Qian (Heaven) is strong; motion within strength. The bottom line moves upward to join the three strong lines above. Adopting the disposition of Heaven—blending with natural forces—allows one to further one's intentions, just as life's energies move under Heaven in the spring, reflected in the creative activity of nature as plants and animals sprout and grow.

Following (Sui): Thunder (movement) below and Lake (joy) above. The hard below the soft. Strong and active thunder follows Lake's gentle joy and, by following, can initiate movement at the right time. Rather than using direct force, one seizes the moment, choosing an alternate course or path to follow in order to prevail. By adapting to the moment, by following, one gets others to follow and perform their functions correctly and with pleasure.

■ PALACE OF MOUNTAIN

The following eight hexagrams contain Mountain as the inner trigram. In each situation, the top yang line in the Mountain trigram stops or slows upward/forward movement. The Mountain symbolizes stillness, inner reflection, and humility; biding one's time for movement to begin again.

Withdrawal/Retreat (Dun): Mountain pushes upward and Heaven retreats. This is like winter coming and darkness growing; the light retreats and living things draw back, preparing to go into hibernation before they return in the spring. The dark yin lines advance and grow in strength. Therefore the yang lines retreat, so as not to exhaust themselves. Through retreat, success is achieved. By slow, measured withdrawal one avoids a life-and-death struggle and can prepare for counter-movement at the right time.

Restraint/Keeping Still/Mountain (Gen): Mountain over Mountain, or linked mountains, symbolize stillness and restraint. When movement comes to its natural end, there is rest before new movement begins. The yang lines have moved to the top and stopped in each trigram. One is quiet inside and outside. Restraint is performed "with the back," conveying the idea of turning one's back so the object of desire or the goal is out of sight. When the goal is out of sight, restraint happens automatically and naturally; it is not forced. Keeping still prepares the body, mind, and spirit for progress when the time comes to move forward.

Gradual Advance (Jian): Wood on top of Mountain. On the Mountain a tree grows slowly and therefore it is firmly rooted in the Mountain, unlike a fast-growing plant with shallow roots. After keeping still, movement begins again slowly; advancing step by step, gradually, with the firmness of the Mountain at the root of the moment. The yang line in the third position moves upward slowly. Xun (Wind), the outer trigram, represents penetration. Within is the tranquility of the Mountain; without are the penetration and insight of Wind, which make progress possible.

Minor Excess/Minor Superiority (Xiao Guo): Thunder on the Mountain. The strong middle lines are surrounded or enclosed by the weaker lines above and below. Although there is strength within, only the weaker elements are mediating with the outside world. Strength is lacking to achieve great success. Prudence is necessary, and only small matters should be undertaken at this time. Achieve superiority in small matters and things will go smoothly.

Obstruction/Adversity (Jian): Water on top of Mountain represents two obstructions; hardship on top of hardship. The third yang line halts, confronted by danger ahead. One is surrounded by danger: a watery abyss in front and a high Mountain behind. When faced with danger, the Mountain inner trigram is the key to extricating oneself and overcoming obstructions in one's path. Premature advance, pushing against the obstruction, is risky. In order to prevail, persevere, pause, turn attention inward and reflect, waiting for the proper moment to advance.

Modesty/Humility (Qian): A Mountain is high because it stands above the Earth. Here, the Mountain is beneath the Earth. The third yang line stops, allowing the yin lines to rise above it. The third line gathers the yin lines together by exercising humility. This raises the earth, usually in the lower position, upward. To establish order the extremes must be equalized. Decreasing where there is too much (the Mountain) and adding to where there is too little (the Earth) creates balance. Thus modesty accords one respect, and allows one to keep one's position and prevail.

The Wanderer (Lu): The Mountain is still, while a Fire burning on the mountain travels on to new fuel. In traveling or moving ahead, one loses one's place and looks for something to cling to. The third line can represent strength overreaching itself through arrogance, but it is moderated by the fourth line, a strong line in a weak position, indicating humility and flexibility are necessary. Overreaching can also be symbolized by the top yang line, fire imbalanced, burning itself out. One should not be reckless, but with Fire's clarity and Mountain's stillness, should attach to or connect with the right places and people.

Influence/Mutual Attraction (Xian): Lake (soft) is above and Mountain (hard) is below. These two mutually attract and stimulate each other. One is still and passive (Mountain—youngest son), the other (Lake—youngest daughter) is joyous. Keeping still with sensitivity, while experiencing joy, prevents overreaching and allows interaction and reciprocity. The yang lines in the fourth and fifth places represent sensitivity and feeling reaching the heart. The man below the woman symbolizes the leader who receives others with humility and self-effacement. Through this reciprocity, the leader influences the hearts of others.

■ PALACE OF WIND

The following eight hexagrams contain Wind/Wood as the inner trigram. In each situation, the top yang lines move from high pressure to low pressure (like air), and so the movement of wind is downward, outward, and upward. Wind pushes gently and constantly, penetrating everywhere, touching everyone and everything.

Decay/Remedying the Ill (Gu): The gentle compliance of the lower trigram (Wind) combines with the rigid inertia of the upper trigram (Mountain). Wind cannot penetrate Mountain's stolid stillness. The yielding lines in both trigrams are stuck under solid lines that restrict upward movement. In order to prevent this stagnant situation from decaying and degenerating, one must take the initiative and correct the problem, using Wind's penetrating insight to get to the root of things.

Well (Jing): Water over Wood/Wind. Wood is like the pole and bucket used to lift the water out of the well. The well supplies nourishment, yet is inexhaustible. Wood draws water upward, both in the well and within plants and trees. The fifth line symbolizes the well lined with stone or tile so that the water is pure and clear. This requires effort. The well cannot be used during this time, but cultivation through hard work leads to a positive result. Self-development, insight, and organization bring benefit. If ignored, things will degenerate.

Pushing Upward/Ascending (Sheng): The image is of Wood pushing upward through the Earth; Wind's gentle penetration combined with Earth's receptive obedience. The upward movement of the yang lines is unobstructed. The soft and the weak, represented by the first line, can climb upward out of obscurity at the proper time. Like a tree, growing slowly, accumulating in small things to become large and great. One must be like Wind/Wood to accomplish this; flowing, adapting, and growing around obstacles.

Penetrating/Gentle (Xun): This is Wind/Wood doubled. The penetration of Wind depends on it being unceasing. In the Wind trigram the yielding line is humble and compliant under the two strong lines. Humility and compliance are not necessarily weak or inferior. Build small successes one upon the other by being steadfast and firm. The effects are gradual and inconspicuous; pushing continuously but gently, like one breeze following upon another, using patience to prevail. To carry things through to completion requires reiteration and reinforcement. If, on the other hand, one is too compliant, too humble, or overthinks the situation, there is no forward movement, no advancement.

Cauldron (Ding): Fire (Li) is above and Wood/Wind below. The image represents a cauldron heated by a fire that is kindled by Wood and Wind. Wood is the nourishment for the flame fanned by Wind. The bottom line represents the legs, and the three yang lines represent the belly of the cauldron; the fifth line, the knobs/handles. The top line represents the carrying ring. The cauldron cooks things, transforming and changing them without destroying them. This is controlled change. The penetration and compliance of Wood/Wind follow fire, feeding it to produce light and clarity.

Great Excess/Great Superiority (Da Guo): Lake over Wood. The Lake rises above the trees. The four strong yang lines in the middle also represent a ridgepole supported on two weak ends. It sags and can break. Things that are too big can get out of control and if they are too heavy and firm, can break. Yet there is strength in the center that can prevail through the gentle penetration of Wind. Taking correct action in this situation relies on combining strength with knowledge and pliability.

Duration/Perseverance (Heng): This is gentleness (Wind) within, and movement (Thunder) without. Both imply movement, but as paired phenomena they complement each other. Movement here is softened so that it lasts. It is self-contained and self-renewing. The movement in both trigrams comes and goes, and through the coming and going it endures; just as the four seasons come and go in an endless, self-renewing cycle. Thunder's action and movement occur with the reflection and insight of the softer element, wind. Actions performed in this way transform things, and create enduring effects that last.

Coming to Meet/Encountering (Gou): The one yin line is able to rise, met by the strong lines at the top. Wind under Heaven is the Wind blowing over the Earth, touching everything, everywhere. The commands of the leader are made known, carried by the Wind. Wind also represents the leader taking note of the condition of those he leads. However, the yin line at the bottom can also represent a negative element that makes an entrance, and as it grows it can displace things, creating instability. Its low position makes it seem harmless; it is easy to assume it can do no harm, but it may contain the seeds of disruption. Hence, the penetrating insight of Wind is necessary in order to avoid difficulty.

■ PALACE OF LAKE

The following eight hexagrams contain the Lake as the inner trigram. In each situation the stillness of the Lake—representing self-reflection, inner knowledge, and inner strength—prevails. The Lake also represents joy, relating to the world with an outward gentleness and inner strength. Joy is represented in the two strong lines of the trigram, with the softer line above. Outwardly yielding and gentle, joy is firm and strong within.

Treading/Conduct (Lu): Heaven above the Lake. The third yin line is in a yang position, which could be dangerous; this yin line treads on the yang lines below it, as on a tiger's tail. However, the yin line harmonizes the strong yang lines with its gentleness. When people gather together, rules of conduct are created. For Lake to be below Heaven is natural. Things should be in their proper places; follow the natural order. When a group gathers together, conduct and propriety develop. Taking risks (treading on the tiger's tail), must be done cautiously, with awareness and attention.

Marrying Maiden (Gui Mei): The implication here is that the Lake, youngest daughter, marries the oldest son (Thunder). This implies she is the second wife, subordinate to the first wife. The third, fifth, and sixth lines potentially block the movement of the yang lines. In this situation, one cannot attempt to supplant those above, but must act with humility, caution, and reserve. In a relationship or a collaboration, one must often subordinate personal desires and goals and try to do one's best, perform to the best of one's ability, remaining mindful of the end or goal.

Limitation/Restriction (Jie): Water above and water (Lake) below; a Lake filled with water. The water is restrained from overflowing. The second and fifth yang lines contain the yin lines. Control, action to be measured and meaningful. By limiting action, one does not squander resources and reserves. Discipline and regulation are necessary, if applied appropriately, with an underlying joy. Too much limitation or control can cause damage and can lead to resistance, bitterness, and rebellion.

Decrease/Reduction (Sun): The implication here is that the third (originally strong) line has moved upward to the top. The foundation is weakened to strengthen the facade. The Mountain is above and gets bigger because the Lake becomes deeper. Another way to look at this: the Lake is evaporating, decreasing to benefit the Mountain, which is nourished by it.

Those above profit at the expense of those below. This can be positive: subordinates working contentedly for those above; but it can also be negative: emphasis on externals rather than what is fundamental.

Approaching/Overlooking (Lin): The two strong lines at the bottom are moving upward, unobstructed. In a time of joyful and hopeful progress, one should not wait, but should respond immediately to take advantage of opportunity. The Earth overlooks the Lake from above. The higher position responds to and oversees the lower position by yielding and allowing things to grow and expand. Oversee and respond to subordinates appropriately by nurturing and encouraging their abilities. This hexagram is also associated with the beginning of spring, when the latent spring energies are beginning to rise and become manifest.

Inner Truth/Sincerity (Zhong Fu): Wind above the Lake; wind blows across the Water. The penetrating power of Wind moves the water; the invisible wind manifesting visible effects. The two broken or empty lines in the center of the hexagram represent an open and sincere heart. Sincerity and generosity uphold the trust placed in you by others. Assess whether people can be trusted before going along with them. Similarly, by inspiring trust and demonstrating sincerity, people will follow.

Opposition/Separation (Kui): Here, opposition refers to polarity. Water (Lake) goes downward and Fire goes upward. The two trigrams also represent the middle and youngest daughter. They live in the same house, but do not have the same goals and aspirations. When people are moving in different directions it is difficult to come together for a common undertaking. However, small things can be undertaken successfully if common ground can be found. Diversity and differences can complement each other and create opportunity if judgments and distinctions are not made harshly.

The Joyous (Dui): Lake doubled. Outwardly yielding and gentle, joy is firm and strong within. Truth and strength dwell inside, while gentleness is employed in social intercourse. Without the strength inside, joy can turn into self-gratification and pursuit of pleasure. Without the softness outside, strength and hardness inside can become stubbornness. Joy in work helps people ignore the toil; encountering difficulty or danger with joy lessens fear. In dealing with people and changing events one must be firm but gentle, strong, and stable, not stubborn and unable to change.

■ PALACE OF WATER

The following eight hexagrams contain Water as the inner trigram. In each situation there is difficulty or danger, represented by Water. Adapting to the situation and taking the path of least resistance allows one to retain the fluidity of movement that will enable one to prevail in the end.

Conflict/Contention (Song): Heaven has an intrinsic upward movement, while Water innately moves downward. The two sections of the hexagram moving away from each other signifies conflict. The strong fifth line implies that if one is clear-headed and strong, the opponent can be met halfway, thereby avoiding conflict. One must be prudent and handle conflict at its inception when latent differences begin to manifest. If conflict is allowed to grow, it can easily go to its endpoint—open hostility.

Deliverance/Relief (Jie): Thunder above and Water below indicate Thunder and rain. Thunder is movement and Water is danger. In this situation, movement is the way to escape danger. Through movement, one avoids danger and finds a safe place; the fourth line moves upward, away from danger. In this hexagram, the thunderstorm clears the air, bringing relief from the dangerous situation. The obstacle has been removed, and complications have begun to ease. Once one is out of danger, one can cautiously move forward.

Water/The Abyss/Sinkhole (Kan): Water above Water is danger twice or a double pitfall. The image is of falling into a dark pit; the yang line has fallen between the two yin lines. Water shows us how to flow onward, through and around difficulty. The yang line in the center of the Water trigram represents sincerity and strength within; one can move through danger by staying centered and sincere, while adapting to the terrain (the circumstances). In dealing with danger one must move forward, to transform a dangerous situation into something positive. Remaining in danger, or seeking danger, is not advisable.

Youthful Folly/ Childlike Ignorance (Meng): Water under the Mountain; the image of a spring flowing out of the base of the Mountain. Keeping still on top and danger beneath. The spring is like youth finding its way; not knowing where to go. Water needs to move on, but it must find a path. The youth must recognize their lack of experience and seek out an experienced teacher to guide them. Spring Water must fill up the hollows in the ground (gain experience) in order to move on. The student must seek the teacher, but the teacher must be patient and tolerant, like the Mountain, in dealing with youthful ignorance.

≡≡ The Army (Shi): The army refers to the masses, the people. Water beneath Earth represents the ground Water stored under the Earth. Danger is below—masses of people are a powerful force, but just as Earth holds the Water, this powerful force can be guided by discipline and obedience (represented by Earth). The strong second line is the general or commander. The yielding lines are subordinate to the general. He is not in the fifth place (that of the ruler) but resonates with it. The rising of the masses can be dangerous unless organized and disciplined like an army. With collective action and joint effort one will prevail. However, the leader or general must not abuse his position.

≡≡ Dispersing/Dissolution (Huan): Wind blowing over the Water disperses it. In people, rigid minds and hearts lead to separation from others. The top trigram is also interpreted as Wood made into boats and paddles, carrying people across the water, dispersing them outward. Wind/Wood, with its persistent penetration, its ability to touch everywhere, is the key to overcoming obstacles and separation. Open communication—Wind penetrating, reaching, and connecting—can bring people and things back together. Vigorous action at the outset, without ulterior motives, can overcome disunion.

≡≡ Before Completion/Not Yet Fulfilled (Wei Ji): Fire above and Water below. Fire moves upward and Water moves downward. They move in opposite directions and do not integrate. Although they are separated, they are in their proper places. They are unfinished, unsettled, continuing to move and develop. If they can be brought to the right place, these two forces can have their desired effect. The fifth yin should not directly oppose the strong lines around it. Care, preparation, and good judgment are required to bring events to the desired conclusion.

≡≡ Oppression/ Exhaustion (Kun): Water is below the Lake. The Lake is empty, drained away or dried up. One's energy has been exhausted or drained away. The yang lines are surrounded and hindered by the yin lines. Although there is adversity, success comes from remaining strong and retaining the capacity for joy represented by the Lake. Complaint will not bring success and can make things worse. Acceptance of the situation, and approaching it with faith and resolve, prepares one to be ready for the moment the situation begins to change.

■ PALACE OF FIRE

The following eight hexagrams contain Fire as the inner trigram. One's inner Fire (truth and clarity) must attach or cling to the surroundings. This can bring both coherence and cohesion. In each situation (whether successful, prosperous, or dangerous), Fire represents the clarity, discrimination, and steadfast adherence to truth that are necessary to cultivate proper relationships with others, and with our work and our life.

Fellowship (Tong Ren): Fire below flares up toward Heaven. What is below rises up to associate with what is above. The weak second line unites the other strong lines. There is light and clarity in the inner trigram and strength in the outer. The second weak line resonates with the fifth line, the ruler. Strength is exercised through civility, clarity, and enlightenment, rather than through military force. Modest guidance and management bring people together in a voluntary unity.

Fullness/Abundance (Feng): Thunder above and Fire (lightning) below represent movement and clarity; movement without, guided by clarity within. There is tremendous energy when Thunder and lightning act together. The true leader acts with enlightenment and clarity and thus can extend themselves to the utmost. Everything flourishes and blossoms. To extend abundance one should share prosperity with others, act responsibly and clearly, and be appreciative of what one has created.

After Completion/Fulfillment (Ji Ji): Water flows downward and fire flares upward. In this way, Water and Fire interact and aid each other. This gives the image of boiling Water in a pot. The lines are in the proper places. A perfect equilibrium has been achieved. *Ji Ji* also refers to ferrying the people across the river, as in rescuing them from a flood or disaster. All have been ferried across, even the smallest and weakest are not left out. Everything is fulfilled. Therefore, one should be prepared for this perfect balance to shift and be ready to adapt and guide things in a new direction, so that the balance is not destroyed.

Grace/Adornment (Bi): Below the Mountain is Fire. The Fire illuminates the beauty of the Mountain. This refers to the innate inner form and clarity. The external adornments of success and prosperity are not the essential thing; they are the exterior form. The exterior form is the adornment, the culture and enlightenment brought about by deeper patterns.

Heaven's strong second line has risen to the top, representing the climax of adornment leaving a yielding line between the two strong lines in the lower trigram. The top line can also represent adornment becoming too extreme and turning into ostentation and pretense.

Light Suppressed/Darkening of the Light (Ming Yi): Fire is below Earth. The light is suppressed and hidden under Earth's three yin lines. Ignorant, unwise leadership damages the light. In this situation, it is best to be outwardly compliant and tractable, while inside one remains uncompromised. One cannot move forward without injury. By yielding on small nonessential matters, one appears compliant, while inside holding fast to one's principles. This hexagram can also mean that the enlightened leader should rule by hiding his or her light. By keeping one's brilliance within, real brilliance can be achieved.

The Family/The Clan (Jia Ren): Fire below generates Wind above. Wind issues forth from Fire. This represents the family or one's personal group. Within a family there is mutual respect and division of responsibilities, each according to his or her place. This is the idea of tending to the familiar with care. By returning to the family, the Fire inside, one can express oneself outside—the arising of Wind. By maintaining cohesion within yourself and your immediate relationships, with honesty and equanimity, you can move forward to accomplish other things.

The Clinging/Fire (Li): This is Fire doubled, representing ascent. The brilliance of Fire can illuminate everything, but Fire's brilliance must cling to something (just as the yin lines cling to the surrounding yang lines) or it will burn out. People associate and work with others, they cling to a way of life, activities, and work. People cling to one another for support. This creates the enlightenment and discernment necessary to ascend in the face of difficulty or danger.

Revolution/Radical Change/Molting (Ge): Fire is below and the Lake above. Fire moves up and Water (Lake) moves down; they attempt to extinguish each other. When Water and Fire fight each other change occurs: the old is abolished so that something new can be created. This is radical change. When there is political or social change, it is necessary to employ clarity, judgment, and enlightenment to negotiate the transition.

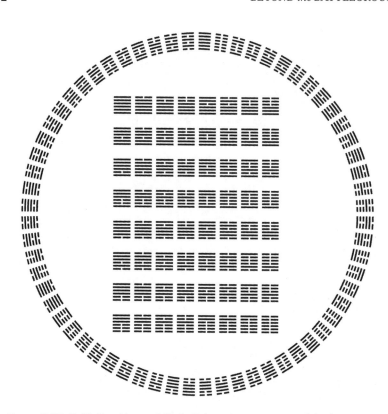

Figure 2.12. Fu Xi (Pre-Heaven) Eight Palace Arrangement of the hexagrams surrounded by King Wen (Post-Heaven) Arrangement

CHAPTER III

Strategy, the *Yijing*, and Ba Gua Zhang

Ultimately makers of strategy must narrow their focus; too much complexity makes the mind seize. At a minimum, they must see clearly both themselves and potential adversaries, their strengths, weaknesses, preconceptions, and limits—through humility, relentless and historically informed critical analysis, and restless satisfaction even in victory. They must weigh imponderables through structured debates that pare away personal, organizational, and national illusions and conceits. They must squarely address issues that are bureaucratic orphans. They must unerringly discern and prepare to strike the enemy's jugular—whether by surprise attack or attrition, in war or in political and economic struggle. And in the end, makers of strategy must cheerfully face the uncertainties of decision and the dangers of action.

  —MacGregor Knox[275]

The many cannot govern the many; that which governs the many is the most solitary. Activity cannot govern activity; that which controls all activity that occurs in the world, thanks to constancy, is the One. Therefore for all the many to manage to exist, their controlling principle must reach back to the One, and for all activities to manage to function, their source cannot but be the One. No thing behaves haphazardly, but necessarily follows its own principle. To unite things, there is a fundamental regulator; to integrate them there is a primordial generator. Therefore, things are complex but not chaotic, multitudinous, but not confused. That is why when the six lines of the hexagram intermingle, one can pick out one of them and use it to clarify what is happening, and as the hard and the soft ones supersede one another, one can establish which one is the master and use it to determine how all are ordered.

  —Wang Bi[276]

The Implementation of Strategy

How is strategy implemented and converted into action? How do the Eight Dispositions/Intentions connect with the ability to generate and implement various possibilities while simultaneously allowing adaptation to constantly changing circumstances? Or to put it another way, how does one capitalize on the potential inherent in a situation, especially a situation that is unforeseen or seemingly chaotic or random? When one considers grand strategy, strategy, operations, and tactics, it is imperative to understand that that these concepts are not linear, but are intertwined parts of a whole. Each informs, influences, and is informed and influenced by the others. Similarly, the Eight Dispositions are an integrated and organic whole, a united and fully integrated system, as opposed to a system composed of separate interlocking parts. Each disposition contains and is contained by the others, and interpenetrates and is interpenetrated by the others.

Colonel John Boyd defines the strategic aim as being: to reduce the opponent's capacity to adapt as an organic whole while improving one's own, thereby improving one's ability to cope with unfolding events while restricting the opponent's ability to do so.[277] Boyd goes on to point out that these kinds of "multi-dimensional interactions suggest a spontaneous, synthetic/creative and flowing action/counteraction operation, rather than a step by step analytical/logical and discrete movement/countermove game." From this kind of thinking specific tactics naturally develop. He adds that the more complex the interaction—technical, organizational, tactical, and operational—the less easily one will be able to adapt to events as they unfold.[278]

Boyd is famous for the creation of the concept of the OODA Loop, a model for understanding how one adapts or does not adapt to the changing circumstances. OODA stands for Observation, Orientation, Decision, Action:

Observation: Observing the environment as a whole and absorbing its potential.

Orientation: A multifaceted, intuitive, or *implicit cross-referencing process* that is interactive and based on one's training, ethnic background, previous experience, cultural tradition, and the unfolding circumstance.

Decision: Reaching a decision.

Action: Acting on the decision.[279]

The OODA loop can diagrammed as shown below.

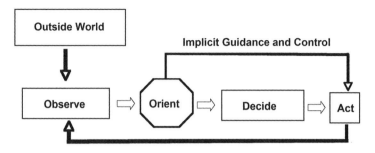

Figure 3.1. The OODA Loop

The key idea here is that orientation *shapes the way we observe and interact with the environment.* Because it shapes the way we observe, decide, and act, we must create patterns, images, and impressions that match our opponent and the world around us, while simultaneously preventing the opponent from discerning the patterns that match with our actions and movements.[280]

The better and more quickly we can do this, the more we can disrupt the opponent's plans, because their observations, decisions, and actions begin to fall behind developing events, and increasingly fail to match what is unfolding around them. We are able to attain freedom of action and the ability to shape and influence perceptions and events and exploit opportunities, while they are distracted, deprived of their freedom of action, and subject to surprise, confusion, and dislocation of their forces, and therefore deprived of the ability to employ their strength. Boyd refers to this as "getting inside the opponent's OODA Loop."[281] Chet Richards describes this as being analogous to playing chess with someone who is a better player, but being allowed to make two moves for every one of theirs.[282]

Both Boyd and Richards use the German blitzkrieg ("lightning warfare") tactics that were employed on the Western front in 1940 to illustrate these ideas. The Germans, by keeping a fast pace and avoiding direct confrontation, kept the larger French forces off-balance, both mentally and physically. The situation changed too quickly for the French. They could not react to the multiple breakthroughs that seemed to happen everywhere at once, so from the outset the Germans controlled the initiative, while

French forces succumbed to paralysis and confusion. The German commanders were trained to think independently and intuitively, and were encouraged to adapt to the situation and exploit opportunities as they arose. In effect, their orientation was such that could they move much more quickly through their OODA loop, thereby allowing them to get inside the French OODA loop.

The movie *The Heart of the Game* is a documentary that follows a Seattle girls' basketball team, the Roughriders, led by their eccentric coach through six seasons of play. This underdog team uses what are essentially blitzkrieg tactics—initiating fast breaks and rapidly changing from one configuration to another as the game unfolds. Rather than using set plays, they are taught to work together to develop and exploit opportunities as they arise, thereby creating confusion in their opponents, who cannot anticipate their actions. In an interview, the coach of a rival team says that she finds it difficult to prepare her team to play the Roughriders, because one never knows what they are going to do. In a sense, the Roughriders are, via their unique tactics and cohesion as a team, able to work inside their opponent's OODA loop.

Arguably, luck is to some degree a factor in any conflict. Events are not entirely predictable, and the unforeseen can always occur. However, warfare and hand-to-hand combat are not sports. Losing the "game" usually means one does not get to play again. Because life is on the line, master strategists through the centuries have sought to remove luck from the equation. The great swordsman Miyamoto Musashi, reflecting back on his many duels with the razor-sharp Japanese sword, felt that his victories up to that point were based on either luck, his own innate abilities, or the inadequacies of his opponent, rather than his skill.[283] This led him to devise a way of strategy that he describes in the *Book of Five Rings*. The Xing Yi boxer Guo Yun Shen similarly advises one not to rely on one's natural abilities or to focus too much on special abilities, as one can then become restricted by those abilities. He advises instead cultivating harmony in the interior, in order to generate qi and spiritual intention so that the body can transform as needed. It is worth revisiting a statement by Sunzi that resonates with Guo's ideas:

> The victories won by a master of war gain him neither fame for his wisdom nor merit for his valor, because he is bound to win as his tactics are

built on assurances of victory. He defeats an enemy already defeated. Thus the skilled warrior puts himself in a position in which he cannot be defeated and misses no opportunity to defeat his enemy. So it is that a victorious army will not engage the enemy unless it is assured of the necessary conditions for victory, whereas an army destined for defeat rushes into battle in the hope that it will win by luck. The skilled warrior seeks victory by cultivating the Way and strengthens the rules and regulations and in so doing gains the initiative over his enemy.[284]

In Ba Gua Zhang, the goal is to change inside, rather than increasing one's natural abilities. It is thought that natural ability or athletic ability can actually impede progress, because it is too easy to rely on it for victory. Although you will be victorious against those with less natural ability, you will always be vulnerable to being defeated by those with more natural ability. In internal martial arts, one trains not to rely on athleticism, but to change one's own internal responses so that they are generated internally by the mind, will, and qi. In arts like Ba Gua Zhang, one must remain alert and internally quiet, ready to respond and adapt to the opponent, while looking for opportunities to control them by hiding your intention, while they reveal theirs.

This strategy relies on the ability to exploit opportunities the moment they begin to develop; the moment before they manifest. For this to happen, the body must perceive and respond intuitively, without conscious thought. This is in some ways similar to Boyd's idea of the *implicit guidance and control* that shortens the OODA loop. Kenji Ushiro, an exponent of Okinawan karate, believes that this occurs in a preconscious moment. If one is attacked and reflexively blocks, Ushiro feels that this is merely a conscious conditioned response. However, if you enter into your opponent as your opponent is about to attack, they are turned back on themselves and the attack instantly stops. Ushiro explains this as a moment that occurs in the half-second gap before the mind recognizes what has occurred.[285]

Sergeant Rory Miller points out that in the OODA loop time is often critically lost in the two middle steps, usually because people try to gather too much information, thereby allowing the opponent to act while one is still orienting and deciding. In the real world, it is necessary to act on partial information. It is impossible to have all the information, even if one had the time to gather it. Having too much information and too many options increases the time it takes to choose and act. Miller adds that novel observations require a reorienting that causes people to lock up rather than act, because it is difficult to make decisions in the face of uncertainty.[286]

> The people I know that consistently do well in ambushes or have often beaten the maxim that action is faster than reaction have one thing in common. They have a group of techniques that form the core of their strategy that they DO NOT SEE AS SEPARATE TECHNIQUES. Mac has hundreds of disarms and counterattacks, but when he is surprised he "defangs the snake." He can and will do it in a hundred different ways, but in his mind it's just one thing. James "does damage." Again, hundreds of techniques that are all one thing in the brain. I "take the center."[287]

In both war and martial arts, one prepares for the unknown and the unexpected. This means one cannot simply learn a set of programmed responses. One cannot rely on techniques or programmed reactions and responses, as it would be impossible to prepare for every possible attack, or every possible situation. Even the same attack, performed by two different people, will present with two different signatures and may elicit very different, but appropriate, responses. In Ba Gua Zhang, one cultivates a disposition that allows one to create possibilities and exploit opportunities spontaneously, while they are still developing. There is no specific plan or response/counter-response programming. One is constantly surprised (as is the opponent) by one's own reactions and responses, and consequently, they cannot be anticipated or tracked. Essentially, they take place in Ushiro's half-second gap. In this way, movements and techniques can "occur" that were not specifically rehearsed or practiced.

Ba Gua Zhang: Exponential Potential for Change

Ba Gua Zhang's congruency with the principles of change expressed in the *Yijing* offers a unique and dynamic expression of the latent energy continuously unfolding in the body's every movement. While the Eight Dispositions and their associated trigrams can express an internal unity of intention

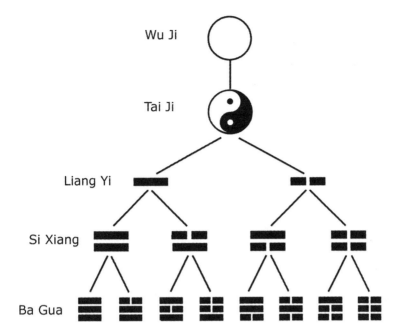

Figure 3.2. Exponential Potential in Ba Gua Zhang and Yi Jing: Diagram I

and strategy, these internal configurations also have a correspondence with external movements and postures. These body patterns / configurations are an active integration of intention (Yi), qi, and physical force, which generates an effective and efficient self-defense methodology and simultaneously acts as a nourishing life *(Yang shen)* practice. For the Ba Gua exponent, each movement or posture is a moment of change, a dynamic internal potential built out of the oppositional forces of the eight trigrams. Each movement, by containing its opposite, allows an endless oscillation from one polarity to another, much like the strategies of zheng and qi discussed in part one of this book. The above diagram is used by Ba Gua exponents to illustrate the exponential potential of these endless changes.

 **Wu Ji** (無 極)

Wu Ji is the place where movement begins. There is no thought, no intention. Movement and stillness are not known. The chest is empty and the abdomen is full. The form is undifferentiated, unfixed.

 **Tai Ji (太 極)**

Tai Ji is created from *Wu Ji*. Once there is even the beginning of a turning / spiraling action inside the body, however minutely, then right and left, yin and yang, up and down are created. Heaven and Earth are also created with man at the center of their interaction. This is *San Ti Shi*, the Three Body Pattern.

Liang Yi (兩儀) and San Ti Shi (三體式)

Liang Yi refers to the two polarities, yin and yang. Liang Yi is manifested in the body by San Ti Shi, the Three Body Pattern. In Ba Gua, San Ti Shi is called *Lao Seng Tuo Bo*, "Old Monk Holds the Alms Bowl."[288] In Xing Yi it is the posture of *Pi Quan*,[289] or Splitting Fist. San Ti Shi corresponds to Heaven, Earth, and Human Beings.

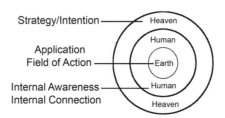

Figure 3.3. San Ti Shi: Three Body Pattern, Heaven, Earth, and Human Beings

San Ti Shi is a pattern that instantly arises out of the spiraling of the Tai Ji, a pattern that manifests yin, yang, heaven, earth, front and back, up and down, right and left. San Ti Shi is the linking of strategy and tactics with internal connection and internal awareness. It is the foundation of movement, a dynamic state of stillness that connects spirit and intention and potentiates movement. In Ba Gua Zhang, San Ti Shi is related to the Millstone Pushing Palm—*Tui Mo Zhang*,[290] the basic posture for turning and circle walking. The circle walking itself is an expression of the simple yin-yang dynamic of the Liang Yi: turning rightward, or turning leftward, feet hooking inward toward the center of the circle / spiral *(Kou Bu)* or swinging outward *(Bai Bu).* Circle walking unites the body in an endless expansion and contraction. Sun Lutang feels that the Liang Yi is the principle of contraction and expansion of the one qi.

> With the One Qi turning, Heaven, Earth, and 10,000 things appear in the body.[291] The hook step and the swing step must be pure. Do not get a twisted step. The body, waist, legs, and knees, each part, must expand and contract and follow together. When you begin to practice, go slowly. After a while, the dantien fills with Qi. When it becomes natural, then you can go faster. Therefore, it is an internal skill. The first emphasis is on the Qi. When the Qi is flowing circularly, then the body's one hundred veins [channels and collaterals; meridians] unfold liberally. The hands and the feet will be agile.[292]

Si Xiang (四象)

Si Xiang means "four shapes or appearances." Once there is turning rightward and leftward while circle walking, there is changing direction and changing the palms. In Ba Gua Zhang, Si Xiang refers to the Single Palm Change or Single Changing Palm, which incorporates four essential oppositional yet complementary movements:

Ning (擰)—Twist
Guo (裹)—Wrap
Zuan (鑽)—Drill
Fan (反)—Overturn

The famous Ba Gua exponent Jiang Rong-jiao describes these four energies as *Gun*-Roll, *Zuan*-Drill, *Zheng*-Contend, and *Guo*-Wrap.[293] Jiang uses these words to refer to the various types of *jin-li* or "energy-strength"[294] encountered during one's practice of the Single Palm Change. From the Single Palm Change all other changes and tactics originate and take shape. Within twisting, there is drilling. Drilling is also piercing (*Chuan*). Therefore, within piercing there is also rolling/twisting, and within rolling/twisting there is piercing/drilling. Contending is sometimes translated as *extending*.[295]

In wrapping, the intention (Yi) and force (Jin) are embraced internally, while in extending/overturning intention and force extend outward. In wrapping there is extending/overturning, and in extending/overturning there is wrapping. Sun Lutang explains this as follows:

> Rising makes drilling. Falling makes overturning. Rising makes crossing. Falling makes flowing. Rising and drilling are piercing. Falling and overturning are striking. Rising is also striking. Falling is also striking. Striking, rising, and falling are like smoothly turning machinery. In practice, you need this method. It is not any different from Xing Yi Quan.[296]

Although methodically trained, Wuji, Tai Ji, Liang Yi, and Si Xiang are not sequential, do not unfold over time, but are instantaneous, the void, intention, and movement occurring simultaneously, in an instant in time. They are directly connected to the eight trigrams (Ba Gua). The Ba Gua expand the scope of possible actions and responses without increasing the number of decisions and choices to be made, beyond turning rightward or leftward, and hooking inward or swinging outward with the feet.

Ba Gua (八卦)

The Ba Gua or Eight Diagrams refer to the trigrams of the *Yijing*. This refers to the Eight Dispositions/Attitudes outlined in Chapter II. In Ba Gua Zhang, the eight trigrams and the Dispositions/Attitudes are linked to eight body forms known as ding shi[297] or "fixed/determined patterns." These eight fundamental body patterns in turn have a correspondence with eight emblematic animals. The association of animal imagery with a trigram and ding shi posture does not imply an attempt to imitate animal movement. The animals act as emblems of an internal configuration or body pattern that transforms the body from the inside out, as it flows from one posture to another—now a crouching tiger, or a cloud-swimming dragon, then a hawk diving and soaring or a snake coiling and twisting. This develops another level of awareness and strategy in performing and applying each body pattern.

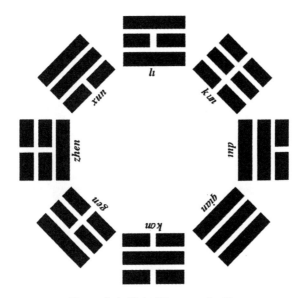

Figure 3.4. Eight Trigrams: Ba Gua

Trigram Image	Trigram Name	Symbol	Ding Shi Body Pattern	Emblematic Animal
☷	Kun	Earth	Downward Pressing Palm	Tiger
☰	Qian	Heaven	Heaven Uplifting Palm	Dragon
☱	Dui	Lake	Ape Offering Peach Palm	Monkey
☶	Gen	Mountain	Mountain Pushing Palm	Bear/Horse
☵	Kan	Water	Yin Yang Fish Palm	Snake
☲	Li	Fire	Touch Heaven Penetrate Earth Palm	Phoenix/Swallow
☴	Xun	Wind	Ball Embracing Palm	Hawk/Lion
☳	Zhen	Thunder	Millstone Pushing Palm	Qi Lin

Notes:
1. In some styles of Ba Gua Zhang, the Horse can be associated with Fire (li) or Heaven (qian).

2. The Qi Lin is a mythical animal that is often translated as the unicorn. The Qi Lin (Kirin in Japanese) however, has the head of the dragon, the body and horns of the deer, hooves of the horse and tail of the ox. Other descriptions depict the Qi Lin with the scales of a carp, the hooves of an ox, the tail of a lion, and the head of a dragon. In some depictions, the Qi Lin has two horns, rather than one.

Figure 3.5. Trigrams and Fundamental Body Patterns

Because all the other changes and methods emanate from the ding shi forms and their manifestation of the principles inherent in the eight trigrams (Eight Dispositions or Intentions), the ding shi can be expanded or transformed into eight linear maneuvers and the circular changes of the *Lao Ba Zhang* form (Old Eight Palms).[298] These dynamic expressions of the fundamental forms and principles in turn produce countless changes and potentials within the Six Sides (up-down; front-back; turning right–turning left) and the Eight Directions.

Trigram Image	Trigram Name	Symbol	Linear Plam	Lao Ba Zhang Palm
	Zhen	Thunder	Upward Striking Palm	Single Changing Palm
	Kan	Water	Yin Striking Palm	Covering Palm
	Dui	Lake	Opening Palm	Body Turning Palm
	Kun	Earth	Windwheel Chopping Palm	Chopping Palm
	Li	Fire	Heaven Earth Palm	Opportunity Seizing Palm
	Xun	Wind/Wood	Ten Ton Weight Falls to Earth Rhinoceros Gaze at Moon Palm	Step Following Palm
	Gen	Mountain	Insert Flowers in Armpit Phoenix Enters Nest Palm	Soft Body Palm
	Qian	Heaven	Face Slapping Palm	Flat Penetrating Palm

Figure 3.6. Trigrams, Eight Linear Palms and Eight Palm Changes

A final association of the trigrams is with Ba Gua Zhang's eight basic movements. Wang Shu Jin lists them as follows (Fig. 3-7).[299]

In fact, these eight fundamental movements are contained within each of the ding shi, the Eight Palm Changes (Lao Ba Zhang), and the Eight Single Linear Movements. One is always and continuously hooking, splitting, moving, entering, leading, pushing, holding up, and carrying. The following schematic (Fig. 3-8) shows how seemingly disparate techniques and methods are all one method, one technique.

Trigram	Movement	Yi Jing Image
☰	*Tui* (to push)	Heaven
☷	*Pi* (to split)	Earth
☵	*Tuo* (to uphold)	Water
☲	*Kou* (to hook)	Fire
☳	*Ling (*to lead)	Thunder
☶	*Dai* (to carry)	Mountain
☴	*Ban* (to move)	Wind
☱	*Jin* (to enter)	Lake

Figure 3.7. Trigrams and Basic Movements

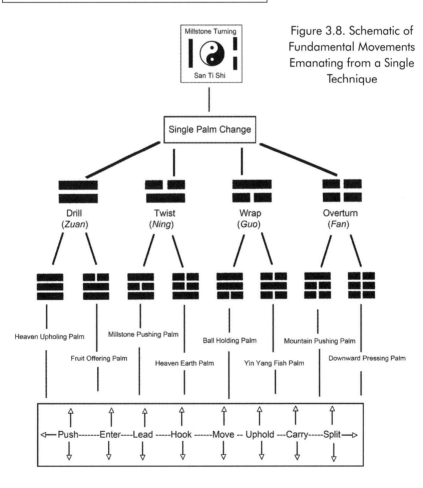

Figure 3.8. Schematic of Fundamental Movements Emanating from a Single Technique

Liu Shi Si Shou (六十四手)

The Sixty-Four Hands or *Liu Shi Si Shou* are generated by the eight trigrams and their associated body patterns, movements, and changes. Linked in sequences of eight, the Sixty-Four Hands can be understood to correspond with the sixty-four hexagrams in the Eight Palace configuration (see Chapter II). Each sequence of eight movements presents a series of moves and countermoves that logically follow one upon the other. Although it is impossible to follow a set sequence against a real opponent, the sequences begin to teach one to change fluidly with the opponent's changes. This is reminiscent of Mao Zedong's idea that when fighting the first battle, you must have an idea of how the second, third, and even the final battle will be fought, what will occur in each case should you or the enemy prevail, and how that will affect the next battle. Although the predictions will not be certain, and will not turn out exactly as planned, by thinking out the possible changes that can occur in the general situation, we can reduce uncertainty.[300]

But the Sixty-Four Hands are not just a set of idealized combat sequences. Each of the Sixty-Four hexagrams contains the "energy" or pattern of two of the trigrams. In Ba Gua Zhang, each of the Sixty-Four Hands can then be understood to contain the body patterns that correspond to two trigrams. Therefore, each of the movements of the Sixty-Four Hands can generate multiple changes, potentially transforming into numerous possibilities depending on the opponent's response. Looked at in this way, the Sixty-Four Hands are not so much specific applications as they are combinations of the primal patterns or "energies" of the Liang Yi, Si Xiang, and Ba Gua. In effect, the Sixty-Four Hands are simply higher-order archetypes that are combinations of the basic archetypes set out earlier in the exponential growth pattern shown above in Diagram I. This creates an expanded diagram on opposite page.

The arrow on the right shows that there is movement in both directions—exponential potential outward, but potential that also constantly recurs back to the beginning. Multiples of sixty-four possibilities are too complex to be useful. As Boyd and Miller pointed out earlier, the more complex an interaction is, the harder it is to adapt to changing events, because the OODA loop becomes drawn out in time. Through constant

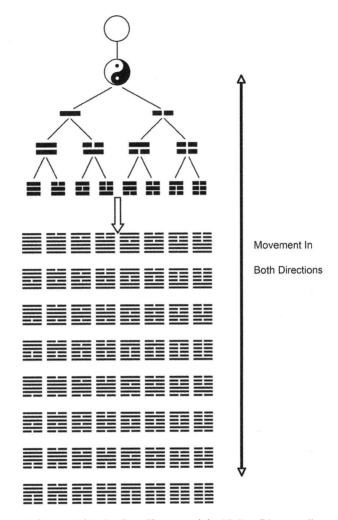

Figure 3.9. Exponential Potential in Ba Gua Zhang and the Yi Jing Diagram II

recursion back from the sixty-four to the eight, from the eight to the four, from four back to the two, to the Tai Ji, to the Void/Wu Ji—multiple possibilities become nothing more than variations of one or two choices. Having at most two choices to make, no matter what the situation, allows movement through the OODA loop to be virtually instantaneous. Hence, the famous saying in Ba Gua Zhang: *From one change, a thousand changes and transformations.*

When looked at in this way, each of the Sixty-Four Hands can be understood in a number of ways. What appears to be a strike could be a throw or a lock, and a step can be a kick or a throw. When preconceptions and limitations are removed, the sixty-four movements are reduced to being combinations of eight postures; the eight postures are reduced to different versions of wrapping, twisting, drilling, and overturning, which in turn reduce to turning right and left, hooking inward and swinging outward. In this way, the body manifests a limitless potential for change and adaptation.

If the Sixty-Four Hands are really body patterns that manifest an innate potential for change, then ultimately change can also occur internally, reflected only subtly in the external body pattern or form. Wes Tasker, a colleague of mine who is an expert in many styles of martial arts, likened this idea to heuristic theory:

> If heuristics are defined as "intuitions that appear suddenly in consciousness, whose underlying reasons we are not fully aware of, and are strong enough to act upon," or "a method that is particularly used to rapidly come to a solution that is reasonably close to the best possible answer, or optimal solution," then what you are describing is simply Ba Gua's Heuristic Decision Making Tree. This then shrinks the first three parts of the OODA loop. If we already have in place advanced decision making trees (heuristics) based on the congruency of the Sixty-Four Hands, Lao Ba Zhang, Eight Single Movements, and the Ding Shi—then we have in place a process that rapidly moves through the Observation, Orientation, and Decision parts [of the OODA loop] and moves (seemingly) straight to Action before the opponent can possibly catch up. So, in a more general sense, what is a "martial art" except a set of basic tools that are then formed into decision making trees (forms and/or drills) that are practiced until they become readily available to the unconscious? Thereby accelerating the first three stages of the loop.

A "Black Swan" as defined by Nassim Nicholas Taleb is "an event with three attributes: 1—it is an outlier in that it lies outside the regular realm of expectations. 2—it carries an extreme impact. 3—in spite of its outlier status, human nature makes us concoct explanations for its occurrence after the fact, making it explainable and predictable. In other words—any fight is a Black Swan, and integral to negotiating through a Black Swan would be heuristics[301]."

Another version of Ba Gua's heuristic decision making tree is pictured below. It is perhaps the most accurate of the various schematics presented, because the circular pattern provides an organic image of many layers operating simultaneously.

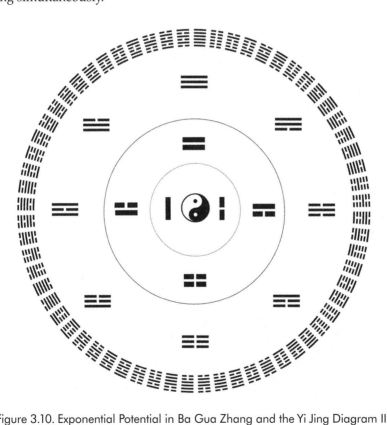

Figure 3.10. Exponential Potential in Ba Gua Zhang and the Yi Jing Diagram III

Ba Gua Straight Line Eight Diagram Sixty-Four Palms

直趟八卦六十四掌 *Zhi Tang Ba Gua Liu Shi Si Zhang*

First Line: Palace of Thunder 第一趟

1. Step Forward with the Uplifting Palm
   進步挑掌 *(Jin Bu Tiao Zhang)*

   THUNDER
   Thunder ䷲ Quake / Thunder (Zhen)

2. Lion Rolls the Ball
   獅子滾球 *(Shi Zi Gun Qiu)*

   WIND
   Thunder ䷩ Increase (Yi)

3. Entangling Hand Hidden Strike
   纏手掖撞 *(Chan Shou Ye Zhuang)*

   EARTH
   Thunder ䷗ Return (Fu)

4. Crouching Tiger Leaps the Ravine
   臥虎跳澗 *(Wo Hu Tiao Jian)*

   MOUNTAIN
   Thunder ䷚ Nourishment (Yi)

5. Punch Under the Elbow
   肘底看捶 *(Zhou Di Kan Chui)*

   FIRE
   Thunder ䷔ Bite Through (Shi He)

6. Turn Over the Arm Splitting Strike
   反臂劈捶 *(Fan Bi Pi Chui)*

   LAKE
   Thunder ䷐ Following (Sui)

7. Double Whip to Press the Elbow

雙鞭壓肘 *(Shuang Bian Ya Zhou)*

HEAVEN

Thunder ䷘ No Falsehood (Wu Wang)

8. Step Forward with the Cutting Elbow

進步截肘 *(Jin Bu Jie Zhou)*

WATER

Thunder ䷂ Difficulty at the Beginning (Zhun)

Second Line: Palace of Water 第二趟

1. Blue-Green Dragon Extends Its Claws

青龍探爪 *(Qing Long Tan Zhua)*

WATER

Water ䷜ Sinkhole / Abyss (Kan)

2. Brush the Sleeves and Strike Continuously

抹袖連捶 *(Mo Xiu Lian Chui)*

EARTH

Water ䷆ The Army (Shi)

3. Cloud Dragon Offers Its Claw

雲龍獻爪 *(Yun Long Xian Zhua)*

THUNDER

Water ䷧ Deliverance / Relief (Jie)

4. Move Away the Clouds to See the Sun

撥雲見日 *(Bo Yun Jian Ri)*

HEAVEN

Water ䷅ Conflict / Contention (Song)

5. Pat the Chest and Pounce with the Elbow
   拍胸補肘 *(Pai Xiong Bu Zhou)*

   MOUNTAIN
   Water ☵ Childlike Ignorance (Meng)

6. Turn the Body and Butt with the Elbow
   轉身頂肘 *(Zhuan Shen Ding Zhou)*

   LAKE
   Water ☵ Exhaustion (Kun)

7. Punch the Ear with a Penetrating Strike
   貫耳穿捶 *(Guan Er Chuan Chui)*

   WIND
   Water ☴ Dispersing (Huan)

8. Hungry Tiger Tears Open the Heart
   餓虎扒心 *(E Hu Ba Xin)*

   FIRE
   Water ☲ Before Completion (Wei Ji)

Third Line: Palace of Lake 第三趟

1. Step Forward Unite and Strike
   進步團撞 *(Jin Bu Tuan Zhuang)*

   THUNDER
   Lake ☳ Marrying Maiden (Gui Mei)

2. White Ape Offering Peach
   白猿獻桃 *(Bai Yuan Xian Tao)*

   LAKE
   Lake ☱ Joyous (Tui)

3. Wind Wheel Overturning Elbow

   風輪反肘 (*Feng Lun Fan Zhou*)

   WATER
   Lake ䷻ Limitation/Restriction (Jie)

4. Immortal Watches the Chess Board

   仙人觀棋 (*Xian Ren Guan Qi*)

   MOUNTAIN
   Lake ䷨ Decrease (Sun)

5. Golden Thread Brushes the Eyebrow

   金絲抹眉 (*Jin Si Mo Mei*)

   FIRE
   Lake ䷥ Opposition/Separation (Kui)

6. Jade Maiden Throws the Shuttle

   玉女穿梭 (*Yu Nu Chuan Suo*)

   WIND
   Lake ䷼ Inner Truth/Sincerity (Zhong Fu)

7. Step Back and Lead the Sheep

   退步牽羊 (*Tui Bu Qian Yang*)

   EARTH
   Lake ䷒ Overlooking (Lin)

8. The Overlord Sends Off the Guest

   霸王送客 (*Ba Wang Song Ke*)

   HEAVEN
   Lake ䷉ Treading/Conduct (Lu)

Fourth Line: Palace of Earth 第四趟

1. Departing Horse Turns Back
   走馬回頭 (*Zou Ma Hui Tou*)

   THUNDER
   Earth ䷏ Enthusiasm / Contentment (Yu)

2. Two Immortals Preach the Dao
   二仙傳道 (*Er Xian Chuan Dao*)

   MOUNTAIN
   Earth ䷖ Splitting Apart (Bo)

3. Body Overturning Splitting Strike
   翻身劈捶 (*Fan Shen Pi Chui*)

   HEAVEN
   Earth ䷋ Obstruction / Standstill (Pi)

4. Wild Horse Crashes through the Trough
   野馬撞槽 (*Ye Ma Zhuang Cao*)

   WATER
   Earth ䷇ Union (Bi)

5. Great Roc Spreads Its Wings
   大鵬展翅 (*Da Peng Zhan Chi*)

   WIND
   Earth ䷓ Contemplation / View (Guan)

6. White Robe Scythes the Grass
   白袍鍘草 (*Bai Bao Zha Cao*)

   EARTH
   Earth ䷁ Receptive / Responding (Kun)

7. Zhou Cang Shoulders the Broadsword[302]
   周倉扛刀 *(Zhou Cang Kang Dao)*

   FIRE
   Earth ䷢ Advance/Progress (Jin)

8. Liu Quan Advances the Melon
   劉全進瓜 *(Liu Quan Jin Gua)*

   LAKE
   Earth ䷬ Gather Together (Cui)

Fifth Line: Palace of Fire 第五趟

1. Escape the Body and Transform the Shadow
   脫身化影 *(Tuo Shen Hua Ying)*

   WIND
   Fire ䷤ The Family (Jia Ren)

2. Stroking Hand, Slicing [Kick], and Trample
   捋手蹁 踩 *(Luo Shou Pian Cai)*

   HEAVEN
   Fire ䷌ Fellowship (Tong Ren)

3. Advancing Step Bumping Strike
   進步撞捶 *(Jin Bu Zhuang Chui)*

   EARTH
   Fire ䷧ Light Suppressed (Ming Yi)

4. Head On Spring Kick to the Knee
   迎面彈膝 *(Ying Mian Tan Xi)*

   LAKE
   Fire ䷰ Revolution (Ge)

5. Sweep the Ear with a Single Strike
   掃耳單捶 *(Sao Er Dan Chui)*

   WATER
   Fire ䷾ After Completion (Ji Ji)

6. Arm Overturning Charging Strike
   反臂衝捶 *(Fan Bi Chong Chui)*

   FIRE
   Fire ䷝ The Clinging (Li)

7. King of Heaven Holds Up the Pagoda
   天王托塔 *(Tian Wang Tuo Ta)*

   THUNDER
   Fire ䷶ Fullness/ Abundance (Feng)

8. Queen Mother Winds Thread
   王母拐線 *(Wang Mu Guai Xian)*

   MOUNTAIN
   Fire ䷕ Adornment (Bi)

Sixth Line: Palace of Wind 第六趟

1. Thousand Kilo Weight Falls to Earth
   千斤墜地 *(Qian Jin Zhui Di)*

   EARTH
   Wind ䷭ Pushing Upward (Sheng)

2. Sun and Moon Advance Together
   日月並行 *(Ri Yue Bing Xing)*

   LAKE
   Wind ䷛ Great Superiority (Da Guo)

3. Golden Cicada Sheds Its Skin
   金蟬脫殼 *(Jin Chan Tuo Qiaoi)*

   WATER
   Wind ䷯ Well (Jing)

4. Lean on Mountain Squeezing
   倚山擠靠 *(Yi Shan Ji Kao)*

   MOUNTAIN
   Wind ䷑ Decay (Gu)

5. Pull the Hand and Bump with the Knee
   捋手撞膝 *(Luo Shou Zhuang Xi)*

   FIRE
   Wind ䷱ Cauldron (Ding)

6. Lazy Dragon Lies on the Pillow
   懶龍臥枕 *(Lan Long Wo Zhen)*

   HEAVEN
   Wind ䷫ Coming to Meet (Gou)

7. Twist and Lift the Hand to Slap Upward
   扭手提撩 *(Niu Shou Ti Liao)*

   WIND
   Wind ䷸ Penetrating / Gentle (Xun)

8. Step Forward with the Downward Pressing Palm
   進步塌掌 *(Jin Bu Ta Zhang)*

   THUNDER
   Wind ䷟ Duration / Perseverance (Heng)

Seventh Line: Palace of Mountain 第七趟

1. Thrust Flower Under the Elbow (Into the Ribs)
   插花掖肘 *(Cha Hua Ye Zhou)*

   HEAVEN
   Mountain ䷠ Withdrawal/Retreat (Dun)

2. Lone Phoenix Enters the Nest
   單鳳投巢 *(Dan Feng Tou Chao)*

   WATER
   Mountain ䷦ Obstruction (Jian)

3. File Inside and Stamp Outside
   裡挫外踩 *(Li Cuo Wai Duo)*

   LAKE
   Mountain ䷞ Mutual Attraction (Xian)

4. Cover the Elbow Push the Mountain
   掩肘推山 *(Yan Zhou Tui Shan)*

   MOUNTAIN
   Mountain ䷳ Keeping Still (Gen)

5. Wind the Elbow and Wave the Lotus
   纏肘擺蓮 *(Chan Zhou Bai Lian)*

   WIND
   Mountain ䷴ Gradual Advance (Jian)

6. Turn Around and Beat the Waist (Like a Drum)
   轉身擂腰 *(Zhuan Shen Lei Yao)*

   THUNDER
   Mountain ䷽ Minor Superiority (Xiao Guo)

7. Ape Climbs the Pole

   猿猴爬杆 (*Yuan Hou Pa Gan*)

   FIRE
   Mountain ䷲ The Wanderer (Lu)

8. Bend the Bow to Shoot the Tiger

   彎弓射虎 (*Wan Gong She Hu*)

   EARTH
   Mountain ䷲ Modesty / Humility (Qian)

Eighth Line: Palace of Heaven 第八趟

1. Four Dragons Drawing Water

   四龍取水 (*Si Long Qu Shui*)

   THUNDER
   Heaven ䷡ Great Strength (Da Zhuang)

2. Embrace the Moon to the Breast

   懷中抱月 (*Huai Zhong Bao Yue*)

   LAKE
   Heaven ䷪ Resolution (Kuai)

3. Immortal Sifts the Rice

   仙人簸米 (*Xian Ren Bo Mi*)

   HEAVEN
   Heaven ䷀ The Creative (Qian)

4. Stroking Hand Plays with the Pearls

   捋手戲球 (*Luo Shou Xi Qiu*)

   WATER
   Heaven ䷎ Waiting (Xu)

5. Zhang Fei Steals a Horse (by Trickery)[303]

   張飛騙馬 *(Zhang Fei Pian Ma)*

   FIRE

   Heaven ䷌ Great Holding (Da You)

6. Slice Two Revolving Doors

   片旋兩門 *(Pian Xuan Liang Men)*

   WIND

   Heaven ䷈ Small Accumulation (Xiao Xu)

7. Wind Wheel Splitting Palm

   風輪劈掌 *(Feng Lun Pi Zhang)*

   EARTH

   Heaven ䷊ Peace (Tai)

8. Lone Goose Leaves the Flock

   孤雁出群 *(Gu Yan Chu Qun)*

   MOUNTAIN

   Heaven ䷙ Great Accumulation (Da Xu)

CHAPTER IV

Patterns of Change:
The Order of the Hexagrams

All things between heaven and earth follow these rules: When something has reached its extreme, it starts to develop in the opposite direction; when something has waxed full, it then wanes. . . . Flourishing and fading succeed each other. This is exemplified by the four seasons. Something prevails, only to be prevailed over. This is exemplified by the Wu Xing, or five elements. No living being can escape the cycle of life and death. That is the nature of life itself. Capability and incapability coexist. That is in the nature of all things. Advantages and disadvantages exist side by side. That is in the nature of all situations.

—Sunzi[304]

Patterns of Change: The Order of the Hexagrams

The order of the Hexagrams show us there is constant change. Even when there is apparent stillness or stoppage, it is momentary in the greater scope of the pattern. Life does not stop, it rises and falls endlessly. Things manifest and dissapear, coalesce and dissolve, only to reemerge and reform again and again. New things are beginning to manifest as old things end. To be aware of the new while it is still invisible allows one to prepare for its coming, to be ready to meet it. This requires all the qualities of the trigrams themselves: intention and planning, adaptability and sacrifice, stillness and humility, movement, stimulation and renewal, penetration and sensitivity, reflection and joy, yielding and responding, insight, unity and clarity. Within the changes there are also moments of apparent stillness, of waiting, during which things gather and coalesce. Stillness within movement, and movement within stillness take place within the endless changes.

In the hexagram order, each even-numbered hexagram is the inverse of its predecessor. The yin and yang lines are reversed. This reflects the natural tendency of phenomena, situations, and occurences to change into their opposite when they reach their peak.

1. The Creative (Qian): Heaven above Heaven. Yang is the creative principle. The strong yang lines move ahead to completion.

2. Receptive/Responding (Kun): This is Earth above Earth, the opposite of the previous hexagram. The yin lines yield and respond to the yang lines. Only by this combination of complementary opposites can movement, growth, and development take place.

3. Difficulty at the Beginning (Zhun): When yin and yang, the soft and the hard interact, things are born. Water (the abyss) blocks Thunder's upward movement, represented in the first yang line. There is difficulty at the beginning (birth throes).

4. Youthful Folly/Childlike Ignorance (Meng): As things begin to develop, they are in an immature state. The hexagram consists of a dangerous place (Water) below a Mountain. Behind is danger, ahead is the closed door of a Mountain. One must find one's way.

5. Waiting (Xu): Water above Heaven. Danger (the abyss) lies ahead. The strong yang lines of Heaven (below) stop, stay away from danger, and wait for the right moment to move ahead. When things are in an immature state, they need to bide their time. In waiting there is nurturing—the promotion of growth.

6. Conflict/Contention (Song): Heaven above and Water below operate in contrary ways. Promoting growth leads to contention and conflict. Growth and need are tied to instincts of ownership that can lead to conflict.

7. The Army (Shi): When there is conflict, there is sure to be a rising of the people (like Water gathering within the Earth). Hence, the army is formed. The yang line in the second position, representing the general, gathers the other lines around it.

8. Union/Holding Together (Bi): Water on the Earth; water and Earth mutually support each other. The yin lines are drawn together by the yang line in the fifth position, representing the leader. When people band together (the Army), a group develops. Groups involve closeness and union. If people mutually assist one another, things can develop.

9. Small Taming (Xiao Xu): The yin line holds the five yang lines, just as Wind in the sky (Heaven) gathers clouds. When there is union and mutual assistance, there is development; a group gathers together and little by little things begin to develop.

10. Treading/Conduct (Lu): For the Lake to be below Heaven is natural. Treading means that things should be in their proper places; follow the natural order. When a group gathers together, conduct and propriety must necessarily develop. The single yin line can harmonize and hold the yang lines together with its gentle conduct.

11. Peace (Tai): When one's conduct is correct, things proceed smoothly. Heaven moves upward and Earth downward, so they interact. This is Heaven on Earth; there is peace and tranquility.

12. Standstill/Obstruction (Pi): The opposite of the previous hexagram. The yang lines go upward and the yin lines move downward. Heaven and Earth move apart. There is no interaction. Things cannot be tranquil and smooth forever. That is why standstill and obstruction follow peace.

13. Fellowship (Tong Ren): Heaven above Fire. Fire burns up to connect with Heaven. Obstruction cannot last. Five yang lines respond to the single yin line. This is the opposite of obstruction. When obstruction to movement occurs, people must cooperate with one another in a spirit of fellowship and shared goals in order to advance.

14. Great Holding (Da You): Fire above Heaven. The yin line unites the forces of the yang lines. When there is fellowship with others, and the clarity of vision symbolized by Fire, possessions and/or attainment naturally yield themselves up to the group. This is Great Holding.

15. Modesty/Humility (Qian): The Mountain is underneath the Earth rather than above it. The third line pulls the other lines together through humility and modesty. When one's possessions are great, one should not indulge in pride, but should be modest and share both hardships and achievements.

16. Enthusiasm/Contentment (Yu): Earth is below Thunder. The yang line is in the position of strength. Earth is content to respond to the outward action of Thunder. To have possessions, attainment, and humility leads to delight and contentment.

17. Following (Sui): Thunder is below Lake. Lake is gentle and Thunder's active movement follows Lake's gentle contentment. When people are content, they follow out of joy rather than coercion.

18. Decay/Remedying the Ill (Gu): Wind is below the Mountain. The Mountain stops movement. This combined with the compliance of Wind creates stagnation. When there is contentment and compliance, it can give way to complacency. This can lead to decay.

19. Approaching/Overlooking (Lin): In this situation the two yang lines are advancing, moving forward, becoming great. Earth, above the Lake, oversees it. Oversight remedies problems that may arise. When things are flourishing and advancing, one must be wary of sudden difficulties or potential decline.

20. Contemplation/View (Guan): The two yang lines in the previous hexagram have reached the top. The image represents a tower from which one can see all around, like Wind blowing over the Earth and touching everything. Only when something is great (fully developed) can it be viewed and contemplated. By both setting an example and observing carefully, one can prevail.

21. Bite Through (Shi He): Fire above Thunder represents inner movement combined with clarity of thought. Through observation and contemplation, there can be differentiation. The hexagram looks like teeth coming together to bite through something between them that is obstructing their union. This implies that direct action (Thunder) and judgment/differentiation (Fire) are necessary in order to achieve success.

22. Grace/Adornment (Bi): Fire under the Mountain symbolizes Fire revealing and enhancing the Mountain's beauty. When things come together, they cannot be combined arbitrarily. There is order, organization, and culture. This creates adornment and grace.

23. Splitting Apart/Falling Away (Bo): The yin lines are about to push out the yang line. The Earth is under the Mountain, but cannot support it, so the Mountain is about to collapse. When development reaches its ultimate limit, symbolized in the previous hexagram, the inner substance can fall away, leaving behind ostentation and superficiality.

24. Return (Fu): Thunder (movement) under the Earth represents a renewal, a new beginning, like the coming of spring after winter. The single yang line moves forward unobstructed. Things cannot fall away forever and cease to exist. When falling away reaches its limit there is a return, things rise again.

25. No Falsehood (Wu Wang): Thunder under Heaven. When the movement of renewal and return is in accord with natural law (represented by Heaven) rather than human desire, everything is correct without error.

26. Great Taming/Great Accumulation (Da Xu): Mountain over Heaven. When there is no error, Heaven's forward movement is restrained by Mountain's calm firmness. Then there can be a great buildup with the strength and creative energies stored at the top.

27. Nourishment (Yi): Mountain (stillness) and Thunder (movement). Regulated movement—a balance of movement and stillness. Movement and desire combine with cultivation and regulation. The hexagram looks like an open mouth. When there is great accumulation and storing, there is also nourishment of the body and of the spirit.

28. Great Excess/Great Superiority (Da Guo): With the regulation of movement and nourishment comes excess. The waters of the Lake above have risen above the trees (Wind/Wood). The center of the hexagram is strong, but the ends are weak, meaning that there is danger of collapse, but with Wind's penetration in the form of observation and caution success can be achieved.

29. Water/The Abyss/Sinkhole (Kan): Water over Water; double danger; the sinkhole or the abyss, signified by the weak yin lines in the middle and at the ends. A state of superiority and excess cannot endure forever. What goes up eventually comes down. Great superiority encounters pitfalls, but if one can adapt like Water to conform to the situation, one can prevail.

30. The Clinging/Fire (Li): Fire over Fire. The yin lines cling to the surrounding yang lines. As falling reaches its limit it is converted into something to cling to. Success in the abyss, the dark comes from finding one's way by employing clarity and insight.

31. Influence/Mutual Attraction (Xian): Lake over the Mountain. The Mountain and the Lake are a pair that enhance each other. The nature of the Lake is that its water collects and nourishes the Mountain. The nature of the Mountain is to accept this nourishment. Rain on the Mountain also fills the Lake. When things go together and have cohesion, there is mutual attraction and reciprocity.

32. Duration/Perseverance (Heng): Thunder and Wind complement each other. Like the Mountain and Lake in the previous hexagram, they are paired phenomena. Movement outside and gentleness within. When there is reciprocity and attraction, things endure. When movement is softened it is not worn down, but is enduring and persevering, like Thunder and Wind coming and going together endlessly.

33. Withdrawal/Retreat (Dun): Mountain under Heaven. The Mountain rises up to Heaven, while Heaven retreats. Yin advances while yang retreats. What endures must eventually withdraw or retreat. Success gained through withdrawal at the right time.

34. Great Strength (Da Zhuang): Thunder above Heaven; strength within and movement on the outside. Now yang is flourishing as yin retreats. After withdrawal and decline, strength flourishes again. One will prevail through the correct application of strength.

35. Advance/Progress (Jin): Fire above Earth. This can symbolize the sun rising and advancing over the Earth, and Earth's hollow lines receiving the sun's light and energy. Great power and strength do not stand still. They move and advance with progress and clarity.

36. Light Suppressed/Darkening of the Light (Ming Yi): This is the reverse of the previous hexagram, Fire under the Earth. In advancing there is eventually damage or suppression. When the strong are injured, the weak and petty are in control. To prevail in this situation, one's comes brilliance should be kept hidden within the ordinary, the plain (i.e., within Earth's receptivity).

37. The Family/The Clan (Jia Ren): Wind arises from Fire and Fire is intensified by Wind. Fire in the inner trigram represents Fire from within, Fire returning home. Powerful action begins inside and provides mutual generation; the inner and outer generating each other represents the family. When light is suppressed, when there is injury, as in the previous hexagram, it is necessary to go inside. This is a return to the family; a return to what one knows.

38. Opposition/Separation (Kui): Fire above and the Lake below. Fire moves upward and Lake downward. This represents opposition, things separating, going different ways. When the family is exhausted or comes to an end there is separation and discord.

39. Obstruction/Adversity (Jian): Water over Mountain. Surrounded by obstacles: the Mountain is behind and Water (the abyss) in front. Disharmony and opposition lead to adversity and obstruction. Keeping still and steadfast (like the Mountain) is the key to prevailing in this situation.

40. Deliverance/Relief (Jie): Thunder above Water; movement outside of danger (the abyss)—movement removes one from danger. A thunderstorm clears the air, the obstacle has been removed. Eventually there is a relief from a difficult situation, a return to the normal order. It is movement that brings success here.

41. Decrease/Reduction (Sun): Mountain above the Lake. The third yang line has moved to the top, decreasing what is below; the inner foundation gives to what is above. The Mountain can become unstable if the foundation is decreased to increase the Mountain. With relief there is relaxation and neglect, which can lead to loss and reduction.

42. Increase (Yi): The strong lower line of Heaven in the upper trigram has sunken down to fill the bottom of the lower trigram, creating wind above Thunder. When the outer or upper gives to the lower or inner, this is an increase. The foundation is strengthened. When things decrease, eventually there is a turning point and things increase again. Thunder and Wind increase each other. Increase in the bottom or inner trigram initiates movement.

43. Resolution (Kuai): Lake above Heaven; water from the Lake rises to Heaven and there is a cloudburst. Eventually increase resolves. When increase continues without stopping, there is a breakthrough, like water filling a Lake until there is overflow. The yang lines move up to push out the yin line in order to break through and resolve the situation.

44. Coming to Meet/Encountering (Gou): Heaven above Wind. The soft and pliable encounters the hard and strong. Wind touches and encounters everything. Wind carries Heaven's intentions everywhere and simultaneously brings information back. When increase stops and there is resolution, there is also loss and separation. Eventually things must come together again, and new opportunities are encountered as yin at the bottom encounters yang. There must also be caution and awareness—when yin moves forward it can grow and overcome yang.

45. Gather Together (Cui): Lake above Earth. This is water in the Lake gathering and rising. The two strong lines gather the other lines together. When things meet or come together, they gather, like people meeting and congregating. Precautions should be taken, because when water gathers it can overflow its boundaries, and when people gather there can be strife.

46. Pushing Upward/Ascending (Sheng): Wind / Wood under Earth. Plants in the Earth grow upward. When things gather, there is accumulation. As things accumulate and gather, they push upward and outward; they grow. Power here comes from the root. Just as with a plant, progress that is steady and without haste leads to successful growth.

47. Oppression/Exhaustion (Kun): Lake above and Water below. When Water is below the Lake, it means the Lake is dry. Water has leaked out. Upward growth expands strength. If climbing upward does not stop, there is eventually exhaustion and oppression. When there is adversity, it is necessary to connect to and preserve one's inner strength in order to prevail.

48. Well (Jing): Wood is below and Water above. A wooden bucket is used to bring up Water from the well, just as plants draw water up from the Earth, or air pressure (Wind) pushes Water out of the Earth (a spring). When exhaustion sets in, things cannot go upward anymore. There must be a return to the beginning, to the bottom, like drawing up Water from the well. The well is inexhaustible, but it takes knowledge and discipline to make use of it.

49. Revolution/Radical Change/Molting (Ge): Inside the Lake there is Fire. Their incompatibility—Lake can extinguish Fire, and Fire can turn the Lake into vapor—creates change. After a long time, the well needs to be renovated and purified. Revolution is transformation, changing the old for the new. Adjust to the changing circumstances and you can change and transform inside so as to adapt to external changes.

50. Cauldron (Ding): Fire above Wood / Wind. The flame, kindled by Wind and Wood, cooks and transforms. This is the full realization of the previous hexagram. The cauldron is the image of transformation and change, because it transforms things. This can symbolize the realization of something new, a new state. Cooking in a cauldron symbolizes controlled change; combining and transforming to produce the new, but without totally destroying the old.

51. Thunder/Quake (Zhen): This is Thunder doubled. The first strong yang line moving upward is augmented by the yang line in the upper trigram. There is movement inside and movement outside. Transformation and change, the new, are movement that shock. This shock activates the inactive or complacent yin lines, arousing them to action.

52. Restraint/Keeping Still/Mountain (Gen): Mountain over Mountain, or linked Mountains, represents stopping and restraint. The yang lines have now moved to the top and stopped. Movement cannot continue forever. Eventually things stop. Then they move again. Movement and stillness generate and contain each other.

53. Gradual Advance (Jian): Wind/Wood on the Mountain. Things that stop must move again. Restraint cannot last forever. Eventually forward movement and growth begin again. The yang line in the third position moves upward slowly, like a tree growing on a Mountain. Gradual advance means that the movement is orderly. This can only occur with the discerning penetration of Wind/Wood on the outside.

54. Marrying Maiden (Gui Mei): Thunder over Lake. Thunder stirs the waters of the Lake. This is the image of a man marrying a younger woman, the woman following the man and responding to him. Things are moving toward their proper places, but are not yet there. The third and fifth yin lines are not in their proper place. They can potentially block movement. In this case, orderly movement leads to attainment of the goal.

55. Fullness/Abundance (Feng): Thunder (movement) on the outside above Fire (clarity inside); the interaction of clarity and movement signifies abundance. One can extend oneself to the utmost and prevail. Everything is in its proper place, so growth is possible and there will be abundance and greatness.

56. The Wanderer (Lu): Fire on the Mountain; Fire burns and moves on to new fuel while the Mountain remains still. When abundance comes to the end of its flourishing, one must move on to start a new cycle, in order to avoid stagnating. This means giving up one's position. That is why abundance is followed by the Wanderer. The strong line in the fourth place means that one should not overreach or be reckless, but exercise reserve and clarity during the journey. The Mountain within also symbolizes this reserve and restraint.

57. Penetrating/Gentle (Xun): Wind inside and outside. To wander means to give up one's place. To be taken in, to enter, to find a new place requires gentleness and compliancy. Wind doubled symbolizes this gentle entrance, but gentleness and compliance do not signify weakness or being ineffectual. The penetration of Wind comes from its unceasing nature, prevailing gradually and inconspicuously like breezes blowing one upon the other. On the other hand, too much compliance, humility, or overthinking prevents advancement.

58. The Joyous (Tui): Lake doubled. Joy is represented in the two strong lines in each trigram: strong inside and gentle outside. Two Lakes replenish each other. In the previous hexagram, the penetration of Wind provides entrance, helps one to find one's place. Having entered, there is delight and joy. Involvement with others brings pleasure.

59. Dispersing/Dissolution (Huan): Wind above water. Wind blows over the Water's surface, spreading and dispersing it in all directions. Joy has an expansive energy; when people are joyous their energy expands outward and disperses. There is no restraint. This can create a sense of dissolution and separation. Success in this situation comes because the strong second line enters, but is not pressed by the yin lines on either side of it. Also, the fourth yin line cooperates with the strong yang above.

60. Limitation/Restriction (Jie): Water above the Lake. The Water must be restrained from overflowing; it must be contained by the Lake. The second and fifth yang lines contain the two yin lines in the center. Things cannot disperse and separate forever. There must be a limitation. Limitation means that there are restrictions and people must exercise discipline. Limitation must not be too bitter or harsh or it will not have the desired effect.

61. Inner Truth/Sincerity (Zhong Fu): Wind over Lake represents compliance and joy. The soft yin lines are in the center, surrounded by the strong yang lines. The softness within represents an open and sincere heart. When there is proper discipline and limitation, people above and below have open hearts. They trust the regulations and maintain them.

62. Minor Excess/Minor Superiority (Xiao Guo): Thunder on the Mountain. Thunder is close, meaning that nearer, smaller things must be attended to. The yang lines are enclosed by the yin lines, which are in the position of strength and mediate with the outside world. This is the opposite of the last hexagram. Trust and compliance create a small excess, which means one can engage in small undertakings. The image resembles a bird. The bird should not fly too high or it will overextend and endanger itself. To prevail, achieve superiority in minor things.

63. After Completion/Fulfillment (Ji Ji): Water is above Fire, Water moves downward, and Fire moves upward so that they commingle and join, thereby completing each other. The strong lines and weak lines are all in their proper places. Once there is minor superiority, things can reach their climax. Because the yang and yin lines are in their proper places, perfect equilibrium is reached, but small details must be attended to or things will pass the point of equilibrium and become chaotic.

64. Before Completion/Not Yet Fulfilled (Wei Ji): Fire is above Water. Fire and Water are moving in opposite directions (Fire upward and Water downward), so they do not integrate. Once things are settled and completed they end. In this situation, things are not yet completed. They continue to develop and create, because they are unfinished and unfulfilled. This is a new beginning. When things are unsettled, and beginning anew, it is best to be prudent, hence the fifth yin line does not oppose the strong lines around it.

CHAPTER V

Applying Principles of Strategy and Change in Daily Life

Strategy is a system of expedients: it is more than mere scholarly discipline, it is the translation of knowledge to practical life, the improvement of the original leading thought in accordance with continually changing situations. It is the art of acting under the pressure of the most difficult conditions.

—Field Marshall Helmuth von Moltke[305]

The Book of Changes *is pragmatic. Its focus is on this world, not the next. Its purpose is to help people lead meaningful and fulfilling lives in a world full of changes over which they may have only limited control. Its ethical philosophy is rational, practical, humane, and nonfanatical. It is not concerned with the salvation of souls. It is very much concerned with redemption, but only in the sense that people have the ability to turn their lives around and return to the Dao or Way that is appropriate for them. . . . The book seeks to help people attain good fortune and avoid bad fortune, but, as the* Great Treatise *explains at one point, its real purpose is to allow human beings to be without blame; that is, to have done everything they can to live in concord with the world around them while maintaining their integrity.*

—The Laws of Change[306]

Friction Revisited

The Prussian military thinker Carl von Clausewitz referred to friction as "the force that makes the apparently easy seem so difficult."[307] Clausewitz's notion of friction in warfare also applies to us as individuals, particularly when we are trying to get something done, and this friction is magnified as we interact with others, or are part of a group, an organization, or a large enterprise. What affects our actions and derails even the best-laid plans, or keeps us from even making coherent plans, is the fact that we are always dealing with a changing environment and therefore are always to some degree acting in ignorance. Not only do we have limited knowledge to begin with, but we also have to cope with unpredictable events that can never be completely anticipated. This situation is made worse by the imperfect transmission and processing of information. Even the things that theoretically can be known are not completely reliable, because they are subject to personal opinion and emotion, opposing agendas between individuals, mistakes, and or even the inability to process the volume of information. Emotion and stress can also affect our ability to negotiate life smoothly, or to get the outcomes we want in our work and personal life.

This kind of subjectivity can lead to actions that are based upon selected temporal aspects of a situation, rather than identifying the more general trends and circumstances of which the situation is but a single part. It can also lead to an orientation that causes underestimating or overestimating what is possible in a given situation. In the words of Michael Handel, former professor of strategy at the U.S. Naval War College, "Particularly in military affairs, reality is surprisingly elusive. In fact the higher the level of decision making, the more reality is likely to be distorted by wishful thinking, political considerations, ideological biases, poor intelligence, past experience, partial information, and individual and organizational interests."[308] Mao Zedong felt that only by extensive objective analysis of the situation at hand could the reality of the moment be understood and factored into one's long-term strategy. Is this possible?

In his book *The Art of Action*, Stephen Bungay uses the nineteenth-century Prussian army, commanded by Field Marshal Helmuth Karl Bernhard Graf von Moltke ("Moltke the Elder"), as an example of strategic thinking and organization that operated successfully in uncertain circumstances at an uncertain time. Bungay returns to Clausewitz's problem of friction: the gaps between plans and actions and between actual outcomes and desired outcomes. We make plans that do not always result in actions, and the actions that do occur are not always those desired, nor do actions always result in the outcomes anticipated. Bungay identifies three distinct gaps that explain why in plans, actions, and outcomes there is often a mismatch between what we desire and what we achieve.

1. **Knowledge Gap:** the gap between outcomes and plans
   Our plans are imperfect because we lack knowledge. We either don't know, or we have interpreted what we do know incorrectly. We may have made false assumptions about what is happening or overestimated our capabilities or those of others. In terms of the future happenings, we can never know everything.

2. **Alignment Gap:** the gap between plans and actions
   We have not aligned our plans with what is actually happening. Actions take place too early or late. Others involved may have different priorities and time frames that are not congruent with ours.

3. **Effects Gap:** the gap between actions and outcomes
   Even with knowledge and timely, appropriate action, the effects may not match up with our desires. Chance and unpredictability are fundamental in a constantly changing world. There are countless events occurring simultaneously. We cannot have knowledge of all of them, let alone control them, and we cannot predict with certainty how they will interact.[309]

Bungay goes on to point out that when uncertainty makes us uncomfortable, we often try to get a handle on it by trying to gather more data (knowledge), by micromanaging (alignment), or by increasing control (effects). *These natural reactions do not simply fail to solve the problem, they make it worse.* More information creates more noise, micromanagement slows everything down, and trying to control everything creates further slowness, rigidity, and inability to act.[310]

Bungay terms his solution "directed opportunism." It involves abandoning the linear model of simply developing a plan, acting on it, and then observing the results. Instead, one employs cycles of doing or thinking. "The horizon within which actions are planned is limited, the effects of the actions are observed, reflected on, and new action is initiated. So the thinking-doing loop becomes a learning-adapting loop."[311] This allows a person, an army, or an organization to act rapidly as events unfold, but at the same time maintain the capacity to adjust to changing circumstances. Under von Moltke, the Prussian army was reorganized into a military organization that could operate in this fashion, with a flexibility and effectiveness that its opponents could not match. This model is not unlike John Boyd's OODA loops (see Chapter III).

Strategic Perspective and Orientation

John Boyd's writings on strategic thinking build on the ideas of von Moltke and Bungay by looking more closely at our orientation: the way we observe, interact with, and interpret the world around us. For Boyd, one's individual strategic perspective or orientation has three basic components:

- Physical: the world of matter, energy, and information that we live in and move through.
- Mental: our emotional and intellectual activity, which is generated to adjust to and understand the physical world.
- Moral: our cultural orientation and the codes of conduct and standards of behavior that constrain, as well as sustain and focus, our emotional and intellectual responses.[312]

According to Boyd, the art of success lies in looking beyond reliance on our own personal experiences and mental subroutines. This means looking at other disciplines and activities and connecting them to what we know from our own experiences and the strategic world we live in. It means *physically interacting* by opening up and maintaining channels of communication with the outside world. It means *mentally interacting* by selecting information and alternative channels of knowledge, in order to generate mental images and impressions that match up with the events and circumstances unfolding in the surrounding world. *Morally,* we interact "by avoiding mismatches between what we say we are, what we are, and the world we have to deal with, as well as by biding by those other cultural codes and standards we are expected to uphold."[313]

Boyd's conclusion is that if the purpose of strategy is to adapt and to shape changing circumstances as they unfold so that we can live and prosper on our own terms, then we cannot be isolated, but must analyze and synthesize information and ideas across competing channels of information and cultural backgrounds. This generates potentially "new" images and impressions that match up and relate to the changing world as it unfolds around us. Such an approach requires forging new patterns of orientation, through insight, imagination, discovery, and innovation. We may be forced to unlearn, relearn, adapt, and change.[314]

Neither Boyd nor Bungay define strategy as a set of plans, machinations, or movements. Strategy is intention, a will to achieve a certain outcome or series of outcomes, and our intention vis-à-vis those outcomes will also be subject to change and adaptation. Bungay takes this a step further by telling us that intention and strategy are less a plan than a direction.[315]

The *Yijing* and Personal Life Strategies

The *Yijing* echoes Boyd in his approach to this difficult problem. The central premise of the *Yijing* is that the world as we experience it is constantly changing. We are born, age, mature, grow, decline, and die. People, organizations, and countries rise and fall, what goes up comes down, and what is reduced eventually increases. Things expand, reach a limit, and then contract inward to another limit, only to grow and expand again. This constant change and rise and fall produces uncertainty, and that uncertainty, while it can give us hope that things will go well, also produces a disquiet that they may not go well. Our lives and fortunes will change as the world we live in experiences change. To prevail, to experience good fortune, requires having the ability to ride the changes with equanimity, poise, and attention. We must be able to understand the nature of the times and change our behavior accordingly. This requires that we be alert, aware, and proactive. Like the experienced general, we must understand the shape and flow of events so that we can arrange things in our favor.

If at this point you feel that this kind of "strategic thinking" is too calculated or that it does not apply to your life, let's drop the idea of military strategy for a moment and look at change from the standpoint of individuals making their way through the uncharted sea of life, with all of its richness, beauty, excitement, danger, doldrums, sunrises and sunsets, storms, tempests, and uncharted reefs. How does an individual move through life with all its unpredictable summits and depths as smoothly and gracefully as possible? "People should strive to understand the nature of the world with complete clarity and without illusion or wishful thinking. They must accept the world for what it is and not as they would like it to be. And they must adapt to changing circumstances. The past is past, and we must continuously move on in accord with the flux of events. Wise people try to understand the nature of the times and move in harmony with the world instead of vainly striving against circumstances."[316] This does not mean giving up who you are, but understanding who you are, your intentions and orientations and how they shape you, because this will have an effect on how you move in the world.

Change is part of who we are, and it is, to some degree, what makes us who we are. "Change confronts us and shapes our identities. It requires us to clarify our values. Thus adaptation to change is not simply clever strategy. It is also a process of self-cultivation and self-education. Through dealing with change, one comes to understand who one is and what one truly believes in."[317] Our intention shapes our interaction with the changing world and, in turn, intentions themselves are also shaped by that interaction.

The *Yijing* has a very practical orientation in its approach to change. It teaches us about change and engages with the many facets of human life, in order to help us understand, adapt to, and flow with uncertainty and change. Although the *Yijing* is a book of vast depth, and has been subjected to extensive commentary and interpretations—which sometimes confound as much as they elucidate—recurring themes and ideas permeate the text. These can be understood as general principles of living life in an ever-changing world. For purposes of simplicity and utility these principles can be reduced to five:

- Change is always composed of yin and yang forces (aspects). Relationships between things and between people are both contradictory and complementary.
- Every effect has a cause, and every effect is also a cause.
- Change has underlying patterns and currents.
- Change has identifying signs and warnings.
- Specific qualities, psycho-spiritual orientations or outlooks, can be identified that help one adapt to change.

1. Yin and Yang: Opposition and Compatibility; Contradiction and Agreement

   Situations, things, and people are driven by yin and yang forces. One must understand, harmonize, and accept these oppositional forces in order to adapt and act effectively. Relationships between things and between people are both contradictory and complementary. Embracing both opposite and compatible views broadens the scope of one's orientation to uncertainty and change. An unfavorable, seemingly contradictory situation can be changed into a favorable one if one can see the situation from all angles and orientations.

2. Causes and Effects

   Actions can lead to specific effects, but it must be kept in mind that these effects then become the cause of other sets of circumstances that may not have been foreseen. Hence, any strategic outlook must constantly adapt, as one's very actions and their effects create a continuously changing landscape that must be navigated with insight, courage, and wisdom.

3. Patterns and Currents of Change

   The *Yijing* shows us that although events may seem random and unpredictable, they do follow discernable patterns that can be generally understood. The *Yijing* reveals that change in the world around us, although on the surface complex and random, often repeats in patterns that have fractal-like regularities. Change is circular. Pattern emerge, disappear, and reappear again. Things may never change in exactly the same way twice, but transformation often follows similar patterns that can be identified. Peace is often followed by obstruction and opposition, and when something reaches an apogee of success and magnificence, its inner substance can fall away, resulting in the superficial and ostentatious (see Chapter IV).

4. Identifying Signs and Warnings

   Change can be sudden, but often it starts slowly and almost imperceptibly. If one can identify that the situation is shifting before events unfold completely, it is possible to adapt to events and even shape them when they are small and easier to handle. Once the changes are fully underway, it is more difficult to adjust to and shape them. Through the awareness, flexibility, and cultivation of the Eight Dispositions (see

Chapter II), one can prepare and lay the groundwork for the adaptations we must make.

5. Specific Qualities and Outlooks that Make Adaptation Possible

To be proactive and ready to adjust to change in our lives, we must develop an awareness and an inner strength that will carry our intention and vision through difficult times. Further, one must cultivate a mental attitude of observation, planning, adaptation, adjustment, and readjustment that is ongoing and flexible in nature. The *Yijing* introduces the notion of the Superior Person, who may also be understood as a leader or statesman. Throughout the *Yijing*, the Superior Person's behavior pattern and mental attitude are held up as an example of how to avert misfortunate and obtain benefit from situations as they change. Many of these qualities are those espoused by the Ba Gua adepts and the great generals of history.

Qualities of the Superior Person: Cultivating the Strategic Mind-Intention

The key qualities of the Superior Person, as expressed in the *Yijing*, can be summarized, because they reoccur in different ways throughout the text. Understanding these qualities can help you cultivate an outlook, awareness, and "mind-intention" that allows strategic thinking to unfold naturally in your life. This strategic mind-intention and behavior exhibits a blend of the following qualities and attributes.[318]

- Perseverance and patience.
- Modesty without servility.
- Tolerance without indulgence.
- Decisive but not obstinate. Listens to the advice of others.
- Takes the initiative. Is active but not reckless.
- Knowing when to move and advance and when to stop or retreat.
- Knowledge of what is enough and what is too little.
- Knowing when to show brilliance and when to hide it.
- Knowledge of how to gather people together in order to realize a shared intention.
- Knowing how to lead and how to follow.

- Willingness to help and educate others.
- Respect for others.
- Able to balance opposition and compatibility and contradiction and agreement.
- Understanding the cycles of change and the interplay between yin and yang.
- Adaptability to changing circumstances.
- Thinking ahead while having awareness of past events.
- Bold and decisive, yet calm and cautious.
- Aware of danger in moments of peace and prosperity and optimistic in difficult times.
- Keeps resources in reserve for future (unseen) needs.
- Cultivates inner strength and inner harmony.

Perseverance and Patience

Perseverance is an attribute that is stressed repeatedly in the *Yijing*. Perseverance includes the ability to adapt to changing circumstances. Proceeding slowly in small steps is advocated in the *Yijing,* as is waiting, not acting until the right moment. This requires patience, and the fortitude to hold to one's intention, direction, and ultimate goal while adapting to the circumstances as they unfold. You don't have to change your goals and intentions, but you may have move toward them via circuitous route.

Perseverance should not be confused with being unchanging or obstinate. Perseverance by itself, without awareness of change and growth, is not healthy and can lead to stagnation and frustration. Taking things step by step without being dissuaded is a good thing. However, one must be able to take advice from others and change if one is on the wrong path.

Hexagram 32 is translated as Perseverance, Constancy, or Duration. It is composed of Thunder above and Wind Below. These are paired phenomena. Both Wind and Thunder represent movement. Each aids the other: Wind carries Thunder farther and Thunder strengthens Wind. Thunder is yang excitement, while Wind stands for yin gentleness. Together, these two create a state of balance and sustainability that has the potential to create enduring things that last. Thunder also represents the importance of being able to change and find a new path, rather than obstinately sticking to a path that will not reach fulfillment.

Perseverance/Constancy   Modesty

Modesty

Modesty does not mean humility or meekness. It refers to doing what is necessary without fuss or ceremony. This means working toward a goal with diligence and without expectation of approval and praise. No aspect of the task is beneath a modest person. They work steadily toward their goal and do not put themselves or their private concerns above others. Modesty requires inner strength and steadiness. Modesty includes tolerance and open-mindedness. It strengthens, rather than weakens, one's ability to lead. The Chinese say that "the belly of a chief government official should be large enough to pole a boat."[319]

Modesty, Hexagram 15, is composed of Mountain under Earth. The Mountain is usually in the higher position, resting upon the Earth. Here, what was in the lower position (Earth) is raised upward through the modesty and restraint of that which was higher (Mountain). This creates balance, which aids one in maintaining one's position. In an organization, this could refer to the leader or manager being open and receptive like the Earth. This has a positive effect on the other members of the group, and on other levels of an organization, so that there is harmony between the different levels. This dynamic is also seen in other hexagrams, such as Peace, Hexagram 11, in which Heaven, normally above Earth, has elevated Earth to a higher position.

Peace

Tolerance

Tolerance does not mean indulging oneself or others or "suffering fools gladly." Tolerance embodies broadmindedness, acting with patience, restraint, understanding, and flexibility. It also conveys an idea of honesty and uprightness. To act appropriately often requires direct, decisive action, but it also requires an openness to new ideas, and the patience and inner strength to adapt and adjust according to the circumstance.

The Earth hexagram (Hexagram 2), with its six broken (yin) lines, may seem to be in opposition to the six solid (yang) lines of Hexagram 1 (Heaven). Earth represents receptivity. This does not denote passivity or weakness, but action that is in accord with the situation. This receptivity is the natural complement to the dynamic, decisive direct action of Heaven. True strength and direct action also require flexibility, patience, and tolerance, the ability to act within the constraints of the real world, to act as the situation demands, rather than trying to impose our will upon it. One can prevail through direct action, but one can also prevail through acceptance and tolerance, through nurturing a particular situation, rather than taking hold of the reins directly.

Earth   Contentment   Union   Gather Together

In general, the hexagrams in the Palace of Earth convey a sense of achievement, success, and contentment through the receptive tolerance of Earth. Earth has the ability to sustain, embrace, and nourish Heaven's vision by gathering support from capable people who are attracted by the upright honesty, adaptability, and acceptance of Earth. Hexagram 16, Contentment and Joy, is symbolized by Thunder over Earth—movement and action built upon the support and teamwork of others, trusting in those around you. The cooperation, trust, and tolerance of Earth is also reflected in Hexagram 8 (Union: Holding Together), in which Water above is channeled and directed by the Earth below. In Hexagram 45 (Gather Together), Earth provides foundational support for the Lake, which rests above.

Knowing how to gather people together in order to realize a shared intention reflects a balanced yin-yang dynamic. An example of this is Hexagram 35 (Advance; Progress), in which Fire is over Earth, symbolizing the sun rising over the Earth. Progress comes from cooperation, mutual support, and recognition of the contributions of others. The leader recognizes and rewards the work of those he or she leads, and they in turn respect both the leader and their comrades. The sun brings clarity and light to the Earth. Insight and clarity bring cohesion to an enterprise—progress and forward movement are connected to the efforts of others who participate in and share a common vision. Even with help and support (Earth disposition), for progress to occur there must be a directed intent, and clarity of vision (Fire disposition) that shapes change and progress.

Advance

Leading and Following

To lead effectively one must also know how to follow. This means those leading and those following should have a harmonious relationship. When following others, one must do so for the right reasons, not simply for one's own personal ambition or for immediate gain. To properly follow others, one must have faith and trust in the quality and importance of their beliefs, goals, and methods. This will bring out your best efforts and enrich the interaction, your own life, and the lives of the others involved. To lead, one must know how to adjust oneself to those that follow and adapt to their needs. This requires modesty, tolerance, and trust on both sides. Those who lead also follow. They may follow a person, an idea, a vision, or a principle. The effective leader adapts to the situation, as do his followers. The leader listens to others' opinions with respect and with a willingness to change his or her opinion. Both the leader and follower are open to the achievements of others.

Hexagram 17 (Following) is composed of Lake over Thunder. This is the image of following. Thunder is movement and incitement, but here, rather than leading, it follows Lake's gentle enthusiasm. The strong lines in both trigrams are below the yin lines that they follow. This symbolizes adaptation to the needs of others and adaptation to the changing circumstances, while preserving one's direction and goals, allowing one to get a fresh view of the situation. The text of the *Yijing* describes this as "one's self control having the capacity to change directions and leaving one's own gate to relate to others in a way that achieves merit."[320]

Following   Great Accumulation

Similar ideas about following and leading appear throughout the *Yijing*. In Hexagram 14 (Great Accumulation), Heaven is below Mountain. Heaven's limitless strength is stored through the stability of the Mountain. The fifth yin line is surrounded by the five yang lines. This yin line represents the enlightened leader whose modesty and receptivity gathers talented people around him or her. This creates a powerful combination of strength, clarity, and accord. The Army (Hexagram 7) also contains this dynamic. The Army is composed of Earth over Water. This represents Earth containing, supporting, and guiding the power of Water. The second line is the only yang line. It represents the general who leads their troops, inspiring them and instilling esprit de corps while at the same time exercising authority and enforcing discipline. Water is adaptable and changeable and follows the contours of the Earth. Thus, the leader is adaptable to the changing terrain and the changing situation. Water will seek the low ground. The army, led by an able commander, fulfills its duties and follows through to the conclusion of the conflict.

Army

Education: Learning from Others

When one encounters difficulties or roadblocks to progress, it is often necessary to seek counsel from others. It is impossible for one person to have all the answers in a complicated situation. Rather than pretending to have all the answers, one should see this situation as an opportunity for growth, an opportunity to expand one's knowledge and experience. Hexagram 4 (Youthful Inexperience) is composed of Mountain over Water.

This is keeping still with danger underneath; in a difficult situation where one cannot move ahead, but waiting may also be dangerous. One should seek counsel from someone more experienced or someone with the specific knowledge required to resolve the situation. On the surface, the hexagram refers to an inexperienced person seeking wisdom from someone more experienced. However, knowledge and exchange go in both directions. One who teaches in one area must be open to being a student in others. The teacher also learns from the student. Teaching and learning form a two-way interactive process.

Youthful Inexperience

Learning from others and taking advice requires an open mind and a kind of innocence, hence Hexagram 4 is also referred to as "Youthful Folly." This implies that a person knows what to do, or is told what to do, but he or she does not like the answer and refuses to accept the reality of the situation. We may get answers that we don't like, but we must be open to seeing them as possible solutions. Teaching also requires an open mind, as well as tolerance and compassion. The teacher cannot be quick to judge and criticize. This attitude often pays off, because others will respond to this generous attitude of sharing.

Stillness, Stopping, and Waiting: Adaptation and Movement

The Mountain trigram symbolizes stopping, stillness, restraint, and control; the reining in of something that is going too far; knowing when enough is enough. Action for action's sake is not good. Waiting is not "doing nothing." It is preparation that is psychic and also material in nature. To wait and then move at the appropriate time and place requires awareness both of the changes around us and of our own internal changes. Many of the hexagrams in which Mountain is below, forming the inner trigram, express different aspects of this idea.

Trigram 39 (Obstacle and Adversity) is composed of Water above Mountain. Water can symbolize Danger, and like Mountain, it can be an obstacle to forward progress. Mountains behind and a watery abyss ahead block movement. The key to extricating oneself from this situation lies in the disposition of the Mountain. Stop and free yourself from entanglements. Refresh your strategy and wait for the right time and place to begin again. Trigram 33 (Retreat) takes this strategy a step further by counseling a strategic retreat to a position of strength. Retreating from a situation at the right time requires correct timing and a calm, cool-headed attitude. A tactical retreat can enhance your power by extracting you from a situation that is working against you and not serving your best interests. A timely withdrawal allows you to view things more objectively and wait for the right time to take a new direction.

| Obstacle | Retreat | Stillness | Gradual Advance |

Hexagram 52 (Restraint and Stillness), Mountain over Mountain, symbolizes stopping at the right time and place. This calms the situation. Once stress and turbulence are lessened, one can assess the situation with clarity. After stopping and assessing, one knows when to move and in what direction. This is symbolized by Hexagram 53 (Gradual Advance). Gradual Advance is composed of Wind / Wood over Mountain—a tree growing slowly and steadily, supported by the solid stillness and patience of the Mountain. Laying a firm foundation is the key to efficacious movement. Wind's gentle penetration and insight are also important here. Proceeding with caution, knowledge, and insight makes gradual progress possible.

Bold Decision and Forward Movement

The three strong lines of the Heaven Trigram represent a powerful force that moves forward and upward. Sometimes situations require bold, decisive action. When the time is right, one should seize the initiative and move forward like a fearless general. Hexagram 1 (Heaven), composed of six strong yang lines (Heaven over Heaven), symbolizes exactly this situation. Everything is favorable and one must boldly move forward. However, you must put your plans into action carefully by prioritizing what is important. Avoid expending energy needlessly. Harmonize conflicts and you will gather others around you who will aid you in fulfilling your vision.

Hexagram 11 (Peace) symbolizes this harmony. Earth moves downward to connect with Heaven's upward movement. This represents the interaction of people, or the parts of an organization, harmoniously coming together to achieve a shared goal. There is concord and prosperity. This does not mean one can relax. Times of peace and harmony should be enjoyed, but they are also periods where the groundwork can be laid for future enterprises by forming alliances and creating new ideas. One must also watch for the inevitable change in the situation, so that one is prepared to adjust accordingly.

In the *Yijing*, harmony is followed by its opposite, Standstill and Obstruction (Hexagram 12). Standstill represents disruption of the previously harmonious communication. If you have built sufficient strength and resources in times of peace, then you will be prepared. With clarity, insight, and understanding one will be able to surge forward again. Hexagram 14 (Great Holding) symbolizes this, with Fire's clarity of purpose and internal cohesion placed over Heaven's strength. Opportunities unfold and success is achieved through one's inner purpose, magnanimity, and generosity, symbolized by the fifth yin line (in the position of the leader) that attracts the five yang lines to it.

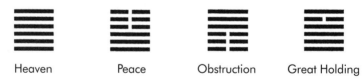

Heaven   Peace   Obstruction   Great Holding

The Zhen Trigram symbolizes movement, renewal, and opportunity. This movement is qualitatively different than Heaven's steady, powerful advance. The movement and creativity expressed by Zhen is sudden, sometimes shocking, bursting out in new, unexpected directions. Hexagram 51 (Shock; Quake) is composed of Thunder over Thunder—Thunder doubled. There is danger, but there is also movement that is unexpected and therefore opportune. Danger and opportunity shock you out of your routine, so that you look in new directions. Zhen's force can also be seen in Hexagrams 27 (Nourishment) and 21 (Biting Through). In Nourishment, Mountain above slows Zhen's powerful upward movement, stopping it before it can overreach itself. In this hexagram, Mountain also symbolizes stillness and self-cultivation, which sustains one's progress. In Biting Through, Thunder combines with Fire. Fire's clarity combines with the powerful energy of Thunder to burst through obstructions. To succeed in this situation, one should take prompt and powerful action that is precise and clear. When Thunder and Fire combine, lightning (clarity and power) is produced.

Shock   Nourishment   Biting Through

Adaptation to Change

Adaptation to changing circumstances is a central theme in the *Yijing*. Water's adaptability, its ability to take the shape of a container, or to flow and "leak" around obstructions, effortlessly exploiting the terrain, makes it a perfect metaphor for adaptation and change. Hexagram 29 (The Abyss) is Water over Water—Water doubled. This is also danger doubled—Water rushing rapidly through an abyss. One must push on through this danger with sincerity, courage, and fortitude, but one must also employ Water's fluidity to "ride the rapids" to their conclusion, deftly negotiating the terrain and adjusting one's course with faith and perseverance. Hexagram 40 (Deliverance and Relief) depicts Thunder above Water. This situation is likened to a thunderstorm clearing the air. The tension and difficulty have finally broken open and dispersed. Things are moving in the right direction after a time of difficulty and danger. It is time to clear the air, make changes, mend fences, and create harmony so that things go smoothly in the future.

Abyss   Relief

Cohesion: Bringing People and Ideas Together

In China, the family was traditionally the model for people coming together in political or social organizations. The family represents leaders who look out for their followers and members of groups coming together to help one another. Fire's clarity, brilliance, and cohesion represent this aspect of human interaction. Fire also represents the human heart's ability to see through the fog of illusions and recognize the truth. Human life and human endeavors require these qualities to succeed. Hexagram 37 (Family) depicts Wind above, issuing forth from Fire below. You can move forward and spread outward over the earth like the Wind because you are supported by others, by your family. The lines in this hexagram also depict the family members (the lines of the hexagram) in their proper places, each comfortable in his or her role and harmoniously working together for the common good. In Hexagram 13 (Fellowship), there is a similar dynamic. Heaven's strength and endurance are sustained by Fire's sincerity and enlightened thinking. The five yang lines come together around the yin line in the second position. This unity creates the potential to follow through and succeed. Instead of forming cliques, the leader in the second position unites others so that all can benefit.

Family   Fellowship

Increase and Decrease

There are cycles of plentitude and scarcity. As yin and yang fluctuate, there is movement in both directions. If there is an increase or excess in one direction there is a decrease or deficit somewhere else. Hexagram 41 (Decrease) is followed by Hexagram 42 (Increase). In Decrease, Lake is below and Mountain is above. Decrease is generally understood as coming from Hexagram 11 (Peace). The third (yang) line in Peace moves upward to the top position. What is below has decreased while what is above has increased. This can be positive or negative. If a building is too heavy on top, it can collapse. This is like a heavy Mountain on top of a Lake. The Lake cannot support the Mountain. Similarly, if only the interests of those at the top of a social structure benefit, at the expense of those below who support that structure, then there is an imbalance and potential for strife.

Decrease can also be positive and natural—giving up nonessentials to move ahead or sacrificing something to gain something else. This is the

Lake evaporating and nourishing the Mountain, which, through this benefit, is able to flourish and reciprocate—renewing the Lake through Mountain streams and rainfall. In a social order, decrease is harmonious when everyone benefits and gains compensate for losses. This requires delicate judgment and timing. Decrease can also be seen as a method of self-cultivation: reducing ego, self-centeredness, self-indulgence, and self-importance and subsuming the ego in order to promote inner clarity and balance. This applies to individuals or social groups.

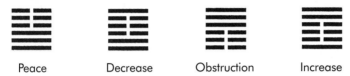

Peace   Decrease   Obstruction   Increase

Hexagram 42 (Increase) is created from Hexagram 12 (Obstruction). In Hexagram 12 Heaven and Earth are splitting apart and moving away from each other. Heaven moves upward and Earth moves downward. The fourth (yang) line of Hexagram 12 moves downward to the lower trigram so that the lower trigram benefits. This is represented by Wind over Thunder, two forces that naturally combine and augment each other's power. This is a "win-win" situation in which people are actively helping one another and cooperation brings success. Those in more powerful and influential positions act to benefit those below, who have less status and power. When people feel that those in power have their interests at heart, they cooperate to achieve difficult tasks and ambitious projects. Everyone benefits. Increase also provides further insight into self-cultivation in individuals and social groups. Strength and attention move from above (outside) to below (inside). This means focusing on the fundamentals and foundations of the situation rather than external, peripheral concerns. It also teaches the value of reciprocity. Benefiting and uplifting others inspires them to work with you, or for the good of the group you all are part of. In the end, this generosity of spirit will be rewarded.

The Message of the *Yijing*

The recurring and overlapping themes of the *Yijing* weave a tapestry of images centered around negotiating our lives as human beings in all areas of human interaction. The *Yijing* does not always distinguish between groups. Although it often talks about the family or the ruler and the state, these models are interchangeable. Therefore, *Yijing* principles can be applied to any social group from the individual, to a family, to business and social organizations of varying sizes and degrees of complexity, or even to governments and states. In Robert John Lynn's introduction to the *Yijing*, he eloquently sums up its importance and utility:

> [The issues the *Yijing* concerns itself with are] the interrelatedness of personal character and destiny; how position defines the scope of action; how position and circumstances define appropriate modes of behavior; how the individual is always tied to others in a web of interconnected causes and effects; how one set of circumstances inevitably changes into another; how change itself is the great constant—and flexible response to it the only key to happiness and success. There is a core of insights here that can speak to this and any other age—if we but allow it to do so.[321]

Harmony and Balance

The *Yijing* stresses maintaining harmony and balance in even the most difficult situations. The lines in the hexagrams are rarely perfectly and evenly balanced. This occurs in a very few situations (hexagrams). Perfect balance that is static and unchanging becomes stagnant and decays. Balance is actually an ongoing dynamic equilibrium that must be monitored and attended to. Balance, at its heart, is straightforward. We walk along a crowded street or keep our car within its lane through a constant series of small adjustments that are ongoing. Both of these actions require monitoring our speed, drifts to the left and right, and our proximity and position relative to others. This requires a harmony of opposites: left, right, too close, too far, too fast, too slow, etc. Ongoing observation and monitoring, adjusting, acting, and reacting in walking and driving generally happens smoothly, and to some degree automatically. A skilled driver or walker negotiates all of this seamlessly, without sudden stops and starts, noticing openings in the flow of movement just as they emerge and moving around obstructions before they completely manifest. This requires knowledge and experience, which are implicit and always operating under the surface—a kind of body wisdom.

Wisdom

Implicit wisdom can be seen in many areas of human endeavor. It is what Ba Gua training attempts to instill in a martial artist. It exists in the intuitive brilliance of great military commanders and captains of industry, in successful organizations and businesses, and in an individual's harmonious relationships. Wisdom requires knowledge. However, knowledge alone or knowledge in the form of information is not enough. Reliance on this type of knowledge and on formal decision making can be paralyzing, because as Stephen Bungay pointed out earlier, more information creates more noise and more uncertainty.[322] This is in contrast to wisdom—an implicit "knowing how." Hence the saying, "Knowledge is the source of wisdom and wisdom makes knowledge flourish."[323] Taking the right action at the right time requires wisdom.

Self-Cultivation

Balance and wisdom are the product of many things, but at their heart they are rooted in an ongoing inner cultivation. By cultivating ourselves, we prevail and succeed in life. Life and its changes can seem chaotic, and there are many factors that prevent desired outcomes—what Clausewitz calls "friction" or the "fog of war." Uncertainty, the "fog," is, to some degree, the result of our own turbulent emotions. Piercing through it requires asserting the human qualities that master those emotions.[324] While we cannot always control the world around us, we can control our reactions to it—our emotions and ways of thinking. By cultivating inner strength, we can prevail against stagnation or difficulties in life. This requires sincerity and cultivation of inner truth—understanding who you are and where you are headed.

Specific Applications of Strategy to Life

The *Yijing* elucidates many principles of the art of change and the general mind-set one must cultivate in order to successfully blend with change and uncertainty. Military strategy provides examples of how great commanders negotiated moments of danger and opportunity, and Ba Gua

Zhang offers a body-mind discipline that engages with change and transformation. But how do we apply these ideas more specifically in our lives, our relationships, and our work? In order to further understand strategy, specific examples of application are helpful. To this end, it is helpful to examine strategy and change in relation to the following three areas of life and social interaction.

1. Business and Work
2. Social and Family Relationships
3. Self-Fulfillment and Life Path

When looking at these three areas, there will necessarily be much repetition and overlap, as these arbitrary divisions are ultimately all part of the larger pattern of change. The business of life includes the business of the marketplace, and business ultimately involves relationships between people. I leave it to the reader to apply ideas in any one of these three areas to the other two.

1. Application of Strategic Principles to Business and Work

In Asia, the marketplace is often described as a battlefield and the writings of strategists like Sunzi, Zhuge Liang, and Miyamoto Musashi are studied and interpreted for their application to business trade. Zhuge Liang's Fifteen Rules for Generals (see Appendix II) have been reinterpreted as strategies for the art of management by more than one author.[325] The *Yijing* has also been studied with the goal of improving outcomes in business and management. This trend is also true in the West, where the successes and failures of great military commanders are often related to business and finance. What can we learn from these diverse sources?

The following discussion will not present business strategies in the context of a battlefield contested by large corporate entities. There are many other books on this subject, which discuss taking control of markets and undermining the competition. While these concerns might be of interest to CEOs of large companies, they are not as useful to the average person. The approach here will be to look at the basic principles of managing and directing business on a smaller, operational scale, with equal applicability to an individual, a small business, or a larger cooperative effort.

Visions, Plans, Directions, and Goals

Any enterprise proceeds from a vision or a direction. The question is, should that vision be converted into specific plans and goals? There is no easy answer to this question. The traditional approach is to make a business plan with steps and follow through to a goal. However, all too often this does not work. Long-term business planning is difficult, if not impossible, a fantasy. There are just too many factors that are out of our hands, including the economy, changing market conditions, customer needs, political decisions that affect your business—the list goes on. Some business strategists like software entrepreneurs Jason Fried and David Hansson are dismissive of plans, seeing them as little more than guesses:

> When you turn guesses into plans, you enter a danger zone. Plans let the past drive the future. They put blinders on you. "This is where we're going because, well, that's where we said we were going." And that's the problem: Plans are inconsistent with improvisation. And you have to be able to improvise. You have to be able to pick up opportunities that come along. Sometimes you need to say, "We're going in a new direction because that's what makes sense today." The timing of long-range plans is screwed up too. You have the most information when you're doing something, not before you've done it.[326]

Many business experts agree in principle with this approach. Stephen Bungay feels that we should focus on our intentions rather than plans, because from intentions a general direction can be plotted. Bungay draws on the experience and writing of Field Marshall Von Moltke, who believed that military strategy must be understood as a system of options and expedients. Von Moltke felt that it was only possible to plan at the very beginning of a military operation. He is famous for saying, "No plan of operations can look with any certainty beyond the first meeting with the major forces of the enemy."[327] Von Moltke stressed extensive preparations and training of officers in order to create a foundation and command structure that could adapt to a series of constantly changing and unpredictable outcomes.

In 1870, during the Franco-Prussian War, this approach to strategy allowed him to surround the French army at the Battle of Sedan. This, for all intents and purposes, ended the war and resulted in the capture of the

Emperor Napoleon III. Bungay applies von Moltke's ideas to business strategy by creating an operating system that is essentially an ongoing process of adaptation. This requires alignment of purpose (intention creating cohesion) among those involved and a process of assessment—and evaluation, briefings, and back briefings that are ongoing. This in turn creates an "operating rhythm" that is constantly reassessing what is happening so as to maintain momentum and be prepared for adaptation and change.[328]

Chet Richards, a disciple of the late Colonel John Boyd, takes a similar approach to business operations, which is derived from Boyd's definition of strategy: "a mental tapestry of changing intentions for harmonizing and focusing our efforts as a basis for realizing some aim or purpose in an unfolding and often unforeseen world of many bewildering events and many contending interests." [329] This viewpoint led Richards to eschew a "how-to" approach to business strategy, and embrace one that is action-oriented.

- Keep focus on the customer, while having an eye on the competition and the field of action (the strategic environment).
- Provide the team with a continuing stream of options.
- Enable rapid switching between options.
- Encourage initiative at all levels.
- Harmonize efforts internally and externally in order to realize our intentions.[330]

Of course, this kind of actualized intention requires that you are aligning your intention with the marketplace and with your own internal capabilities and constraints, all the while keeping in mind that these external and internal factors are subject to change and revision. Intention and direction often get confused with specific goals. Goals are stepping stones along the way to realizing one's intention(s). Some goals are long-term ones, and in hindsight may seem the same as intentions. More often, specific goals need to change as circumstances change. Goals are useful, unless they become written in stone and adhered to at all costs. A vision and intentions that stem from that vision drives the creation of goals. A good vision allows immediate goals to be articulated and written down. A "vision document" should be short, concise, and open-ended.

For the vision document to have any power, it must consolidate ideas from many other places. It should absorb the key thinking from research, analysis, strategic planning, or other efforts, and be the best representation of those ideas. Any vision for a team is a failure if understanding it requires the reader to do even half the work of the author. For this reason, it's best to separate out the goals and directives from all of the supporting arguments and research behind the plan.[331]

Plans will naturally flow from the original intention-direction and articulated goals, but plans even more than goals are subject to change. Any plan may turn out to have no relationship with reality and may need to be discarded. Therefore, writing out a big detailed plan is usually not useful, as it is subject to change the moment it is implemented. Often these kinds of documents end up in a file cabinet.[332]

Project manager and Microsoft veteran Scott Berkun lists five important qualities of a good vision.

- It is simple and clear.
- It is intentional (directional) in nature.
- It consolidates the ideas.
- It is inspirational. It has charisma.
- It is memorable and resonates.[333]

Operating Systems and Unified Practices

If we look at intention and direction as a kind of grand strategy, then using the military model, business practices and modes of operation unfold on the Operational Level. Both Chet Richards and Stephen Bungay use the operational culture of the German army as models for emphasizing the operational level of an action-oriented strategy. The Mongol army of the thirteenth century also operated in a similar fashion. An operational culture involves pre-training before the operation begins. In the German army this involved creating a shared doctrine and experience that inspired creativity, problem solving, and flexibility. Von Moltke emphasized the development of an officer core that could take initiative and exercise independent judgment in battle. Decentralization of the decision making process allowed responses to changing events to be initiated quickly. This in turn allowed German units to react more quickly, getting inside the opponent's decision making loop (OODA Loop). Similarly, in business, decisions need to be made quickly, as changes unfold. This is difficult in a centralized top-down command structure. Such a structure can lead to micromanaging.

A plan that is not exactly a plan can seem disorganized or indecisive. However, if one has created an operational code and rhythm in which operations people are briefed, and rebriefed, so that feedback and reaction to feedback is ongoing, then many decisions can be competently made at the operational level. This requires discussion, debate, and checkpoints, to see if tasks are done and to rethink actions that did not get the expected results. In this way, a frame of reference is created for whatever is happening and various alternatives can be explored.

Writing things down is an important part of an effective operational code. It prevents the loss of valuable ideas that came up in the decision making process so they can be reconsidered later. It also allows one to move ahead because ideas and decisions have been documented, so one's attention can then turn to other things, secure in the knowledge that whatever was discovered, discussed, and decided can be returned to when necessary.

Decisions and Actions

It is easy to make decisions, but not easy to make effective decisions. We like to think that decisions are made on the basis of knowledge—one gathers information, studies the options, and then makes a logical, rational choice. However, if we are honest, most of us recognize that we don't actually make decisions this way. Why is that? The answer is at least four-fold.

1. We often make decisions based on past decisions and the perceived results of those decisions. This is the past driving the future. What worked before may work again, but basing today's decisions on yesterday's successes can prevent improvisation and interfere with the ability to respond to changing events. The ebb and flow of situations and configurations shown in the order of the hexagrams (see Chapter IV) shows how easily situations can change and even reverse themselves.

2. We make decisions based on the group or organizational culture we are a part of. Decisions are often related to the orientation of that culture. If

the orientation of the group prizes innovative solutions to a problem, the problem may be approached that way. If the culture is nervous about new ideas, decision making will be approached more conservatively.

3. We make decisions based on emotions—what others will think, to protect our reputation, win praise, etc. Even very "business-like" people have emotions that influence their decisions, and they may or may not be aware of this.

4. We make decisions based on implicit knowledge, reasonable assumption, quick projections, and "gut instinct" for the situation.

Information is almost always imperfect. We can never have enough information to make absolutely certain that our decisions are correct. If we wait too long to gather information, then opportunities may be lost. We are often forced to work with the information at hand and make projections based on how that information lines up with the situation requiring a decision. How can we do this effectively? Through feedback that occurs before, during, and after the decision and action. John Boyd's OODA loop provides a very useful model of the decision making process. The OODA loop is not just about making speedy decisions. It involves developing and reshaping one's orientation to events and decisions as they unfold, by observing matches and mismatches between events that are anticipated, those that are observed, and those that require an action or reaction. Part of this is involves maintaining an ongoing engagement with shaping the environment in which one is operating. This includes shaping one's intentions and aims so that they are attractive to others who are participants in the process. This engagement can happen on many levels and involves response and feedback from all levels.

In short, one needs to start by *doing something* and by having in place an orientation, ethos, and operational organizational system that has feedback and adaptivity at all levels. This requires a cohesive operating orientation with a balanced team that is willing to ask tough questions, and recognizing that it is better to make mistakes by acting, than through indecision and inaction. One does not always need to act, in the usual sense of the word. The *Yijing* frequently counsels that there are situations in which it is better to wait, to gather strength and to adjust your orientation in order to better align yourself with unfolding events. This kind of "not-acting" is a decision made in relation to a particular set of circumstances, as opposed to inaction, which can stem from complacency *(Tomorrow will be the same as today)*, or failure to act.

In order to effectively employ the model of the OODA loop, you must train yourself to exploit your intuitive knowledge or "feel" for the situation—what Boyd refers to as implicit knowledge. This is not magical thinking, but rather training oneself to see the whole of the situation, from fragmented observation and limited understanding of seemingly chaotic configurations. This kind of training, whether it is learned individually, or as part of an organization's internal operational orientation, can bypass the slower, more formal decision making process that must analyze and choose from multiple alternatives.[334]

Making decisions and acting on them means that one will make mistakes. There will be failures, but they are temporary. What goes down will rise again, as long as one is attentive to what went wrong. Be willing to act and make a mistake, rather than not acting for fear of making one. Mistakes instruct. Take responsibility for the mistake, even if was not your fault. Taking responsibility to correct errors is an opportunity for growth and part of the process of developing implicit knowledge and wisdom.

Cultivating a Balanced Outlook

The *Yijing* repeatedly counsels accepting advice from others, and being open-minded. The collective dynamic of a group is far more powerful than a single individual. Although great military commanders are celebrated for their genius and creative approaches to difficult situations, they are supported by capable subordinates who combine diverse skills. Different people are suited to different tasks, but with a unified vision and common purpose great things can be achieved. This means having balanced thinking. Any team or group profits from having people of diverse backgrounds who bring different skills and viewpoints to the table. A team composed of people who are obedient and agree with the leader or groupthink will not get the advantage of stimulation and input from different areas of expertise and different orientations. Critical thinking is often diluted when members have similar values and viewpoints. A heterogeneous team is more likely to generate new ideas and fresh perspectives, ask tough questions, and consider hybrid choices.

To build this kind group dynamic requires tolerance and modesty. This means not putting yourself before others, being open to other viewpoints, and avoiding the formation of cliques and factions. Dissenting opinions are useful. Constructive disagreement can help clarify things, if people know they will not be punished for speaking their mind. This requires trust and unity of purpose. If you are not part of a team, it is important to find ways of seeking other viewpoints.

Whether you work alone or with others, one way to train yourself or your team is to avoid language that interferes with and suppresses creative problem solving. For many years my father had a poster entitled *99 Idea Killers* on the wall of his office. It is a good place to start in understanding how interactions with others can promote effective responses to changing events, or can have the opposite effect, of undermining innovation. Some examples of "idea killers" are:

1. It doesn't grab me.
2. They'll never buy it.
14. It's not in our image.
15. It's not our style.
16. It sounds too simple.
33. It turns me off.
43. That's not consistent with the way we do things here.
44. I've heard that one before.
45. Get a committee to look into it.
46. Take a survey.
96. That's very provocative, but. . . .
97. That's very interesting, but. . . .
98. That's really fantastic, but. . . .
99. Yes, but. . . . [335]

Respect and Appreciation

Zhuge Liang, the master strategist of the Three Kingdoms period in China, understood people. He had much to say about relationships between people, which project managers in China have applied to business.

To be able to understand others, the leader should be perceptive. However, to be perceptive, one should pay attention to the motive of each of his immediate subordinates. A leader needs to be extremely careful in deciding what is right and what is wrong. The basic principle of viewing and listening is to be able to see minute matters and hear soft sounds that are produced. This is because small matters are often missed and soft sounds ignored. A wise leader must, therefore, be able to pick out details from very small matters and be able to identify grievances behind a simple complaint.[336]

Zhuge Liang also felt that in any organization talented people should be treated with respect and benevolence. This entails trust, which flows from consistent behavior and fair treatment. When there is trust and consistency there is commitment at all levels, which in turn allows delegation and decentralization of authority. To trust others, you have to trust yourself. If you often work alone, trust in yourself gives you peace of mind not to doubt every decision you make.

The *Sunzi (The Art of War)* is now being frequently applied to business. Rewriting the text word for word so that the words apply more directly to business and management produces interesting results. Below is a passage in which Sunzi discusses types of terrain. The passage has been interpreted so that the work environment is the terrain:

> In some work environments workers are very productive.
> People feel free to criticize each other.
> These are open work environments.
> Everyone shares access to the same areas and resources.
> Those who are better at cooperation will be more productive than others.
> This is a shared work environment.
> People can be very productive at solving problems.
> In doing so, however, they can create enemies. This is a risky work environment.
> There are stupid rules.
> There are foolish restrictions.
> There are meaningless goals.

Everyone runs into these problems in the organization. These are bad work environments.[337]

Communication and Meetings

To be effective, communication must be precise, short, and action-oriented. Nothing wastes more time than inefficient communication, which slows decisions and forces one to go over the same ground several times. In warfare, bad communication is deadly. In business it costs time and money. Field Marshall von Moltke is famous for his brief, yet clear directives, and officers in the Prussian army were trained by Moltke himself to draft effective orders. Directives and orders should have the following qualities:

- Short
- Clear
- Logically arranged in short sentences
- Precisely convey the intentions of the superior
- Complete—delineating each part of the task(s) to be performed[338]

Zhuge Liang had similar ideas about orders and directives. In many of his engagements he gave precise orders to each commander so that they knew how their tasks must unfold in time and space. Zhuge Liang felt that the commander must be strict with themselves and enforce self-discipline, and that this in turn would lead to efficient and clear directives. Communication is not just writing orders, but involves talking to people at all levels of involvement and responsibility. Through conversation, not only will you get better compliance, but you will get useful information and ideas from unexpected sources.

Meetings are also a form of communication, but there is a reason why many people hate meetings. Meetings can interrupt important work if they are not conducted properly. The authors of Rework, entrepreneurs Jason Fried and David Hansson, present many of the negative aspects of meetings without mincing words.

Meetings are toxic. The worst interruptions of all are meetings. Here's why:

- They're usually about words and abstract concepts, not real things.
- They usually convey an abysmally small amount of information per minute.

- They drift off-subject easier than a Chicago cab in a snowstorm.
- They require thorough preparation that most people don't have time for.
- They frequently have agendas so vague that nobody is really sure of the goal.
- They often include at least one moron who inevitably gets his turn to waste everyone's time with nonsense.
- Meetings procreate. One meeting leads to another meeting leads to another. . . . [339]

Meetings are, however, necessary and useful, if they are held judiciously and not too often. Von Molke's criterion for directives can easily be adapted to meetings. Meetings should be short, with a clear topic and agenda that everyone understands. Go directly to the specific problem that needs to be solved. Set a time limit, and end with action plans and assignments to implement those plans.

Information and Metrics

Information is useful and vital, but its importance is often overrated. Information has been likened to a flashlight in a dark room.[340] It reveals some things while others are hidden in the shadows. Information illuminates and this can help you to understand the possible choices. Getting good data and good intelligence can help accelerate a decision by highlighting or potentially eliminating certain choices. But data and metrics can be tricky. Numbers can be misinterpreted. For example, just because lots of people are looking at a product does not mean anyone is buying. Information needs to be interpreted to be useful, and data can be cherry-picked and shaped to support a viewpoint. Data that does not support an idea is easily left out or ignored. "Objective testing" can be used to bolster choices of parties that have vested interests. Even good data only reveals certain things: the information that is being measured. This also can mean that only goals that can be easily measured are achieved, and nothing else. At any moment in time, metrics are imbalanced, because the situation itself is usually imbalanced and difficult to measure accurately, much like hexagrams in the *Yijing*, which are always in the process of becoming something else.

Metrics can be helpful, but often it can be more useful to talk to people and find out what is going on directly. If we know the intention and the direction we are heading in, it is then possible to align ourselves and our capabilities with this direction and with developing situations in the outside world (the marketplace). Then we can make decisions and take actions that will bear fruit, as long as the decisions we make are subject to change and revision as events unfold. You will garner more useful information by doing something that is aligned in purpose, and congruent with the knowledge you do have, than by waiting for more data. Eventually, according to Stephen Bungay in his book *The Art of Action,* "something unexpected will happen, which sooner or later it will. At that point everything depends upon people. Metrics give us information. Interpreting the information can impart understanding. Taking right action requires wisdom. Only people can have that."[341]

2. Application of Strategic Principles to Relationships

Relationships between people is a large topic. All too often discussions of this kind are reduced to pseudo-psychological advice that does not provide insight into the underlying patterns of interaction between people. These patterns of interaction and their ongoing modification and transformation are the focus of our discussion here.

The *Yijing* is a remarkable tool for helping us to understand universal patterns of interpersonal relations, because at its heart the book is about relationships between people, their relative positions and roles in society, and its various social structures. You can be a leader in one context, and subordinate in another context. Women can be both mothers and daughters, men both fathers and sons. As the *Yijing* suggests, the social dynamics of a family have application to an organization, a business, or a nation. Understanding and relating to other people is difficult. It is difficult to know what we think, let alone what others think. And what people say often has a disconnect with what they do. If there is a fog of war, there is also a fog of understanding between people.

We are all connected to others in the societies in which we live, and to some degree our social roles, position, and circumstance define appropriate modes of behavior. We are all, as individuals, always tied to others in a web of interconnected causes and effects. This is neither good nor bad, but it can and does create friction and perpetuate the "fog," which makes easy things so difficult. In his book *The Righteous Mind*, social and moral psychologist Jonathan Haidt presents evidence that indicates the importance of the development of groups in evolution. People tend to see and define themselves as members of a group, whether a discrete and obvious group such as a religious organization or a specific company, or a larger, more amorphous group like liberals or conservatives. Haidt feels that "moral capital" is the resource that sustains these communities. He defines moral capital as:

> The degree to which a community possesses interlocking sets of values, virtues, norms, practices, identities, institutions, and technologies that mesh well with evolved psychological mechanisms and thereby enable the community to suppress or regulate selfishness and make cooperation possible.[342]

Research in moral and social psychology indicates that an individual's reasoning tends to align with the community of which he or she is a part, and that this reasoning is often intuitive and based on self-interest and reputation, more than logic or a quest for truth. However, there are also indications that if individuals come together in the right way, with a common bond or a sense of "shared fate," then the "truth" of the individual can be balanced by the diverse opinions of others. When this happens, a more balanced reasoning is cultivated, and positive actions and decisions are more likely to result.[343] This is a good definition of group and organizational self-cultivation.

Qualities for Cultivating Effective Relationships

Earlier we looked at the qualities of the Superior Person, as they are presented in the *Yijing*. These qualities allow the natural unfolding of a strategic disposition that is of service in all aspects of one's life. Most people don't want to think of their relationships with their spouse, children, family, and friends as involving strategy. It seems a bit cold and calculated, and when the discussion is about relationships the term "Superior Person" seems a bit, well, superior. So, in this context, perhaps these qualities should be thought of as a disposition for cultivating effective and rewarding relationships. Some of the qualities already discussed were:

- Perseverance and Patience (in relation to Hexagram 32)
- Modesty (in relation to Hexagram 15)
- Tolerance (in relation to Hexagrams 2, 16, 8, 45, and 35)
- Learning from Others and Education (in relation to Hexagram 4)
- Cohesion: Bringing People Together (in relation to Hexagrams 37 and 13)

These qualities interconnect many attributes and behavior patterns that make for smooth social interactions and open, productive communication between people. They embody broadmindedness, acting with patience, restraint, understanding, and flexibility. They also encompass thoughts about honesty and upright behavior.

Forming Relationships: Mutual Influence (Hexagram 31)

A good starting point for taking this discussion further is Hexagram 31. This hexagram is variously called Reciprocity, Mutual Influence, Wooing, Interaction, Conjoining, Sensing, and Feeling. It is composed of Lake over Mountain. On a basic level, Mountain symbolizes stillness. The Mountain slopes are nourished by the Lake. Mountain and Lake are also opposites. To some degree, this hexagram is about the attraction of opposites—stillness and joy. The Mountain is not a steep peak that causes water to run off it. It contains an open space where rainwater collects. Mountain and Lake mutually influence each other, like two people courting. They meet because the Mountain rises up, and the water of the Lake sinks downward. Dui-Lake traditionally represents the youngest daughter, and Gen-Mountain the youngest son. When they meet, there is mutual joy and attraction, courtship, and love. These two kinds of material forces (Qi) stimulate and respond to each other.[344] The stillness of Gen-Mountain symbolizes a mind that is innocent and selfless, the basis for proper interactions with others. The result of this kind of interaction is joy, symbolized by Dui-Lake.[345]

Reciprocity—Mutual Influence

Mutual Influence also symbolizes conjoined thinking: attracting others who have a similar way of thinking, or swaying them to your thinking, not through manipulation but through a reciprocal give and take. Then the relationship, whether it be friendship, romance, a business relationship, or family relations, is likely to be satisfying and to endure. This hexagram also teaches us about what attracts and what is attracted. In the words of *Yijing* scholar Jack Balkin: "What kind of company do you keep and what kind of people do you pursue? If your relationships are unhappy, perhaps it is because you are attracting (or pursuing) the wrong sort of people, or perhaps it is because of some unhealthy vision you have about yourself. Good relationships bring out the best in ourselves and in others. Consider what your relationships are bringing out in you and in the people you are connected to."[346]

The line commentaries for the first three lines of this hexagram reference the toes, calves, and thighs. The toes represent the beginning of attraction and mutual influence—a new idea or meeting someone new and experiencing a sense of attraction. Movement in the calves symbolizes wanting to move ahead, to follow the impulse of the feet. This image implies that you are not in control of either yourself or the situation. Instead of being led into a situation you don't understand and have not thought through, one can use Mountain's stillness and restraint to slow down, so that you do not act prematurely. The thighs symbolize impulse and sensation, which can lead to rash action. Avoid forcing your ideas and emotions on others, and avoid readily accepting the enthusiasms of others, unless they mesh with your own inner sense of self. Enthusiasm is positive, but it can also lead you into situations and relationships you are unprepared for.

The fourth line is the ruling line of the hexagram. The line commentary promises that "perseverance brings good fortune and regrets disappear." This line relates to the heart. The Heart-Mind and your true self are engaged with the interaction. The commentary goes on to say, "When the quiet power of a man's own character is at work, the effects produced are right. All those who are receptive to the vibrations of such a spirit will then be influenced."[347] In China, "heart" (*xin* 心) refers to mental processes and feelings, hence *xin* is often translated as "Heart-Mind." The Heart-Mind, according to Yanhua Zhang, is a "system of functions that forms a continuing process of being or becoming a person."[348] This conception includes physiological, psychological, and sociological dimensions, which are not separate. Emotions, morals, and the bodily sensations that arise from them and give rise to perception are not separated from thinking. The Chinese conception of the Heart-Mind points to the importance of our emotions and passions, and the necessity of understanding them in relating to others. In this hexagram, the references to parts of the body in juxtaposition to relationships confirms our innate sense that thoughts, feelings, and implicit communication are as important as, or even more important than, conscious, reasoned thought when we react and respond to others. Zhang goes on to say that these considerations are both cultural and situational in nature and are in a constant state of transformation. "When much planning and calculations fail to lead to a solution, worries and anxiety can arise; on the other hand, when actions taken at the critical moment transform a dangerous situation into a favorable one, happiness arises." What is particular about this "process-centered Heart-Mind physiology is that it commits to an unobstructed process of transformations in accordance with a given social context and environment."[349]

The last two line commentaries for Hexagram 31 reference the neck and back and the mouth and jaws. Line five is the back of the neck, which is firm and strong and conveys the idea that integrity and strength of conviction are important in connecting with others. However, there is also an implication that this firmness can be carried too far and transform into an unattractive rigidity. The final yin (broken) line relates to the mouth and conveys the idea of "empty words" not backed by the real intention of the Heart-Mind. In the commentary there is no indication of a result, either positive or negative, because cheap talk has no significance.

Intuition and Reason: Overcoming Differences

Social psychologists have found that in decision making, intuitions tend to come first and strategic reason comes later.[350] Confirmation bias, the tendency to make verbal arguments support our existing viewpoint, is powerful and stronger than we like to think. In *The Righteous Mind*, Professor Jonathan Haidt points out that gut feelings can be useful in making interpersonal judgments, but can be problematic in larger social groupings and in the making of public policies. He compares an individual to a single neuron, which is able to fire a pulse along its axon. It reacts and responds. Put neurons together and you get something larger, a system that is much more flexible than a single neuron. Haidt says an individual, like a single neuron, is good at finding evidence to support a position he or she already holds for intuitive reasons. This is often the problem in relationships—when we listen to and observe other people, we often only see and hear the things that confirm an intuition or feeling we already have, even if that feeling is not entirely rational. However, if you put individuals together in the right way, their reasoning powers can be enhanced and modified by others in a positive and more balanced way.[351]

We tend to unconsciously conflate different behaviors and words. For example, arguments can easily become connected to a person you have a relationship with, so that an expression on their face, or even just their presence causes you to react as though they are disagreeing with you or arguing with you. You react, they respond, and "the argument" begins anew. The reaction may be silent, but the underlying feelings and emotions are conveyed. Tai Ji exponent David-Dorian Ross relates this to Hebbian theory.[352] "The general idea is an old one, that any two cells or systems of cells that are repeatedly active at the same time will tend to become 'associated,' so that activity in one facilitates activity in the other."[353] These elevated states of activity that have become associated then maintain a low-level dysfunction that is difficult to break by logical reasoning. Haidt's premise, that we need the intervention of other points of view to break through these kinds of patterns, makes sense in the context of relationships between people. In China this is called "seeking identical points by allowing different points of view."

Sustaining Relationships: Constancy-Perseverance (Hexagram 32)

"Perseverance" means "long-lasting and enduring." This hexagram is the inverse of its predecessor Mutual Influence. Zhen-Thunder is above and Xun-Wind is below. Thunder is carried further by Wind and Wind is strengthened by the power of Thunder. Thunder and Wind are usually transitory, but that which produces them, Heaven and Earth and nature's cycles, are enduring. Thunder represents power and motion manifest. In this hexagram, Wind symbolizes the eldest daughter and Thunder the eldest son.

This is an older couple, who experience the enduring relationship of husband and wife. Relationships between people endure because each person is comfortable in their roles. This idea can be applied to any relationship. Relationships endure not because they are unchanging and fixed but because they change, grow, and evolve. What persists and is constant is the self-renewal. As one thing ends, a new thing begins. "What endures renews itself and its effects through continuous activity. What endures does so through change, not in spite of change."[354] Change and uncertainty test relationships, but they also provide the stimulus for the relationship to grow and become stronger. Thunder is the directing force of change. It is supported by Wind (the Gentle) on the inside, representing softness and flexibility. Endurance and perseverance require flexibility, like bamboo bending in the wind.

Mutual Influence and Constancy tell us much about relationships. These hexagrams reveal the implicit forces at play in our interactions with others and offer ways to engage with these forces to produce harmonious and beneficial relationships. Here the *Yijing* goes to the core of the matter—a centered and sincere Heart-Mind is the key element that allows one to participate in and maintain harmonious relationships with others that grow and transform over time.

How Relationships Move Apart and Renew Themselves

Change is what aids enduring relationships, but it is also change that leads people to move away from each other. This is highlighted by the inter-transformation of the Peace (11), Obstruction (12), Decrease (41), and Increase (42) Hexagrams.

In Peace, Heaven is below Earth. This seems to invert the natural order of things, but Heaven's strong yang lines have an upward movement while Earth's yin lines move downward. This configuration allows these opposing but complementary forces to interact and harmonize. Even as this hexagram forms, the lines flow into one another and a transformation unfolds. What is below moves upward so that the inner trigram decreases and gives to the outer trigram above. Gradually Obstruction (Standstill) appears. Francois Jullien compares this to an amorous relationship: "Between lovers, what is at first a fleeting divergence at the heart of their complicity starts to be underscored, or perhaps it begins with the first silence, which is then met

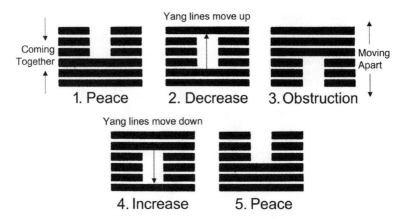

Figure 5.1. Inter-Transformation of Peace, Decrease, Obstruction and Increase

by others; it concentrates, becoming more and more opaque and solid and henceforth becomes immovable. They no longer have a hold over it; they have not noticed it, but a gulf has opened between them."[355]

This transformation from Peace to Obstruction is discrete. It is difficult, almost impossible to perceive the transformation until it reaches a certain threshold. At that point, the result is apparent, but the process of transformation itself is difficult to trace. Jullien points out that this transformation is not driven by the culpability of a guilty party, but arises from the "propensity" of the situation itself, its tendency to flow in a certain direction. The potential for this movement is implicit in the yin-yang polarity of the situation. The potential for reversal is also implicit. From this divide comes increase—what is above gives to what is below, and a new interaction occurs.

The first line of commentary in both hexagrams, Peace and Obstruction, is virtually the same: *When one pulls up the rush plant, it pulls up others of the same kind together with it.*[356] Things get pulled up together because their roots are entangled. Negative features can be brought to light and rectified early on, before seeing the entwined roots that anchor negative aspects of the situation and the evolution that inexorably flows from them. Through vigilance and adaptability one can then steer toward another configuration and even reverse and overturn the situation.[357] The line commentary for the sixth (top) line in Obstruction is: *Here one overturns Obstruction. Before there was obstruction, but afterwards, happiness.*[358]

If Hebbian Theory is right and "cells that fire together, wire together,"[359] then the difficulty in maintaining positive relationships is in the conflation of emotions and expectations, with the perceived or misperceived roles and actions of the others in the relationship. While reason can help untangle these roots, the *Yijing* shows us that once the roots are firmly anchored, untangling them is difficult. However, through awareness and timely action one can create other potential for transformation and even reversal, where transformation flows back upon itself.

Dispositions for Transformation

The *Yijing* invites us to cultivate a disposition for change and transformation, so that we can adapt to what is at hand, rather than fall back on programmed responses. How can one be aware of the almost imperceptible changes that are constantly unfolding in every situation? Francois Jullien points out that we tend to perceive things only when they become "events" that have occurred, which we must now react to, not realizing that a "silent transformation" has been occurring all along. The event often defines the narrative. Therefore, the couple is "suddenly" estranged, having missed the subtle signs that have been unfolding all along. Possibility and wisdom should not be "sought in the detachment of the exceptional and its 'additional' factors that are formed from an event, but, rather, in the incidence of each 'moment,' timely in its arrival and which we need to learn to welcome. In other words, first of all, to maintain equality with others, without privileging one moment or excepting it in relation to all moments, as true as it is that through its patent features there is already perceived—in a latent way—its coming reversal. Consequently *every* moment is the right moment and it never ceases to teach wisdom."[360]

To interact with each moment as it unfolds requires aligning ourselves with the changes internally and externally. In this sense, every moment is a crossroads, an OODA loop feeding back on itself, resulting in configurations that are the outcome of aligning with change, rather than of specific moments of analysis and decision.

As this is a book on strategy, it is perhaps appropriate to end this discussion of human relationships with a quote from the *Sunzi*—to apply Sunzi's advice to relationships. I have simply changed "enemy" to "other person";

"victory" and "defeat" to "harmonious configuration" and "disharmonious configuration"; and "battle" to "encounter":

> *Know the other person, know yourself,*
> *And a harmonious configuration is never in doubt, not in a hundred*
>   *encounters.*
> *He who knows self, but not the other person,*
> *Will suffer one disharmonious configuration for every harmonious*
>   *configuration.*
> *He who knows neither self nor the other person,*
> *Will fail in every encounter.*[361]

3. Application of Strategic Principles to Self-Fulfillment and One's Life Path

Desires and Goals

What fulfills our life and life path? The idea of articulating a "life path" is actually rather difficult, because one's life path can only be traced in hindsight. There are many decisions in life. If every moment is a crossroads, then there are potentially infinite options. Of course some decisions are automatic: Should I brush my teeth before going to bed? Yes, if I want healthy teeth. Should I eat breakfast in the morning? Probably.

What do you want to get out of life? This can be a difficult question to answer, because choices change as we engage with life, and each choice engenders the unfolding of a new set of circumstances. In *The 4-Hour Work Week*, Tim Ferris says that asking someone "What do you want?" does not produce a *meaningful and actionable answer.* He also addresses the typical interview question—What are your goals? Ferris says the most common response is happiness.[362] This is, again, not a meaningful answer, because one still has to define happiness. Even if you can define happiness, is happiness a sustainable state over time? For happiness to exist, its opposite, unhappiness, must also exist. This is like asking for world peace. Peace only exists in relation to war. World peace is unlikely to happen, and even if it did, how long would it last?

Goals are tricky things. You might know what your goals are for a period of time, but won't those goals change over a lifetime? And what happens when you attain the goal—your life is not over, it keeps unfolding in unexpected directions. This is also the problem with things like bucket lists, reading the hundred great books, or seeing the fifty places in the world everyone should visit before they die. These are goals, but they are not really life-fulfilling goals. More, they are not really about you, the you that is constantly changing and reconfiguring itself to align with events in the world around you as they unfold. "I want to be successful." Again, this is too imprecise and usually ends up relating to external factors like wealth and power, which don't necessarily alter your internal relationship with a constantly changing world and limited lifespan.

How many people have fulfilled a goal and then don't know what to do with the result, because they never thought beyond the goal itself? Learning does not end when you receive your college diploma; it is ongoing. There are many people who study martial arts with the idea of becoming a black belt. It is not uncommon for these people to stop training soon after achieving that goal. Why? Because they never thought beyond the goal and therefore did not see that a discipline like martial arts is a process that is ongoing. The satisfaction lies in the process of moving forward. The same thing happens to people who want to have a fancy sports car or own their own house. Often, once the goal is achieved, the person is unhappy. Investing the fulfillment of oneself in an external object is inherently unfulfilling unless it is connected to something larger, the continuous process of becoming.

War and strategy usually aim at producing peace. When rights, notions of pride, religion, perceived interests, and visions of peace are not reconcilable, force is often the natural arbiter. Peace and war are the coming together of opposites. Peace is usually the goal of conflict, but once reached, an inversion inevitably occurs. Peace often becomes the origin of war, much like a hexagram eventually changing into its opposite as the lines change and evolve. Edward Luttwak sees this equation as having historical veracity: "Peace can be the origin of war in many ways, even though peace is only a negative abstraction that cannot contain any self-destructive phenomenon, as war contains the destruction that eventually destroys war itself. Nevertheless, the condition of peace, that is the absence of war, can create the precondition for war by dissuading the peaceful from maintaining persuasive defenses, encouraging potential aggressors to plan war. Often in history, peace led to war because its conditions upset cultural, economic, and social changes that upset the balance of strength that had previously assured peace."[363]

According to philosopher François Jullien, in Chinese military strategy there are no definite or fixed goals: "The general instead evolves so he can exploit the potential of situations in which he recognizes his benefit, or failing that, so he can exploit his adversary's potential by turning the tables on him, transforming the situation. Success is not in the nature of a goal achieved but of a result, like the dropping of ripe fruit."[364] Jullien further describes the skilled general as remaining alert and keenly responsive to the enemy's movements, so that he can not only elude the enemy, but is always able to effortlessly respond by playing off the enemy's actions: "If I remain alert, I elude my enemy's grasp and my extreme responsiveness constantly replenishes my potential. Conversely, my adversary is hampered by the rigidity of his plans and deployments. I maintain myself in the agile posture of the virtual, while the other remains mired in or confused by the actual and thus vulnerable."[365] This agility is the result of vibrant qi and spirit that have been excited into movement, and are generated without effort, because the opponent himself creates them through trying to actualize his own plans and stratagems. In Ba Gua Zhang one attempts to be like the skilled general, maintaining a continuously engaged yet agile mental, physical, and energetic configuration that allows the body to reside in a potentiated state of excitation, so that each change and transformation becomes a platform for the next.

Excitement and Enthusiasm

This indirectly connects to Tim Ferris's original question—What do I want? Ferris gets to the heart of the matter with his next question: "The question you should be asking isn't 'What do I want?' or 'What are my goals?' but 'What would excite me?'"[366] This question brings us back to focus not on fixed goals but on the process of engagement with life through doing and acting. Goals create tension. By putting goals in the back seat, we can open ourselves to the flow of change that stimulates and replenishes our lives. When the tension is gone it is possible to fully engage with life, even in difficult situations.

Hexagram 16 (Enthusiasm) can mean Exciting, Stirring Up, Enjoyment, Delight, or Contentment, depending on the interpretation. This hexagram is Thunder over the Earth. The image of thunder rising out of the Earth is one of spring rain, thunder, and lightning clearing the air. Thunder shocks and wakens, producing a sustained and far-reaching stimulation and excitation. Thunder symbolizes movement. Thunder incites—it provokes, stimulates, and urges things forward. Earth symbolizes receptivity and preparation. The fourth line is the key line. It is the source of the movement and energy. The fourth (yang) line brings the other yin lines together because it is grounded in the receptivity and centralizing harmony of Earth, which in turn allows joy, contentment, and enthusiasm to unfold from the situation.

Enthusiasm

Hexagram 16 is associated with music and the idea of sympathetic vibration, in which a passive string or vibratory body responds to external vibrations to which it has a harmonic likeness. This sympathetic resonance creates an internal arousal of the Qi and spirit that breaks down not only the barriers between people and groups, but also the barriers within an individual that prevent him or her from moving forward and embracing their full participation in growth and change.

This excitation of spirit and its activation of internal potential is also an important theme in *The Art of War*:

> *The skilful warrior's energy is devastating; his timing, taut.*
> *His energy is like a drawn crossbow,*
> *His timing like the release of a trigger.*[367]

Nourishing Life

In Chinese thought the idea of "Feeding Life" or "Nourishing Life" (*Yang Sheng*) has a direct relationship to Ferris's idea of excitement and Hexagram 16. Francois Jullien defines nourishing life as "the ability to maintain one's capacity to evolve by refining and decanting what is vital in oneself so as to develop that vitality to the fullest."[368] In traditional Chinese medicine, disease is, at its core, movement that is blocked or runs counter to its natural flow. Health lies in an ongoing facilitation of the "Qi Dynamic"—the natural and harmonious movements of the vital force and their various interactions. This may involve actual medical intervention, but according to the *Huang Di Nei Jing*, one of the oldest and most important traditional Chinese medical texts, the true men and women of ancient times were able to replenish and engage with their "innate true energy" because they aligned themselves with the changing patterns of yin and yang and the cycles of change in the world around them.[369]

Aligning oneself with the changing patterns of yin and yang is not merely a physical discipline. It is a unitary disposition of body, mind, and spirit. It means not being attached to a single position, and letting go of the distinctions that attach to a single disposition. Attachment to a viewpoint can impart strong decisiveness, but as Francois Jullien points out attachment can also cut one off from other possibilities: "We should not isolate ourselves in a certain position, lest we cut ourselves off from the opposite position and become deaf to calls to free ourselves from the position we happen to be in (so as to continue to advance); the alternative to this is necessity. Stuck in the extreme life ceases to feed itself, because it loses its virtuality, bogs down, becomes stalemated, and no longer initiates anything new."[370]

Hexagram 27 (Nourishment) is the image of an open mouth with the yang lines representing the upper and lower jaws and the yin lines the teeth. The significance of the hexagram is revealed in its pairing of opposites, Thunder at the foot of the Mountain. This is movement within and stillness without. The life force is aroused and urges forward, modified by tranquility, stillness, and contemplation. This prevents one from surging forward recklessly without the ability to adapt and change.

Nourishment

Completion and Renewal: Hexagrams 63 and 64

Hexagrams 63 and 64 impart to us some important, final wisdom about life and change that can help us, as individuals or as groups, to maintain our connection to the excitation and forward movement of life. Hexagram 63 (After Completion) is a further development of Hexagram 11 (Peace). All the lines are in their correct positions and everything is ordered properly. All the yang lines are in the odd places and the yin lines are in the even places. In this way, each line is balanced by the neighboring lines. The structure of the situation is one of complete balance and harmony.

Water is over Fire is this hexagram. Usually they are opposite and antagonistic, but here they are in harmony. Water in a pot, bubbling on a fire creating steam is the symbol of an objective reaching completion. What was desired has been achieved. However, this state of perfect equilibrium cannot be indefinitely maintained. The Water may boil over and extinguish the Fire, or the Fire may evaporate all the Water. Water also signifies danger. The moment something is completed and balanced, the moment such a peak is reached, a shift the other way begins. The question is whether this state of completion and accomplishment is favorable for future development, because success can lead to failure, just as peace can induce war. When any development reaches its extreme, a reverse movement can be expected. The clarity and illumination provided by Fire are necessary to balance the potential danger presented by this situation.

After Completion   Before Completion

In Hexagram 64 (Before Completion), the positions of Water and Fire are reversed. Fire rises upward and water flows downward, indicating that the two forces are moving away from each other. The lines have all switched to less favorable positions. This is the beginning of a new development and a new cycle. However, this is not really the bad situation it appears to be, because it is also a moment of opportunity. When situations are imbalanced and chaotic, there is greater opportunity to create a new strategy, take a new path, and find new ways of bringing opposite elements like Fire and Water into harmony. Once again, this situation requires combining the judgment and clarity of purpose symbolized by Fire and the adaptability and flexibility of Water.

After Completion is not just the final stage of a development as a whole, it is also the beginning of new development. Before Completion is not chaos and disintegration, but the beginning of a new cycle of growth and opportunity. Although seemingly opposite, the two situations are in fact similar. Both configurations present uncertainty that contains a potential for opportunity. Both require the boldness to move, combined with clarity and insight into the situation, and a disposition of flexibility that allows one to adjust to a situation that is in flux.

Sincerity and Inner Truth: Hexagram 61

The *Yijing* advises us to adjust to changing circumstances, but always in relation to who we are. We should not fix ourselves to a single position, but we do not depart from what our own heart tells us. Hexagram 61 (Inner Truth) shows Wind flowing over the Lake. The lines representing Heaven (top two lines) and Earth (bottom two lines) are solid, while those in the middle, representing Man, are open and empty (Fig. 5-2).

Figure 5.2. Hexagram 61, Inner Truth (Zhong Fu)

Wind fills the space above the Lake. Wind is felt, but cannot be seen, except in the movement it creates on the surface of the lake. This interaction of Wind and Lake is represented by the two broken lines of the diagram. These broken lines also represent a human being with an open heart responsive to the movement of Heaven (represented by Wind) and Earth (represented by the Lake). This openness also reflects a receptivity to truth, one's own and that of others.

Inner Truth means that what is on the outside is also inside. Sincerity, trust, and reliability will bring even difficult and contentious groups and people together. These qualities also help to unify opposing forces within yourself. Inner confidence and trust in yourself is the key to adapting to a changing world.

Wind and Lake also symbolize gentleness and joy. Approaching life and other people with a supple flexibility, joy, and enthusiasm is the basis for great achievements. Wind is penetration and insight into things, while Lake symbolizes inner knowledge and inner strength. Wood can be substituted for Wind, symbolizing a boat on a lake. The ability to cross dangerous waters if one is open inside and firm and strong on the outside—these are the basic qualities of sincerity and inner truth.[371]

Ba Gua Zhang: Training a Disposition for Change and Transformation

The practice of Ba Gua Zhang is one way of sensitizing oneself to the process of change and transformation. As a martial art, Ba Gua Zhang embodies the idea of having a guiding intention but no fixed plans, except to change appropriately with the changing circumstances (dictated by the terrain, energy, and specific configuration of a particular encounter), in order to prevail. This ability can only manifest itself when there is internal harmony and alignment. In Ba Gua Zhang internal harmony is attributed to unity of the Heart-Mind and Intention (Yi) with Qi (vital force), and Qi with Jin. Heart-Mind and Qi can be understood as one's internal configuration or disposition. Jin is an extension of the internal configuration, which can be expressed as force and power, energy and spirit. Jin transforms constantly, manifesting differently from moment to moment, changing according to the situation. These interactions occur largely on an implicit level, while the physical body responds in coordination with the internal unity and harmony. In this sense, the Ba Gua Zhang practitioner cultivates a disposition that has correspondence with Napoleon's famous remark—"I have never had a plan of operations." Through this statement, Napoleon implies that human acumen is unable to see beyond a single engagement and therefore the result of each battle becomes the basis for a new strategic decision.[372] In Ba Gua Zhang, each moment of the encounter dictates the next as the opponent's Jin interacts with your own.

As a mind-body discipline, Ba Gua Zhang trains one to experience and sense the continuous changes and transformations that flow from the internal unity of Heart-Mind, Yi, Qi, and Jin. The postures and movements of Ba Gua Zhang arouse and enliven the Qi, so that there is no gap between intention and action, and the energy pathways are open and free-flowing. This creates the basis for developing a sensitized awareness of transformation and change. Flowing with the moment to moment changes in the body allows one to experience and sense the most minute changes in the internal configuration—an ability to sense the first stirrings of a transformation. The changes in our internal body pattern and the configuration of the Qi internally also interact with what is external—the Qi of the surrounding environment, which includes the Qi configurations of the people and things we are interacting with.

Ba Gua Zhang employs arcing steps. Its basic practice is to walk in circles. In circling, one is continuously changing and turning, simultaneously advancing and retreating with every step, always circling back to the beginning. This is not starting over, but rather a series of renewals. Like the turning of the seasons, each return and each renewal is unique, each return brings something new. The necessary disposition for change and transformation is generated internally and expressed externally, constantly renewed and strengthened through endless cycles that never repeat, but continuously loop. What is generated internally is manifested externally, like the fractal geometry diagrammed in the interconnected loops of a Lorenz Attractor (Fig. 5-3). This constant renewal and fine-tuned sensitivity to the subtle changes in the interplay between your internal configuration and that of the people and events around you creates space and opportunity for positive transformation.

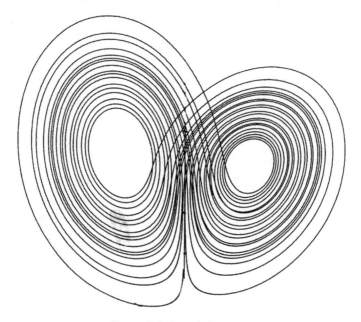

Figure 5.3. Lorenz Attractor

Let Life Decide

No one can know their life path ahead of time, nor can one predict what will fulfill one's potential. Goals, aspirations, and dreams are part of life, but we should not let them constrain us from a full engagement with our potential. The *Yijing* counsels that it is life's movement itself that nourishes and incites our life force to fulfill its potential: "Once we have given up goals and the burdens that go along with them, *life itself* decides how it will go. Once freed of all impediments, life itself is capable of inducing and inciting. . . . There is no need to project the result some distance away or turn it into a fixed finality."[373]

APPENDIX I

Conflict, the Army, and Peace

I am not alone in knowing that the fortune of war is by no means fixed and firm. For many men have been deceived by the hope of victory when it seemed certain that it would come to them, while men who, to all appearances, have met with disaster, have many a time had the fortune to triumph unexpectedly over their adversaries. Consequently I say that men deliberating with regard to peace should not put before them only the expectation of success, but reflecting that the result will be either way, they should make their choice of policy on this basis.

 —Belisarius[374]

Si vis pacem, para bellum.
If you want peace, prepare war.

 —Roman Proverb[375]

No government should ever imagine that it can always adopt a safe course; rather it should regard all possible courses of action as risky. This is the way things are: whenever one tries to escape one danger, one runs into another. Prudence consists in being able to assess the nature of a particular threat and in accepting the lesser evil.

 —Niccolo Machiavelli[376]

Without a full understanding of the harm caused by war, it is impossible to understand the most profitable way of conducting it.

 —Sunzi[377]

Three Hexagrams

Three hexagrams are paricularly important in talking about military strategy and conflict between individuals and nations. They are Conflict, The Army, and Peace. A line-by-line analysis of these hexagrams can aid one in understanding the nuances of conflict and warfare, strategy, leadership, crisis management, and the maintenance of peace.

☰ Conflict/Contention (Song)

Heaven has an upward movement, while Water's movement is downward. The two sections of Hexagram 6 move away from each other, signifying that there is conflict. "Contention arises because of need. This hexagram represents a combination of desire and strength, which leads to contention."[378] Each side has difficulty trusting the other. The strong fifth line implies that if one is clear-headed and strong, the opponent can be met halfway, thereby avoiding conflict. It can also mean finding a wise, impartial arbiter to resolve things. One must be prudent and handle conflict at its inception, when latent differences begin to manifest. If rights and duties are examined carefully, and with sincerity, the conflict can be avoided. If one pushes too hard for a decision, resolution will be difficult. Seeking common ground and not avoiding the expression of differences is one way to avoid conflict. If conflict is allowed to grow, the separation between the upper and lower elements increases. Then it can easily go to its endpoint and lead to misfortune or open hostility. This is not the time to begin new or risky enterprises, because their successful undertaking requires that there be unity of purpose and cohesion of one's forces. It is better to find a secure place from which to operate and attempt to resolve the conflict.

Line 1

The first line is yin. This designates people in a weaker or lower position who cannot bring the conflict to a successful conclusion. Persisting with the conflict will bring trouble. The conflict is in the beginning stage. There may be a slight dispute or criticism, but the trouble will be minor if one does not push the conflict to a decision. People in a lower position cannot generally prevail against those in a higher position. However, guerrilla wars often begin with the weakest, most downtrodden parts of society beginning to resist the injustices of those above. If those above persist in injustice, conflict will grow. Resistance by the weak usually ends unsatisfactorily, unless there is help and guidance from those in a strong position. If resistance strengthens and coalesces into the second strong line, it has a clear path to move forward, unobstructed by the weak third line, and gain in strength. Mao's assessment of the revolutionary power of China's peasants, and his reliance upon them in the struggle for China, is representative of conflict beginning with the weak and apparently powerless.

History shows that in most cases nations or groups in the weaker position rely on outside support and assistance in order to prevail against much stronger adversaries. Americans often forget the important role the French played in the American Revolution. The French not only shipped large amounts of arms, equipment, and gunpowder to the colonial army, but through their navy, threatened Britain's lucrative possessions in the Caribbean.[379]

Line 2

The second line is yang (strong), but it contends with the fifth line, which is in a higher position. Against an enemy of superior strength it is not a disgrace to retreat. If a sense of honor draws one into an unequal conflict it can be disastrous. By returning to "one's home," living modestly and managing one's own affairs, one can defuse the situation. Make concessions to avoid conflict. If one retreats to a powerful domain or position of power, there will still be competition and conflict.

The peace that resulted from the First Punic War was unsatisfactory for the Carthaginians. It reflected Rome's much greater strength, but its heavy-handedness caused great resentment among the Carthaginian leaders, including Hamilcar Barca, the father of the great general Hannibal. Carthage eventually turned to Spain as the place best suited to restore their power, strength, and wealth. Rome became alarmed at the growing strength of the Carthaginian position in Spain and ultimately this led to a second conflict, the Second Punic War.[380]

In 1936 Mao Zedong and other communist leaders led the Long March, an attempt to escape encirclement by the Guomindang forces of Chiang Kai-shek. Piercing the Guomindang perimeter, they passed over wild mountainous regions, fought their way across the Datong river on a pontoon bridge, and marched over snow-covered mountains and bleak marshlands to escape the enemy forces. Finally, in northern Shaanxi province they connected with other guerrilla forces. Only seven or eight thousand of Mao's original eighty thousand followers remained. From this safe and remote base, the Chinese Communist party was able to recover and rebuild its power.

Line 3

The third weak line is surrounded by two strong yang lines and therefore in danger. It cannot contend in the current position. By holding to what one knows, being conservative and in control of oneself without seeking prestige or gain, one can avoid conflict. In that case, one holds on to the merit one has actually earned. Seeking more than that creates friction. Trouble can arise if new undertakings are initiated at this time. This is not time to expand, but time to be cautious and wait. One should not be deflected from one's course by the other lines (i.e., one should not be drawn into conflict with them).

Line 4

The fourth line is strong and not content with its situation. The strength of the fourth line is not balanced. It is insecure, and in wanting to improve its situation it contends with the fifth line, which is in the position of strength. The conflict creates turmoil. By turning back, pausing, and accepting or changing one's position, conflict can be avoided and the natural order can be restored. Sunzi said: "The sovereign should not start a war simply out of anger; the commander or general should not fight a battle simply because he is resentful."[381] By pausing in a situation where one is not strong enough to contend, it is possible to gather strength and put oneself in order.

While Belisarius was contending with the Goths in Italy, Theodebert, leader of the Franks, saw that the Romans and the Goths were both weakened by warfare and viewed this as an opportunity to attack and take Italy from both of them. He advanced with a vast army of one hundred thousand men. He was welcomed by the Goths, who initially viewed him as an ally, but soon changed their minds when he attacked and took Liguria, leaving devastation in his wake. Belisarius had his squadrons shadow the movements of Theodebert's troops and sent the Frankish leader a message advising him that it might be unwise to endanger himself in the *vain hopes* of extending the limits of his possessions.[382] Belisarius knew that the Franks were being overwhelmed by famine. The war-ravaged lands were unable to support their vast host. They were eventually forced to withdraw back into France.

Line 5

The strong fifth line here represents the leader who can arbitrate and resolve conflict. Settling conflict in a balanced and impartial way produces resolution that is good and harmonious. Sun Bin said: "The state prospers when its rulers consistently stick to their words and uphold justice."[383] If one is right and decides well, conflict can be avoided.

After the first Peloponnesian War between Athens and Sparta, there were thirty years of peace. Although both tried to keep the peace, they were eventually drawn into conflict a second time by the complaints and demands of their allies. One of the key issues was that Athens barred Megara, an ally of Sparta, from the harbors of the Athenian Empire—a kind of trade embargo used a measure to dissuade Megara from helping Corinth, another of Sparta's allies. This attempt to avoid direct conflict backfired when Athens refused to revoke its degree against Megara at Sparta's request. Athens misjudged the passion and anger they had provoked in the Spartans and their allies. The Athenians also misjudged their ability to deter the superior Spartan land forces through the defensive strategy proposed by Pericles.[384]

Line 6

The top line is strong and victorious, but has carried conflict to its bitter end. There is victory when the top line contends, but though there may be reward and credit, it will not bring peace, pleasure or respect. One can win, but the prize will be taken away. The implication is that contention will continue; go on and on. Even if one dispute is settled, a new one can arise. There will be no peace.

After defeating the Spanish rebels, the Roman general Scipio Africanus did not take vengeance upon them. He knew that to do so would sow the seeds of future trouble and turn the Spanish into bitter foes. Therefore he did not demand surrender of their arms or take hostages. This showed his confidence and prevented a major rebellion from occurring again.[385]

䷆ The Army (Shi)

Conflict is followed by The Army. Contention and conflict, taken to their endpoint, lead to open conflict, mass uprising, and ultimately war. Thus the army arises out of conflict. The army refers to the masses, the people. Water beneath Earth represents the groundwater stored under the Earth. Danger is below—masses of people are a powerful force, but just as Earth holds the water, this powerful force can be guided by discipline and obedience (represented by Earth). The strong second line signifies the general or commander that draws the yin lines together. These yielding lines are subordinate to the general. He is not in the fifth place (that of the ruler), but he should resonate with the fifth line. From contention comes the rising of the people. This can be dangerous unless there is organization and discipline, like an army under the command of a general who in turn responds to the leader. With collective action and joint effort it is possible to prevail. However, the general must not abuse his position.

In the *Sunzi*, five fundamental factors are critical in examining the army and warfare:

1. **The Way (Dao):** The moral force or moral capital that inspires people to support the leader and the army and to follow through with their support. This includes the morale of the people and the troops.
2. **Heaven (Tian):** The understanding of the conduct of military operations according to seasonal and weather changes.
3. **Earth (Di):** An understanding of terrain in warfare.
4. **Command (Jiang):** The wisdom, ability, trustworthiness, and courage of the commander.
5. **Rules and Regulations (Fa):** The administration, supply, discipline, and organization of the army.[386]

Line 1

A weak line at the beginning means the army must set out in proper order. If the proper order is not established from the beginning, there will be misfortune, even if the cause is just. This first line represents the mobilization of the army. Discipline is necessary to control a large group of people. That is why armies have regulations that must be followed. Losing control of the troops can bring disaster, even if one is victorious. However, merely coercing people into a cause that is not right is also dangerous. There must be an upright moral imperative and mature leadership. The army must be well trained, organized, and disciplined in order for it to succeed.

Scipio Africanus understood that the organization and mobilization of an army required more than just rules and regulations. Liddel Hart describes Scipio's military genius as follows: "His appreciation of the moral factor and of the value of personal observation, two vital elements in generalship was shown in his earliest steps. Before attempting to formulate any plan, he visited the states of his allies and every one of the various parts of his armies seeking by his attitude even more than by his words to rekindle confidence and dissipate the influence of past defeat."[387] Scipio also knew that before an army sets out, it must gather intelligence and devise plans. He gathered information from his commanders, allies, and local people about the logistics of the Carthaginians, where they kept their gold, where their supplies were stored, and at what ports their fleets (their line of communication back to Carthage) docked. In this way, he knew from the very beginning where to position his army and where to strike.[388]

Line 2

This line represents the general. The leader of an army is in the middle of his forces. The other lines yield to the commander. The leader must be in touch with his forces to lead. He cannot lead from a distance, from the fifth position, that of the ruler, but he must have the recognition of the ruler and win the support of other states. This is active yang being supported by yin. The army can only prevail if the leader's authority is respected. The general must thoroughly understand the five factors mentioned in the *Sunzi* above, and he must know his troops. To know his troops he must be among them.

> *Bear the same heat and cold the soldiers do; share their toil as well as their ease.*
> —Zhuge Liang[389]

> *A general should never have to say: "I did not expect it."*
> —Maurice's Strategikon[390]

Napoleon was known for his stirring speeches and his ability to command men and move them to great feats in battle. He had been an ordinary soldier himself, so he knew how to talk to soldiers and how they responded to criticism and rewards. "Napoleon mingled now and then with the common soldiers, recalling their victories, inquiring about their families and listened to their complaints."[391] Napoleon's well-timed promotions, often based on merit, improved morale and created a fierce loyalty among his troops.

Line 3

The third line rides on top of the trigram. It is a weak line and in the wrong place. If an army is run by the troops, or has too many commanders, it cannot succeed. It is not unified if those under the commander seek recognition and status. Zhuge Liang said, "Refusal of the mettlesome to submit to authority, contempt of superiors, or using supplies for personal enjoyment. These things corrupt the armed forces."[392]

Rule by the masses or by committee will bring misfortune. Scipio understood that his subordinate generals who had previously been defeated by the Carthaginians might be jealous of his position. He went to great lengths to treat them with respect, not as rivals.

> *The side which has unity of purpose among its officers and men will win.*
> —Sunzi[393]

Belisarius describes the necessity for cohesion as follows: The scattered battalions of an army, like the limbs of the human frame, should be directed by one pervading spirit, and not attempt various and incompatible movements.[394]

Line 4

The fourth line is weak and in a subordinate position. If faced by a superior enemy, it may be strategic to carry out an orderly retreat. In the *Sunzi:* "If you are fewer than the enemy retreat, if you are no match for him, try to elude him."[395] The army must be kept intact so it retreats in good order to find a more suitable position. This refers to strategy and tactics in general. Sunzi also said, "To operate an army successfully, we must avoid the enemy's strong points and seek out his weak points. As water changes its course in accordance with the contours of the terrain, so a warrior changes his tactics in accordance with the enemy's changing situation."[396] One of the thirty-six military strategies attributed to Zhuge Liang is to evade the enemy in order to preserve the troops. It is often associated with this line of the hexagram.

The soldiers of Belisarius felt that there was ignominy in retreating before the Goths, whom they viewed as barbarians. They complained about the trumpets used to signal a tactical retreat. Belisarius upbraided them, saying that "even intrepidity must be restrained within certain moderate limits, and when it becomes pernicious ceases to be honorable."[397]

Line 5

When under attack, the army must be directed by an experienced leader. The leader responds only after having suffered aggression. This refers to the moral force of defending oneself and the people from aggression. In the words of Napoleon, "morale and opinion are more than half the battle."[398] The sovereign should not interfere with the administration of the army. Ignorance of the internal affairs of the military will cause confusion among both the officers and the men.[399] The second line–yang (the general) is the person to lead the army. A breakdown in organization and leadership would be disastrous. Either one will be defeated or, even in victory, the army will be out of control and transgress its mission.

Belisarius invaded Italy twice, on both occasions battling the Goths for control of the country. Successful the first time, despite the Emperor Justinian's refusal to send sufficient reinforcements to hold what had been gained, he was suddenly recalled. Justinian was fearful of the personal loyalty and allegiance the troops offered Belisarius. This allowed the Goths to regain control of Italy. On the second occasion, although Belisarius managed to retake Rome and bottle up the Goths, he could not sustain his gains due to lack of support from the Emperor. Belisarius was forced to depart and return once again to Constantinople.

Sun Bin, like Sunzi, feels that one of the factors that leads to defeat is a commander who is constrained by his sovereign.[400] However, Clausewitz reminds us that war is a continuation of policy, therefore there are no purely military judgments.[401] Military matters must necessarily emanate from policy. Clausewitz echoes the Army hexagram when he says that "war is to be regarded as an organic whole from which a single branch cannot be separated."[402] There is tripodal balance between the people, the general and the army, and the government or the sovereign. For war to be successful, these three elements must be coordinated and balanced. Sunzi adds that one way a sovereign can bring disaster to his army is if "he interferes with the administration of the army when he is ignorant of its internal affairs, thus creating confusion among the officers and men."[403]

Political leadership in Germany during WWI allowed itself to be caught up by the opinions of the military, who saw war as inevitable and promised a quick victory on the Western front through the implementation of the Schlieffen plan. "The combination of military self-confidence and public heedlessness nullified all attempts to coordinate Germany's political and military strategies rationally and to direct its operational planning to achievable ends."[404]

The great strategist Zhuge Liang understood the danger that military force represented to the nation. In the *Art of War* he says: "The army is a terrible instrument. The general is in a position of great danger and responsibility. Therefore it is said, the weapon that is too firm can break. The greater the responsibility of the general, the greater the danger. Therefore the good general does not rely only on the power of his troops. Although entrusted with responsibility and power from the sovereign, he does not become arrogant. His heart and soul are bent on safeguarding the nation."[405]

Line 6

The army has succeeded. There is victory. Rewards and offices must be handed out with care, according to merit. Petty people, even if they performed well, should not be employed or given power, as they may create chaos and dissension. Military leaders, although successful in their missions and trustworthy, may not be the best leaders after the war is over, so care should be taken in handing out appointments and positions of power and influence. In evaluating performance, reward the good and dismiss the bad.

Napoleon employed punishments and rewards, very effectively, often with dramatic effect. His personal rebukes, although rare, could be devastating, leaving the individual feeling disowned and outcast, struggling to win back Napoleon's favor. Promotion, public praise, and rewards were usually based on merit and provided an example that motivated and united his troops.[406] Promotions based on merit also created a capable officer corps, which allowed the divisional structure of his army to operate smoothly.

*An enlightened leadership is aware of the good and bad throughout the realm,
not daring to overlook even minor officials and commoners, employing the
wise and the good and dismissing the greedy and weak-minded.[407] Record
even a little good, reward even a little merit, and soldiers will be encouraged.*

—Zhuge Liang[408]

 Peace (Tai):

Earth (Kun), the receptive, stands above Heaven. In this hexagram Earth,
above, moves downward and Heaven, below, moves upward. They meet,
mingle, and are in harmony so all things are harmonious. The weak lines are
departing as the strong lines advance—the spirit of Heaven rules inside man
and his earthy animal nature comes under this influence. This hexagram
represents a time of peace, prosperity, and growth.

Line 1

The first line is the leader. As it moves up, it pulls the other yang lines with
it. This is like a plant that, when pulled up, is connected by its roots to
other plants. As one line moves, they all move; a domino effect. Those with
strength and intelligence are starting at the bottom, in the lowest positions.
When one initiates action, the others follow. Rather than standing alone,
one is aided by one's peers. This is the time to move forward and proceed
toward one's goals.

Line 2

The yang leader in this line is in harmony with the yin line in the fifth
place. In times of peace and prosperity one must carefully attend to things
to effect achievement. Here the second line is the leader, able to effect all-
around cooperation even from difficult and uncultivated people. Factionalism and cliques are avoided through including everyone and not neglecting
the distant and far away. Everything is attended to. Foresight must be exercised to anticipate distant changes. One must not lapse into decadence or
fear in times of prosperity, but be willing to undertake dangerous or difficult tasks (crossing the great river). Government and leadership in times
of tranquility must employ all of these elements in order to be balanced
and orderly.

An observant and perceptive government is one that looks at subtle phe-
nomena and listens to small voices. Thus when you are alert to what people
in the lower echelons have to say, and take it into consideration, so that
your plans include the rank and file, then all the people are your eyes and
a multitude of voices helps your ears. This is the reason for the classic say-
ing—"the people are the sage's mind."

—Zhuge Liang[409]

Line 3

What rises will fall. Tranquility will eventually come to a standstill or meet
with obstruction (Hexagram 12). Change will come again. Heaven and Earth
are subtly beginning to change their positions. One should not be unhappy
or surprised; instead, remain aware of this inevitable change. Avoid complacency. Be mindful of danger even in times of peace. Be steadfast and firm
in order to move toward one's goal.

The Congress of Vienna in 1815, convening at the end of the Napoleonic wars, attempted to establish a system that would preserve peace in
Europe by creating an equilibrium of forces committed to maintaining
peace. Although the general peace was more or less maintained for almost
a century, the turning point began in the late 1840s, when national self-
determination became a key element of political reform.[410] This led to the
Franco-Prussian War and ultimately World War I.

Unexpected changes and shifts of power are the warp and woof of international history. In the fifth century BCE, the father of history [Herodo-
tus] already underscored the inevitable and unforeseeable shifts in the
power of states: "I shall go forward with my history describing equally
the great and lesser cities. For the cities which were formerly great, have
most of them become insignificant; and such as are at present powerful,
were weak in olden time."[411]

Line 4

Peace and tranquility have gone past the halfway point and begun to
change. Yin lines are returning to their place and the yang lines move
upward to theirs. There is cooperation with those above and below. This
yin line is in a yin position over the yang lines pushing upward. Although

it resonates with the first line it must also harmonize with the third line (its neighbor), whose close proximity could create a conflict, unless its opposing energy can be induced to complement and go with the fourth line.

Line 5

The weak fifth line is like the sovereign giving his daughter a blessing to one who is below, the second line. The fifth line may be weak in leadership but resonates with the second line, whose wise and strong support he needs. This can also represent the leader allying themselves with those lower in rank and sharing good fortune and prosperity with them. This leads to success.

Chandragupta, aided by his adviser and vizier Kautilya, ruled India during an age of prosperity in 300 BC. Benefiting from Kautilya's wisdom, great loyalty, and ruthlessness, Chandragupta was able throw Alexander the Great's successors out of India and establish a dynasty that would last for more than 130 years. Under their rule, the organization of government was efficient and peace and prosperity were maintained within the borders of the kingdom.[412]

Line 6

The weak, yielding line reaches the top. Peace is about to end. The actions of the weak and yielding are about to cause a separation. Those above do not extend benefits to those below, and those below do not take orders from those above. The change alluded to in line three is about to occur. The city wall is about to fall back into the moat from which it was dug. One should not use force to try to alter the situation. The Army (Hexagram 7) should not be mobilized, as there will be a lack of communication between the leaders and the people. Mobilizing the army will create disorder. Hold fast to one's intimate circle, be conservative, and examine yourself and the situation. Remain steadfast while waiting for the cycle to change. Then one can move forward.

In 1588 the Spanish Armada began to move against England. Although they were not in an open state of war, the peace between Spain and England had been deteriorating for years. The spread of Protestantism in the Netherlands threatened Spanish rule there, and Philip of Spain plotted against Queen Elizabeth, who ruled over a largely Protestant England.

Elizabeth's foreign policy was largely defensive. Known as the "Virgin Queen," she kept the question of marriage open, using it as a diplomatic ploy. She allowed Philip to think that she would marry him or his son, keeping him waiting while she strengthened her alliances and her military forces. She avoided direct land conflict with Spain, instead supporting the Dutch in their rebellion against Spain. "For years Elizabeth played fast and loose with the Netherlands, shifting her policy with fluid circumstance."[413] Because the English economy was dependent on trade with the Netherlands, Elizabeth supported revolt there in order to keep the Dutch from being defeated, and also to prevent Spain from attacking England. At the same time, she supported Huguenot revolts against the French, and Protestant uprisings against the Scottish Queen, who had ties to France.

Sir Francis Drake and other English privateers raided Spanish trading ships coming from the New World, including attacks on Spain's gold fleet. Elizabeth turned a blind eye to their depredations, as it fattened her treasury while damaging the Spanish economy. She made excuses to Philip when he protested, pointing out that Philip was himself violating international law by aiding Irish rebels. At the same time, she threatened a marriage alliance with France.[414]

> Elizabeth's very indecisiveness served her well. Her statesmanship drove both her friends and enemies to tears. She was maddeningly slow and irresolute in determining policy; but in many cases her indecision paid. She knew how to ally herself with time, which dissolves more problems than men solve; her procrastination allowed the complex factors to settle themselves into clarity and focus.[415] Her motto was "video et taceo" (I see and am silent). Inheriting a nation politically in chaos and militarily in decay, her only practicable policy was to keep England's enemies from uniting against it.[416]

Eventually there was open war, though largely at sea, and the huge Spanish fleet, the Armada, was disabled and destroyed in a series of engagements by a combination of English attacks and storms. Despite this victory, the naval war with Spain continued on and off until Philip's death. In the end, the defeat of the Armada changed the balance of power in Europe, while preventing a war with Spain on English soil.

Zhuge Liang on Strategy and Crisis Management

Governor Liu, cast adrift alone,
By fortune found Nanyang's Sleeping Dragon.
He sought to know the shape of things to be;
Smiling, the master mapped his strategy.

   —Three Kingdoms [417]

Zhuge Liang: The Master Strategist

The Water Margin (also known as *Outlaws of the Marsh*) and *The Romance of the Three Kingdoms* are classical Chinese novels based on historical facts. They've had a profound influence on how the Chinese and Japanese view and implement strategy. Both books were favorites of Mao Zedong and were read by People's Liberation Army leaders during the Chinese Civil War, just as they are today by strategists in the PRC.[418] In the business world, *The Romance of the Three Kingdoms* is frequently quoted and referred to by executives studying management techniques in Tokyo and Beijing.

Zhuge Liang (also known as Kongming) is the master strategist portrayed in *The Romance of the Three Kingdoms*. He is venerated as a man of great wisdom, not only in the military realm, but also in the political sphere. Zhuge Liang commanded troops, but also served as a civil administrator and adviser to the emperor. From these experiences, he was able to pass on practical and profound ideas regarding leadership and crisis management. He is credited with many inventions and innovations, some of which bear his name. In addition to wooden oxen and gliding horses, types of wheelbarrows that he invented to supply his troops with grain, Zhuge Liang is believed to be the creator of the *mantou*, a kind of steamed bun, the repeating crossbow (called the *zhuge nu*), and a hot air balloon used for military signaling (the Kongming lantern). He is also purportedly the author of the *Thirty-Six Stratagems* and *The Art of War* (a different book than the *Sunzi*).

After the collapse of the Han dynasty and the usurpation of power by the brilliant General Cao Cao, Zhuge Liang guided the efforts of Liu Bei, a distant member of the Han imperial family, to defeat Cao Cao and return the emperor to power. In aiding Liu Bei, Zhuge Liang employed many subtle stratagems based on foreknowledge and deception. Psychological knowledge of the enemy was crucial, as it enabled him to predict the actions of his opponent. This allowed him to strike directly at the plans of the enemy and mislead him. This approach is in accord with the ideas of Sunzi. To reiterate: "The best policy in war is to thwart the enemy's plans. The second best is to disrupt his alliances through diplomatic means. The third best is to attack his army in the field. The worst policy of all is to attack walled cities."[419]

At the very beginning of his association with Liu Bei, Zhuge Liang showed his deep knowledge of the military, social, and political situation when he outlined his plan, a complex grand strategy that relied on multiple sub-stratagems. He advised Liu Bei to take and hold Jingzhou, the central province.

> If you sit astride these two provinces, Jing and Yi, guard well their strategic points, come to terms with the Rong tribes on the west, placate the Yi and Viets to the South, form a diplomatic alliance with Sun Quan, and conduct a program of reform in your own territory—then you may be able to wait for the right moment when one of your top generals will be able to drive north to Luoyang by way of Wancheng while you yourself mount an offensive from the Riverlands through the Qinchuan region.[420]

In accordance with his goal—to remove the usurper Cao Cao from power and restore the Han Dynasty to power—Zhuge Liang made an assessment of the situation and the other key players. He noted that Cao Cao, although weaker than his rival Yuan Shao, managed to defeat him due to wise planning and favorable circumstances. He also noted that Sun Quan was in a powerful position as leader of the Southland, but added that though the Southland could become an ally, securing an ally was secondary to the immediate and ultimate objectives. Zhuge Liang then proposed Jing-zhou as an immediate objective because its central position provided a strategic location, a secure base where Liu Bei could wait and take advantage of opportunities as they arose. The Riverlands was one of those opportunities, as its leader was weak. Once it was taken, Liu Bei could set up a triangular balance of power between the Riverlands, Sun Quan in the south, and Cao Cao in the north. Then the north could become the primary objective.

In general, Zhuge Liang attempted to turn the enemy's efforts against themselves, and he used deception and persuasion rather than force to defeat the enemy. "He capitalizes upon most people's tendency to misinterpret information according to their own preconceptions and desires, a trait from which he himself is altogether free. His language is often deceptive in that he anticipates how it will be interpreted and incorporates the results into his own planning."[421] Zhuge Liang used this kind of psychological cunning to stir Zhou Yu, the Southland commander, to join Liu Bei in fighting Cao Cao. Knowing that Zhou Yu could not be approached directly, he first agreed with Zhou Yu that making peace with Cao Cao was a good idea, as Cao Cao's army was vast and powerful. He then suggested that the two beautiful daughters of the Southland patriarch be given to Cao Cao as a kind of tribute, and proceeded to recite a poem about Cao Cao's desires in this direction. In fact, the poem was about something else, but appeared to allude to the two women. This indirect approach drove Zhou Yu into a rage against Cao Cao and he vowed to fight.

In other situations Zhuge Liang used false messages and signals, disguised his troops to join with the enemy's, and let the enemy think that they had outfoxed him. His observant knowledge of terrain and of wind and weather patterns was invaluable in outguessing the enemy. When Cao Cao's much larger army was advancing to attack Liu Bei's forces at Xinye, Zhuge Liang had the population retreat toward Fan for safety. He then gave instructions to the various commanders of Liu Bei's army:

1. He had Lord Guan take a thousand men with sandbags to dam the upper end of the river that Cao Cao's army had to cross, instructing them to break the dam the moment they heard men and horses crossing the river.

2. He told Zhang Fei to hide a thousand men at the lowest point of the river crossing, so that when Cao Cao's men attempted to escape drowning from the sudden breaking of the dam, Zhang's men could attack from an advantage.

3. He ordered Zhao Zilong to divide his three thousand troops into four contingents. Zhao was to station himself outside the east gate of Xinye with one group, while the other three groups covered the remaining gates. Before leaving the city, Zhao's men were to cover the rooftops of the houses with saltpeter and sulfur. By observing the weather, Zhuge Liang knew that a heavy wind would blow from the west at about the time that Cao Cao reached the city. When Cao Cao's men entered the houses to rest, the three groups would shoot fire arrows to start a fire. The enemy would be forced by the fire and wind to run toward the east gate, where Zhao's group would ambush them as they exited.

4. Two other commanders were instructed to station men on a hill thirty *li* (about fifteen kilometers) distant from the city, with a thousand troops under a blue flag and a thousand under a red flag. Cao Cao's troops would encounter them first. At that time they were to run away, one group to the east and one to the west. This would confuse the enemy commanders, making them think the troops were merely decoys. The red and blue groups would then set an ambush and attack as soon as they saw flames over the city.

5. All commanders would then retreat to Fan.

The plan succeeded, and the retreat to Fan was successfully carried out under cover of these attacks, while large numbers of Cao Cao's troops were killed.[422]

Zhuge Liang is perhaps most famous for his *empty city ploy*, making his much more numerous enemy think that he had hidden forces by leaving the city undefended and playing his zither from the battlements. In yet another aforementioned example, he *borrowed arrows from the enemy*. With his army short of arrows, Zhuge Liang employed boats with straw dummies dressed like soldiers to pass down the river in front of Cao Cao's army. In the fog, with drums beating, it seemed as though Zhuge Liang's men were attacking. Cao Cao's archers feathered the straw dummies with thousands of shafts, thereby supplying Zhuge Liang's men with arrows.

An example of Zhuge Liang's prowess in defeating the enemy's plans without a battle and calmly handling a crisis is the ease with which he juggled multiple stratagems to hold off five enemy armies advancing against him simultaneously. First, against the Qiang army who was about to attack Xiping Pass, he sent a great general, who the Qiang regarded as almost unbeatable, to guard the pass. This prevented them from attacking. Second, against the Man army, which threatened the southern districts, he sent another commander, who moved his troops about as decoys. Zhuge Liang, understanding the mind of the commander of the Man army, knew the decoys would make him nervous and he would not attack. The third army's advance was stopped because Zhuge Liang forged a note in the handwriting of Li Dan, a potential ally of that army. The note indicated that he was ill and could not assist in the attack. This weakened the morale of the third army and they did not attack. Fourth, there was an attack on Yangping Pass, a formidable obstacle to assault. Zhuge Liang sent an able commander to defend the pass, instructing him to stay on the defensive and not be drawn out of his impregnable position. This stopped the fourth army. Lastly, the Southland army was advancing. Zhuge Liang calculated correctly that their attack was dependent on the attack of the other four. If those attacks made no progress, the Southland forces would be reluctant to attack. As a backup, he sent an able negotiator to repair the alliance he'd once had with the Southland and convince them that their true interests lay in not joining the others in their attacks.[423]

Zhuge Liang has been compared to Odysseus in the *Iliad*. Both employed guile, force, and persuasion in warfare and statecraft. They both understood strategy and the use of battle formations. Like Zhuge Liang, Odysseus was known for his skill in speaking and persuasion as well as his perceptive powers. Although both were physically brave, they were presented in contrast to the less clever yet fierce warriors that accompanied them—Ajax and Achilles in the *Iliad*, and Guan Yu, Zhang Fei, and Zhao Zilong in *Romance of the Three Kingdoms*. Although bravery has its place, it is Odysseus's strategy of the Trojan Horse that ultimately brought about the sack of Troy—and Zhuge Liang's many stratagems, which almost put Liu Bei in power.

Both men acted as strategy counselors to their leaders. One of the key roles of a strategy counselor in meetings is to be highly observant. He listens and watches body language and behavior, looking for nuances that will reveal weaknesses, true intentions, motivations, and ambitions.[424] Odysseus and Zhuge Liang used this kind of intuition and implicit knowledge as much as they did logic to understand the situation and form their strategies. The Greeks referred to this kind of knowing intelligence as *metis*—"an independent mode of intelligence with complex, but coherent mental attitudes and characteristic intellectual behavior applied to ambiguous situations that are not amenable to rigorous logic or calculation."[425]

Much of Zhuge Liang's success and fame as a military leader had less to do with his skill in warfare than his skill in managing people and events in times of crisis, and his ability to combine diverse types of knowledge to create flexible plans that were adaptable to changing circumstances. He understood the problems with organizations, both civil and military; he understood the nature of leadership; and, most important of all, he understood people. In fact, it was largely his knowledge of people and their motivations and tendencies that made him stand out among the many able commanders in the Three Kingdoms period. In *The Art of War*, Zhuge Liang asserts that while it is hard to see into people's inner nature, there are ways:

> Good and bad are different in everyone. Their outward appearance and internal nature are not the same. Some people are outwardly gentle and kindhearted, but are crafty and treacherous. Some are respectful and modest on the outside, but harbor deceit. Some are brave and courageous on the outside, but at heart are cowardly. Some seem devoted on the outside, but inwardly are disloyal. Even so there are seven ways of assessing people:

1. Sow dissension as a means of observing their ambitions and ideals.
2. Use strong words to intentionally enrage them and observe how their manner changes.
3. Ask their opinion about the specifics of a plan to observe their courage and resourcefulness.

4. Inform them of misfortunes, disasters, and difficulties to observe their courage.

5. Get them drunk so as to observe their true nature and self-restraint.

6. Seduce them with profit and reward to see if they are honest and incorruptible.

7. Give them an important matter to handle to see if they can honor their word.[426]

Zhuge Liang with his Feather Fan, drawing by Virgil Bisio
copied from a portrait by Kuniyoshi Ichiyasai

Leadership and Opportunity

Times of change, crisis, and uncertainty require effective leadership. For Zhuge Liang, opportunity lay in these unexpected and unforeseen moments, but as he pointed out, only the most clear-sighted and discerning can take advantage of it.[427] John Boyd reflects that the very nature of leading through command and control implies that the leader orders and compels, retrains and controls. The problem with this type of leadership is that it does not allow the commander and his troops to effectively adjust to the unforeseen or uncertain. Boyd feels that leadership should have a kind of monitoring ability, a way of sorting and reflecting that produces clear perception and insight. This other mode of leadership, which he terms "appreciation and leadership," cultivates an assessment, discernment, and appreciation of what is being done that does not interfere with what is being done or shaped, but discerns its nature. What is being done is then shaped by the leadership, which is in turn informed by appreciation.[428] Writings attributed to Zhuge Liang discuss leadership in detail. Zhuge Liang makes reference to a concept he calls "thought and consideration," an idea not unlike Boyd's concept of appreciation:

A policy of thought and consideration means giving thought to what is near at hand and consideration to what is remote. Thinking means correct strategy, consideration means thinking of plans for eventualities. Major affairs arise in difficulty, minor affairs arise in ease. Therefore if you want to think of the advantages in a situation, it is imperative to consider the harm; if you want to think about success, it is imperative to consider failure. Danger arises in safety, destruction arises in survival. Harm arises in advantage, chaos arises in order. Enlightened people know the obvious when they see the subtle, know the end when they see the beginning.[429] In difficult situations, Zhuge Liang outlined fifteen points to consider:

1. **Consideration:** One's planning must be careful and meticulous. Seek out intelligence about the enemy's dispositions.
2. **Investigation:** Rigorously check and correlate all information about the enemy in order to accurately assess their situation.
3. **Courage:** Though the enemy's dispositions are large and powerful, do not yield.

4. **Honesty:** Do not be guided by profit but by righteousness (honor).

5. **Fairness:** Reward and punishment should be fair and impartial.

6. **Tolerance:** Be capable of enduring humiliation and hardship in order to complete the mission.

7. **Magnanimity:** Treat people with leniency.

8. **Faithfulness:** Be faithful and trustworthy and keep promises.

9. **Respect:** Talented and virtuous people should be treated with due respect.

10. **Clarity:** Clearly distinguish right and wrong. Do not lend an ear to slander.

11. **Caution:** It is important to be cautious and circumspect and not to violate rules and laws.

12. **Benevolence:** Have love for one's fellow man and have concern and care for one's subordinates.

13. **Loyalty:** Be loyal to one's country. Do not hesitate to do what is necessary (go through fire and water) for the country's interests.

14. **Propriety:** Have a sense of propriety. Be content with one's place and duties. Handle matters to the extent of one's capabilities.

15. **Be Strategic:** Be astute and resourceful. Know oneself and know the enemy.[430]

Zhuge Liang's skill in managing people and capitalizing on the change inherent in times of crisis and uncertainty was not only evident on the battlefield, but also in his role as civil administrator. His views on leadership and management are unique in their precision and scope, as relevant today as they were thousands of years ago. In Asia, principles of strategy are applied to business. The Chinese saying *Shang chang ru zhan chang* ("The marketplace is a battlefield") illustrates the importance of strategy in business enterprises and project management.[431] Zhuge Liang is held in high esteem for his abilities as a statesman by CEOs in China and Japan, who regularly consult or comment on his strategies in relation to the modern business world. In looking at selected sections from Zhuge Liang's *The Art of War* (below), Zhuge Liang's vast experience as a leader is apparent as he delineates the qualities necessary for effective leadership, the nature of opportunity, and the importance of avoiding pitfalls in organization and leadership.

There Are Nine Types of Talented Generals:

1. The general who teaches his troops through his own ethical conduct and morality, who standardizes rules and regulations and shows concern for his troops, sharing in their joys and sorrows, is a benevolent general.
2. The general works wholeheartedly, handling not only present events, but also having foresight for the future; he who is not seduced by profit and is dedicated to honor, rather than suffering humiliation or disgrace, is a righteous general.
3. Although in a high position, this general is not arrogant or inflated with his success. He does not hold himself aloof, and is respectful and polite to those of lower rank, demonstrating good and honest virtue. Upright and outspoken, but also magnanimous, this is a courteous general.
4. Through his unfathomable strategies and constant changes he is able to turn misfortune into fortune and in adverse circumstances, to turn disaster into blessing. This is a wise general.
5. The general who keeps his promises and rewards, who performs meritorious service without delay, whose penalties and rewards are strict, but clear, and without regard to class or rank; this is an honest general.
6. The general who rides skillfully and swiftly charges through the enemy, equally adept with sword or halberd; this is an attacking general.
7. One who can scale the heights, walk into danger, and shoot arrows at full gallop, leading his men in the assault or in retreat; this is a cavalry general.
8. Commanding multiple army forces with his invincible power, careful even in small battles, and brave even against formidable foes; this is a valiant general.
9. One who modestly consults with virtuous and talented people, is willing to openly take advice and suggestions from others, is broad-minded, honest, and fair, but also brave, resolute, and strategically resourceful; this is a great general.

Generals Are Different in Their Temperament and Abilities

- The general who is admired by all for his ability to see through the tricks and ruses of others, and can foresee hidden risks, this is a general of ten soldiers.

- If he works hard day and night, is careful and deliberate with his speech, and observes the situation carefully, he is a general of one hundred soldiers.
- If he is dedicated and honest, circumspect and farsighted, and also brave and skillful in battle, then he is a general of one thousand soldiers.
- If he is powerful and awe-inspiring, yet has warmth and sentiment, and can recognize the diligence and efforts of others, if he has concern for the hunger and suffering of others, then he is a general of ten thousand soldiers.
- If he openly recommends talented people, and in his own conduct is honest, generous, and reliable; if he can deal with chaotic situations skillfully, then he is a general of one hundred thousand soldiers.
- If his humanity extends to all who are under his command and if he acts in good faith with neighboring countries; if he understands astronomy and geography, as well as human affairs, and regards the whole world as though they are his own family; then he is the general of the whole world.

Undesired Characteristics of Generals

1. Having insatiable greed.
2. Being jealous of virtuous and talented people.
3. Lending a ready ear to slander; listening to the deceitful talk and the flattery of subordinates.
4. Being capable of analyzing the enemy's dispositions, but being unable to assess one's own.
5. Indecision and lacking in determination.
6. Indulgence in drink and womanizing (possessing vices).
7. Being deceitful and timid.
8. Being treacherous and discourteous.

Opportunity

There are three ways to take advantage of opportunity:

1. Occurrence
2. Situation
3. Favorable Advantage

When an opportunity occurs and one does not take advantage of it, then one is not considered wise. When the situation changes, one is not considered astute if there is no strategy to deal with the changing situation. When one has a favorable advantage and one does not react to take advantage of it, then one is not considered brave. The wise general seizes the opportunity to achieve victory.

Nine Pitfalls in the Organization and Leadership of Troops

1. Failure to seek out detailed and accurate information and to disseminate the information properly.
2. Inability to carefully follow orders, thereby adversely affecting military actions and losing the opportunity.
3. Inability to follow proper order of deployment and move as coordinated whole.
4. Disregard for subordinates. Concentrating only on profit and gain.
5. Using one's position to profit at the expense of one's subordinates.
6. Listening to and believing in slander and rumors or trusting the predictions of fortune tellers. This has a negative effect on morale.
7. Allowing subordinates to make trouble for no reason undermines authority.
8. Generals not following the orders and making important decisions on their own.
9. Corruption. Disregard for the law and plundering the property of the country.

These are the nine pitfalls in the organization and leadership of troops. If any one of them exists disaster will follow.

Trusted Aides

Generals should have their own trusted aides and agents. Those who do not have their own trusted aides and agents are like men walking in the dark, not knowing where to put their hands and feet. A general without trusted aides is like a blind man living silently in the dark, unable to move or turn around. Those who have no trusted aides are analogous to famished men eating poisonous food; invariably they will die. Thus, the smart general chooses those who are knowledgeable and wise to be his trusted aides, those who are cautious and meticulous to be his eyes and ears (spies and agents), and those who are bold and intrepid to be his loyal supporters.

National Defense

A state's most important priority is national defense and the primary goal is to promote preparedness among the people. A small discrepancy in national defense leads to a great error—the state destroyed and its armies annihilated. This is irreversible and indeed a terrible situation! Therefore, when a nation faces disaster, the whole state must unite as one, forgoing sleeping and eating, and together formulate a strategy, select those with ability to command the army, and meet the enemy. If one is not vigilant in peacetime, he will not be alerted until invaders are at the doorstep. This is like swallows building a nest on curtains, or fish swimming in a cooking pot; demise is not far off.

The classics say "if accurate plans without error cannot be made, the army cannot be sent out." They also say: "be vigilant in peacetime, make appropriate arrangements to guard at all times against possible misfortune and calamity." From ancient times this was deemed good governance. It is also said that "even hornets and scorpions have poisonous stings to defend themselves, why not a large nation?" If a state recklessly disregards preparation for national defense, even if it has numerical strength, it cannot be relied upon. Preparedness averts peril. Generals and their troops must prepare before setting out for war.

Importance of Training

If the troops are not properly trained, one hundred soldiers would be unable to resist one enemy. If the troops are trained properly, one soldier is able to hold off a hundred enemies. Therefore, Confucius said "to send people to the war without training them is the same as killing them. When commoners are trained by the virtuous and talented men, they can be skillful in warfare. Therefore, if it is necessary for commoners to join in military actions, they must be given proper training. Teach them loyalty and integrity and inform them of the systems of rewards and punishments so that they know how to behave. Train them to stand up, sit down, march forward and back, attack and retreat, assemble and dismiss, so that they act as one. One can teach ten, ten can teach one hundred, one hundred can teach one thousand, one thousand can teach ten thousand. After skills have been imparted and are reinforced by military tactics they can be sent to fight the enemy."[432]

The Thirty-Six Stratagems

Therefore all things and situations with form (xing) can be named and recognized. All that is named and recognizable can be prevailed over. Thus the sages know how to use the characteristics of things to overpower them, and there are inexhaustible ways of overpowering things and controlling situations. War is a contest between dispositions seeking to prevail over one another. All distinguishable dispositions can be prevailed over. The question is whether you always know the right method to overpower a particular disposition. The changes in the mutual checks among things in the world are as everlasting as heaven and earth and truly inexhaustible

—Qi and Zheng.[433]

The Thirty-Six Stratagems have variously been attributed to Sunzi from the Spring and Autumn Period of China, or Zhuge Liang of the Three Kingdoms period. Another view is that the Thirty-Six Stratagems may have originated in both written and oral history, with many different versions compiled by different authors throughout Chinese history.

1. Deceive the Heavens to Cross the Ocean (Yang Contains Yin)
2. Besiege Wei to Rescue Zhao
3. Kill with a Borrowed Knife
4. Wait Leisurely for an Exhausted Enemy
5. Loot a Burning House
6. Make Noise in the East and Attack the West
7. Create Something from Nothing
8. Advance Secretly by Way of Chencang
9. Watch a Fire from Across the River
10. Hide a Dagger behind a Smile
11. Sacrifice the Plum Tree to Preserve the Peach Tree
12. Lead Away a Goat in Passing

13. Beat the Grass to Startle the Snake

14. Find Reincarnation in Another's Corpse

15. Lure the Tiger Out of the Mountain

16. Leave at Large the Better to Capture

17. Cast Out a Brick to Attract Jade

18. To Catch Bandits, First Capture Their Leader

19. Remove the Firewood from Under the Cauldron

20. Muddle the Water to Seize the Fish

21. The Golden Cicada Sloughs off Its Skin

22. Shut the Door to Catch the Thief

23. Befriend Distant States While Attacking Nearby States

24. Attack Hu by a Borrowed Path

25. Replace the Beams with Rotten Timbers

26. Point at the Mulberry Tree but Curse the Locust Tree

27. Feign Madness but Keep Your Balance

28. Lure Your Enemy onto the Roof and Remove the Ladder

29. Deck the Tree with False Blossoms

30. Reverse Positions of the Host and Guest

31. The Beautiful Woman Stratagem

32. The Empty City Strategy

33. Turn the Enemy's Agents against Him

34. The Self-Injury Strategy

35. Linked Stratagems

36. If All Else Fails, Retreat

1. Deceive the Heavens to Cross the Ocean (Yang Contains Yin)

This stratagem refers to engaging in superficial maneuvers that conceal an underlying purpose. By masking your real goals, even "Heaven" is deceived. By making one's actions seem normal or everyday, it is possible to hide one's true intentions and actions. Yang is the obvious movement, yin is the hidden objective or unexpected movement that surprises the opponent. This also refers to combining the use of zheng (orthodox) and qi (unorthodox) strategies.

In Ba Gua Zhang: The "yang hand" makes the direct, obvious, or observed part of an action while the "yin hand" simultaneously performs the subtle, unobserved, hidden aspect.

This strategy references a famous story about the Tang Emperor, afraid to cross the sea to Korea with his army. One of his generals, afraid that the Emperor might change his mind, told the Emperor that a wealthy farmer wanted to speak with him. The Emperor agreed, because he was told that the farmer was willing to supply his troops with food. The Emperor enjoyed dinner at the farmer's house on the waterfront, not realizing that he was already on a ship whose interior had been made to look like a house. By the time he realized he had been fooled, the ship was well out to sea. At that point he decided to continue onward and cross the ocean.

Deceive the Heavens to Cross the Ocean is associated with Hexagram 59 (Huan, Dispersing/Dissolution), Wind/Wood over Water. Wind, with its persistent penetration, overcomes the obstacle presented by Water. Wind can also be interpreted as guiding expectations or controlling the flow of information to conceal one's real intent. Wood can represent the boat that carries people across the Water, as in the story above. Within Water there is a single yang line, representing hidden strength, just as within Wind and Wood there is softness and pliability coupled with yang strength and movement.

2. Besiege Wei to Rescue Zhao

Besiege the base of those who are attacking or besieging another. To aid a neighbor (Zhao) who is under attack by the Wei, rather than attacking Wei's strong force directly, attack Wei's territory and disrupt supply and communication, forcing them to abandon the siege.

The name of this stratagem comes from the Warring States period. The state of Wei attacked Zhao and laid siege to its capital. Zhao asked the state of Qi for help. The general of the Qi army wanted to attack Wei directly, but his adviser, Sun Bin, suggested he attack their weak point as opposed to their main army, which included crack troops. He advised attacking the

Wei capital at Daliang, so that their communication would be disrupted. The Wei army abandoned their siege and turned to fight the Qi troops. They were defeated at the Battle of Guiling.[434]

In Ba Gua Zhang:

The true aim of pointing at the mountain for chipping the millstone is towards the rock, not the mountain, because the rocks are the material for the millstone. Like the tactics of relieving the Zhao state by besieging Wei, the method of making a feint to the east while attacking the west is applied. When this method is applied it is necessary to be calm in the mind and take the tactics of conquering the movement with stillness.

—Li Zi Ming[435]

Besiege Wei to Rescue Zhao can be related to Hexagram 53 (Jian, Gradual Advance). Wind or Wood over Mountain. Rather than recklessly moving forward, one uses Mountain's stillness combined with the penetration of Wind to pick the correct time and place to act. It can also mean moving gradually, accumulating slowly, like a plant growing on the Mountain.

3. Kill with a Borrowed Knife

Attack the enemy through another, rather than using one's own strength. This can be achieved by inducing an ally to attack while you preserve your own strength, by tricking the enemy into an internecine battle through which they damage themselves, or by "borrowing" their supplies and weapons. Other ways to apply this stratagem are to sow discord in the enemy's ranks through bribes, in order to discredit their own officials and create friction among their allies.

Kill with a Borrowed Knife is related to Hexagram 41 (Sun, Decrease/Reduction). The implication here is that the third (originally strong) line has moved upward to the top. What is below has moved upward. The foundation is weakened. One benefits from the decrease suffered by one's opponent.

> *A way of arousing discord and suspicion among the enemy is to refrain from burning or plundering the estates of certain prominent men on their side and of them alone.*
>
> —*Maurice's Strategikon*[436]

The Emperor Tai Zu, who founded the Song Dynasty, wanted to take over the Southern Tang from Li Yu, a complacent ruler. Li Yu's general Liu Ren Zhao was a competent commander and both his aspirations and ability worried Emperor Tai Zu. He had one of his men steal a portrait of Liu Ren Zhao, which he then hung in his court. When an emissary of the Southern Tang visited the court he saw General Liu's portrait and was told that the emperor and General Liu were quite close, and that Liu had sent the portrait to the emperor. Later, he was shown a mansion that he was told had been given to General Liu for his services to the emperor. When the emissary returned to Li Yu's court, he reported what he had seen and Li Yu had General Liu poisoned.[437]

4. Wait Leisurely for an Exhausted Enemy

Make the enemy waste his strength through futile assaults or maneuvers while your troops gather their strength. Avoid battle until it is at the time and place of your choosing. Observe the morale and spirit of the enemy and wait until it is lax or wanes, and then attack. This strategy is also called "Substitute Leisure for Labor."

Wait Leisurely for an Exhausted Enemy is also related to Hexagram 41 (Sun: Decrease/Reduction). The third (originally strong) line has moved upward to the top. What is below has moved upward, weakening what is below. Inducing the opponent to act too much weakens their inner strength, so they can be defeated when they are exhausted.

Observe first in encountering a group of enemies,
It is natural to retreat before advancing.
In retreating, inspect the situation and understand the changes,
To wait leisurely for an exhausted enemy, to lead them effortlessly.
   —*Method 2 of the 48 Methods of Ba Gua Zhang*[438]

At the beginning of WWI in 1914, German colonial authorities in East Africa commanded a small defense force of several hundred European troops and two to three thousand *Askaris,* highly trained soldiers recruited from native tribes and commanded by European officers. They were surrounded by enemy troops: British forces in Kenya, Uganda, and Rhodesia, Belgian troops in the Belgian Congo, and Portuguese troops in Mozambique. Although events in Africa had little effect on the larger war in Europe, the German forces led by Colonel Paul Emil von Lettow-Vorbeck seized the initiative by attacking the British rail lines in Kenya, and then successfully defended the port of Tanga, inflicting heavy losses on the British. Afterward, British caution allowed Vorbeck to escape encirclement and recruit more troops, in order to conduct a ruthless guerrilla war that would tie down allied troops and supplies so that they could not be committed elsewhere.

In 1915, under political pressure to subdue German forces in East Africa, British and other allied forces under the command of General Jan Smuts mounted a large-scale offensive with over seventy thousand men against Vorbeck's fifteen thousand. Smuts attempted to encircle the German forces by attacking on either side of Mount Kilimanjaro, but Vorbeck escaped.[439] As the campaign continued, the Germans and their Askari warriors, masters of bush warfare, drew their pursuers across rugged and thinly populated territory during heavy rains.[440] Using the terrain and the climate they retreated, living off the land, and raiding and stealing supplies from the enemy, whose supply lines stretched back hundreds of miles, requiring thousands of porters and troops to maintain them. By October 1916, the British Allied South African Infantry had lost ninety percent of its effectiveness due to disease, exhaustion, tsetse, mud, rain, supply shortages, and starvation.[441] In 1917 Vorbeck retreated again, invading Mozambique. This enabled him to obtain medical supplies, food, and large amounts of ammunition from the Portuguese, which lasted his troops until the armistice in 1918.

5. Loot a Burning House

Exploit weakness, confusion, and chaos. When a house is burning, a thief can take advantage of the chaos and commotion and loot the house. Similarly, when a country is in crisis, beset by famine or disease, or disrupted by internal conflicts, it is distracted and vulnerable to attack.

Loot a Burning House is related to Hexagram 43 (Kuai, Resolution). The top line is about to be pushed out. While this internal conflict exists, one can take advantage of the situation and seize the opportunity to attack or take action with speed and determination.

In the eighth century the Tang Empire had secured its frontiers and was prosperous and powerful. However, Tang forces penetrated into parts of what is now Northern Pakistan, bringing them into conflict with Muslim Arabs who defeated the Western Tang Army in 1751, thereby breaking China's power in the West. Meanwhile, in the Northeast, An Lushan rebelled with a large army. He first captured Luoyang and then the Emperor was forced to flee from the capital at Chang'an. Much of Northern China was devastated in suppressing this rebellion. Turkish Uighurs were brought in to suppress the rebellion, but they had to be bought off to keep them from plundering Luoyang. Although peace was declared, the frontiers were left defenseless as troops were called in to protect the capital. The Tibetans took advantage of this situation and raided many Chinese-controlled areas, cutting off metropolitan China from Central Asia.[442]

6. Make Noise in the East and Attack the West

Make Noise in the East and Attack the West refers to inducing the enemy to focus his forces in one location in order to attack another, more weakly defended area. "Noise" refers to false moves, so the enemy does not know where to guard; their weak point can then be found and exploited. This stratagem has multiple levels. The enemy may also attempt to make noise in the east to attack the west, so one must not be misled by false gestures; or one can pretend to be misled, thereby turning the enemy's strategy against him. Additionally the "false" movement, if ignored, can become the true attack.

> *The enemy must not know where we intend to give battle, for if he doesn't know where we intend to give battle, he must prepare in a great many places and, when he does that, those we have to fight in any one place will be few in number.*
> —Sunzi[443]

Napoleon invaded Egypt in 1798. To carry out his plan, he needed to evade the British fleet. Napoleon concealed his plans so well that fifty-four thousand men set out with no knowledge of their destination.[444] He led the British and even his own fleet commanders to believe that he was preparing to fight his way out of the straits of Gibraltar in order to attack England. Nelson's fleet took up the wrong position in the west, while Napoleon's troops were quickly transported east to Egypt, where he defeated Egyptian forces in the Battle of the Pyramids.

In Ba Gua Zhang:

Before attacking the west, first feint to the east,
It is necessary to know how to strike the lower, while pointing
*   to the upper.*
> —*From Song 15 of the 36 Songs of Ba Gua Zhang*[445]

Generally, open first before closing.
Without doubt, when you see him open, you must prevent closing.
Faking defeat, and pretending failure, he will return like whirling dust,
Intention is contained in pointing to the east and striking west.
> —*Method 29 of the 48 Methods* of Ba Gua Zhang[446]

After evading east, west comes again,
Swing the body to make changes and avoid by stepping aside.
Repeat continuously left and right,
Pushing forward and pulling backward lies in the arrangement
*   of the waist.*
> —Method 44 of the 48 Methods of Ba Gua Zhang[447]

Make Noise in the East and Attack the West is associated with Hexagram 44 (Gou, Encountering / Coming to Meet). Wind under Heaven represents the Wind blowing across the Earth, penetrating everywhere so that the condition of things everywhere are made known to the leader. The soft first line represents Wind's pliability and softness, finding weaknesses and chinks in the enemy's armor, as well as ascertaining where he is strong and flexible. This line can also represent control of the enemy's expectations. Once the enemy's dispositions and intentions are known, Heaven's power can be applied precisely.

7. Create Something from Nothing

Create the illusion of something's existence when it does not exist—or the opposite, make something appear to not exist when in fact it does. This can be as simple as the previous strategy, making false moves that the enemy will mistake for real ones, or it can imply creating the appearance of something substantial out of something insubstantial, like lighting campfires at night or making large clouds of dust in the distance to create the illusion of vast forces.

The story most often mentioned in relation to this stratagem is Zhang Xun's defense of Yaongqiu in the Tang Dynasty. Zhang's men, under heavy missile attack and having exhausted their own arrows, fabricated more than a thousand straw men, clothed them as soldiers, and lowered them down the city wall at night. The enemy shot thousands of arrows into these mannequins, allowing Zhang to replenish his supply of arrows. Then, on another night, he lowered picked men down the wall. Thinking he was attempting the same trick again, the enemy did not react. Zhang's "dare-to-die" shock troops attacked the unprepared enemy camp, burning their tents and destroying their supplies.

Kun (2), Fu (24)

Create Something from Nothing is associated with two Hexagrams: Hexagram 2 (Kun, Receptive/Responding) and Hexagram 24 (Fu, Return). Kun is Earth over Earth; it represents the tenth lunar month, when Yin Qi peaks, reaching its full expression in frost, snow, and ice. After the winter solstice, yang begins to grow, represented by Hexagram 24; Earth over Thunder, movement beginning again. From the stillness of winter, movement begins, unseen but already stirring. Similarly, from apparent emptiness, hidden movement and power can be generated.

8. Advance Secretly by Way of Chencang

Use a decoy or bait to make the enemy think you are moving in one direction while you come from another. In some ways this is similar to making noise in the east to attack the west.

"Advance Secretly by Way of Chencang" refers to a strategy used by Liu Bang, the founder of the Han dynasty, in his campaign against Xiang Yu. Liu Bang sent troops to repair roads he had destroyed earlier. These roads were the direct, expected route of advance. While Xiang Yu kept watch on these operations, the rest of Liu Bang's army proceeded to Chencang by a secret route, taking Xiang Fu by surprise.

Advance Secretly by Way of Chencang is related to Hexagram 42 (Yi, Increase). Wind above and Thunder below; Thunder and Wind strengthen and increase each other. When they support each other their energy is doubled. Thunder symbolizes firm resolution within. Wind symbolizes penetrating outward action. As the lines in the top trigram push upward, they increase the movement in the lower trigram; decrease above leads to increase below. Wood's outward penetrating movement symbolizes the bait or decoy. It has force but is soft and pliable. Meanwhile, Thunder, hidden within, moves suddenly and unexpectedly.

9. Watch a Fire From Across the River

When one observes discord or crisis ("fire") among the enemy, wait (observing "from across the river") until there is open conflict and upheaval before taking action. Delay entering the field of battle until all the other players have become exhausted fighting amongst themselves. To attack sooner might unify your opponents. Once they are weakened, one can act.

This name of this stratagem is derived from the battle of Red Cliff that takes place in the *Three Kingdoms*. Zhuge Liang and Sun Quan, leader of the southern forces of Wu, used a complex deception (see Stratagem 33) to get Cao Cao to tie the boats of his huge fleet together on one side of the river, across from Red Cliff. Cao Cao fell for the ruse, because being from the northern plains, he was not proficient at marine warfare. Zhuge Liang then used his knowledge of weather patterns to "raise" a wind that fanned a fire attack on Cao Cao's fleet, burning it, while Zhuge Liang watched from across the river.[448]

Watch a Fire from Across the River is associated with Hexagram 16 (Yu, Enthusiasm or Contentment). The upper trigram (Thunder) represents movement while the lower (Earth) is receptive and obedient. Thunder bursts forth in the spring and the Earth shakes in response. The yin lines respond to the strong line in the fourth position. Thunder occurs in spring, when the time is right. Similarly, in warfare, thunder and shock should be applied at the right time and place.

Note: This stratagem is also called "Sit on the Mountain and Watch the Tigers Fight."[449]

10. Hide a Dagger Behind a Smile

A threatened opponent will resist. Similarly, a direct attack causes a defensive reaction. Reassure the enemy by using a soft, or even friendly, approach, so that they relax. When their defenses are down, a secondary hidden attack will succeed. Conversely, peacemaking overtures made by potential opponents, or made during a conflict that is as yet unresolved, should be regarded with suspicion.

Hide a Dagger behind a Smile is associated with Hexagram 57 (Xun, Penetrating/Gentle), Wind over Wind. Getting the enemy to let his guard down so as to penetrate his defenses requires the soft compliance of Wind, which is unseen yet pushes gently to make its entrance. The soft and pliable yin first line in each trigram is backed by the hidden strength and movement represented by the yang lines.

> *If he [the enemy] has suffered no setback and yet sues for peace, that means he has something up his sleeves.*
> —Sunzi[450]

> *Thus before the action starts, appear as shy as a maiden and the enemy will relax his vigilance and leave his door open; once the fighting begins, move as swiftly as a scurrying rabbit and the enemy will find it is too late to put up a resistance.*
> —Sunzi[451]

In the Three Kingdoms period Guan Yu, one of Liu Bei's commanders, orchestrated a series of stunning victories against Cao Cao, ruler of the Wei kingdom. Lord Guan now held Xiangyang and was besieging the city of Fan, thereby threatening the Wei capital. Cao Cao's exclamation "The tiger has grown wings" expressed everyone's fears about Guan Yu's military prowess and the threat he represented. Cao Cao sent a message to Sun Quan, lord of the Southland, who had previously been an ally of Liu Bei and Lord Guan, but now felt threatened by them. He offered to divide Liu Bei's territory with Sun if the Southland troops would attack Guan Yu from the rear while Cao Cao sent troops to stop Guan Yu's advance. On the pretext that Lu Meng, the more experienced commander of the Southland forces, was sick, Sun Quan appointed a much younger, less experienced commander in his place. This new general sent gifts to Guan Yu, accompanied by a reverential letter. Guan dismissed him as being a mere boy and no longer viewed the Southland as a threat, turning his full attention to the siege and Cao Cao. In reality, Sun Quan and Lu Meng still led the Southland forces, which then proceeded to capture cities in Guan Yu's rear. This forced him to lift the siege, and left him trapped without a base of operations, caught between the Southland forces and the northern Wei army. In the end he was captured and executed by Sun Quan.[452]

11. Sacrifice the Plum Tree to Preserve the Peach Tree

Make a small sacrifice so as to gain a major advantage. Sacrifice short-term objectives in order to gain the long-term goal. Loss is inevitable, especially in crisis and conflict. One cannot succeed on all fronts. Allow the enemy to win the battle of your choosing while you win the war. This stratagem also embraces the principle of using a small unit or units to pin down the main part of the enemy's force while you concentrate your forces to attack his weak point.

In the 1960s the North Vietnamese strategy had been based upon defeating the South Vietnamese forces. When American combat troops became involved, that goal became unwinnable and Ho Chi Minh realized that they would have to develop a strategy of protracted war, losing engagements in order to win the war.[453] The Tet Offensive, in which coordinated attacks were directed against cities in South Vietnam, was a large-scale conflict that cost the North Vietnamese many lives. Although American forces regained control of the situation, it drew attention to conflict and galvanized antiwar protest, which gradually led to a weakening of the American resolve as the war dragged on. The North Vietnamese took the long-term view, looking both at the upcoming American election and *at American culture, where support for the war was wide but not deep.*[454] Ultimately, looking beyond the military conflict itself helped them win the war.

Sacrifice the Plum Tree to Preserve the Peach Tree is associated with Hexagram 39 (Jian, Obstruction/Adversity). Danger in front symbolized by Water, and obstruction, symbolized by the Mountain behind. The third line is in the place of danger—it is surrounded on all sides. The direct route will not lead to success. One must hold back and wait, even lose the battle, to prevail in the long term. The disposition of the Mountain, waiting rather than plunging ahead, combines with the disposition of Water, adaptability, allowing one to sacrifice small things in order to prevail in large things. This is the key to handling this situation.

12. Lead Away a Goat in Passing

Take advantage of the slightest flaw and do not pass up even the smallest opportunity. While carrying out your plans, be flexible enough to take advantage of any opportunity that presents itself. This requires constant vigilance and readiness. Do not focus all of your attention on a single concern, but keep yourself physically and psychologically ready to take advantage of the changing circumstances.

Lead Away a Goat in Passing is associated with Hexagram 19 (Lin, Overlooking or Approaching). The Earth overlooks the Lake from above. The two strong lines at the bottom are moving upward, unobstructed. In a time of progress, one should not wait but should respond immediately to take advantage of opportunity. The higher position responds to and oversees the lower position by yielding and allowing things to move and expand.

In Ba Gua Zhang: "Lead Away a Goat in Passing" is called "Step Back and Lead the Sheep," the name of one of the Sixty-Four Hands, the seventh form in the Palace of the Lake. It is also associated with Hexagram 19 (Lin, Overlooking). In this movement, one redirects the opponent's attacking force so that it falls into emptiness (toward the ground).

In 536 AD, after Belisarius had defeated the Vandals in Northern Africa, Roman troops of the Arian faith revolted against the Emperor Justinian. Belisarius drove the rebels out of Carthage and pursued them until they turned to meet him in battle. As the battle began, a wind sprang up and blew into the faces of the rebels, checking their missile fire. They shifted positions, moving toward the flank of Belisarius so that he would have to turn into the wind to face them. The momentary disorder in their ranks caused by this maneuver was immediately seized upon by Belisarius, who quickly ordered his troops to attack. This unexpected move turned a moment's disarray into a rout, and ultimately defeat for the rebels.[455]

13. Beat the Grass to Startle the Snake

Do something surprising to test the enemy's readiness and reaction: by "beating the grass" one provokes a response from the enemy, thereby "startling the snake." In this way, he may reveal his plans and dispositions. By agitating him, you can disrupt his plans. The opposite can also be true. One must often refrain from engagements that alert the enemy for fear of revealing one's own plans and dispositions to the enemy.

Beat the Grass to Startle the Snake is associated with Hexagram 24 (Fu, Return). After the weak lines have pushed the strong lines out of the hexagram, a new strong line appears. It is faint, not drawing attention to itself, while it waits for more strong lines before moving ahead with strength.

Note: "Move Away the Grass to Search for the Snake" is a movement in the *Ba Gua Zhuan Huan Jian* (Eight Diagram Rotating Ring Sword), in which a horizontal clearing action (beating the grass) paves the way for a direct penetrating thrust.

Soon after crossing the Alps into Italy, Hannibal encountered Roman legions for the first time. At Ticinus (Ticino), he briefly skirmished with the Roman cavalry under the command of Publius Cornelius Scipio. When the Romans retreated he did not pursue, but had his cavalry follow and flank their entrenched positions to carefully observe their discipline and military dispositions. His observations led him to understand that the Romans would not be easy to defeat in a pitched battle. Later, Hannibal's forces camped at Trebia. His Numidian cavalry foraged in the surrounding countryside, ravaging the countryside so that the Romans could not procure grain, while the Romans remained entrenched in their positions. As the elder Scipio had been injured in the earlier skirmish between the Carthaginian cavalry and the Roman horse, his more hot-headed cocounsel Sempronius commanded the combined Roman forces. He moved his forces up to the River Trebia, closer to Hannibal's camp, and set up a fortified encampment there. Sempronius sent out Roman mounted patrols, which, upon encountering a Carthaginian detachment returning from a raid, attacked and pursued them until they were reinforced by a larger unit. Sempronius then sent out more of his troops to beat off the Carthaginians. Hannibal let his troops retreat, but he had seen Sempronius's desire for battle. Sempronius's perception was that the Carthaginians were no match for his troops, and his "success" in this minor engagement made him ignore Scipio's warnings and strengthened his resolve to bring the enemy to battle.

Hannibal then sent his Numidian horsemen out to further annoy the Romans, while he laid a trap for them. The Numidians raided in the vicinity of the Roman camp, causing Sempronius to send out first his cavalry and then his entire army. The Numidians skirmished with the Roman cavalry and then, as ordered, feigned retreat and recrossed the Trebia, drawing the Romans after them, thereby leading them into Hannibal's trap. Hannibal separated the Roman wings from their center by clever use of his cavalry, and then unleashed a surprise attack of hidden cavalry that had been concealed in a narrow gully. They attacked the Roman rear, completing the victory. In this case, by waiting and not revealing his own intentions while getting Sempronius to reveal his, Hannibal employed the stratagem of beating the grass to startle the snake, in conjunction with feigned retreats and knowledge of the terrain, to defeat a larger Roman force.[456]

14. Find Reincarnation in Another's Corpse

This strategy has a number of different manifestations:

1. Often it refers to finding something that conveys legitimacy in one's right to lead so as to build popular support. This can mean resurrecting a lineage that ties one to a previous popular leader.

2. Take an institution, a technology, or a method that has been forgotten or discarded and appropriate it for your own purpose. Revive something from the past by giving it a new purpose or bring to life old ideas, customs, or traditions and reinterpret them to fit your purposes.
3. Absorb another's power to build up one's own.
4. Exploit every possible method of overcoming a difficult situation, thereby wresting victory from the jaws of defeat.

Find Reincarnation in Another's Corpse is associated with Hexagram 4 (Meng, Youthful Folly/Childlike Ignorance), symbolized by Kan (Water) under Gen (Mountain). Water under the Mountain; the image of a spring flowing out of the base of the Mountain. This is keeping still on top and danger beneath. The spring is like youth finding its way; it does not know where to go. Water needs to move on, but it must find a path. Water must fill up the hollows in the ground (gain experience) to move on. The student or youth is represented by the yin line in the fifth position; recognizing his or her inexperience, he or she should seek a teacher (find reincarnation in another's corpse).[457]

A famous example of this strategy is the resurrection of Zhuge Liang on the battlefield after his reported death. Sima Yi, leader of the Wei army, pursued the Riverland army as it retreated, believing that their retreat confirmed the reports of Zhuge Liang's death. When he was about to attack, he saw Zhuge Liang in his carriage with his banners raised, surrounded by the commanders of the Riverland army. Sima Yi panicked and retreated, thinking that he had fallen into a trap, only later finding out that Zhuge Liang was indeed dead and that what he had seen was a statue dressed in the famous strategist's clothing. The deception was planned by Zhuge Liang on his deathbed.[458]

15. Lure the Tiger Out of the Mountain

Never directly attack an opponent whose advantage is derived from their position. Instead, lure them away from their position or isolate them from their supporters, so that they are separated from their source of strength.

Lure the Tiger Out of the Mountain is associated with two hexagrams. Hexagram 39 (Jian, Obstruction) is composed of Kan (Water) over Gen (Mountain). The commentary on Jian refers to difficulty and danger ahead: darkness on top of keeping still, or a river on top of a Mountain; something difficult to cross. In military strategy it represents a heavily fortified place, like a fortress on a mountain. The yang line in the third place aspires to be in the fifth place, but that place is already filled. Therefore, the third yang line stops moving and returns to its own place, attempting to lure the enemy out of its superior position.[459]

Hexagram 40 (Jie, Relief/Deliverance) follows Hexagram 39. Thunder above represents movement; Water below is danger. In this situation, danger or tension has passed, like the quiet after the storm. The third yang line has now retreated to the second place, thereby luring the strong yang line in the fifth place ("the tiger") down out of its position of strength to the weaker fourth place.

For an example of this strategy see Stratagem 13: Beat the Grass to Startle the Snake. Hannibal's actions at Trebia employed this strategy, in conjunction with Beat the Grass to Startle the Snake. By using annoying raids, attacks, and calculated and feigned weakness, he lured the Romans ("the tiger") out of their fortified camp.

16. Leave at Large the Better to Capture

Close in on a defeated enemy and he will fight desperately. Follow him closely but do not press him too hard; leave him an escape route. As long as he believes he has a chance at freedom, he is unlikely to turn and fight.

This is reminiscent of Belisarius's speech to his troops when they urged him to attack the retreating Persians:

> The most complete and most happy victory is to baffle the force of an enemy without impairing our own, and in this favorable situation we are already placed. . . . Deprived of refuge in case of defeat, the Persians will fight with all the courage of despair, whilst we, enfeebled by a rigorous fast, wearied with rapid marches, and having by our speed outstripped several of our slower battalions, must enter the field with diminished strength and unequal chances of success.[460]

> *When a populous city is taken it is important to leave the gates open, so the inhabitants may escape and not be driven to utter desperation. The same holds true when an enemy's fortified camp is taken.*
>
> —Maurice's Strategikon[461]

Leave at Large the Better to Capture is associated with Hexagram 5 (Xu, Waiting), which is composed of Water above Heaven. Clouds gathering in the heavens mean that rain will come when it is time, but it cannot be made to come. Water above Heaven also symbolizes danger ahead. When danger is ahead, the firm, strong lines of Heaven wait until the right moment. Strength in the face of danger bides its time, takes precautions, and waits for the right opportunity.

17. Cast Out a Brick to Attract Jade

This refers to obtaining something of value by giving away something of lesser value. Tempt the opponent with profit, and if he disregards precaution to get it, he is vulnerable.

Cast Out a Brick to Attract Jade is associated with Hexagram 4 (Meng, Youthful Folly/Childlike Ignorance). The inexperienced leader in the fifth place moves up to the top position. He becomes arrogant and overreaching; he mistakes the worthless for the valuable.

There are countless examples in military history in which a retreating force abandoned goods and equipment. When the advancing enemy stopped to plunder the discarded equipment, a counterattack caught them with their guard down. In the Three Kingdoms period this was used as a deliberate strategy.

One of the problems that plagued Belisarius is that his commanders and troops would sometimes abandon their missions to search for booty, even when the enemy was nearby. When the Vandals in North Africa retreated, the Romans captured their camp, which contained the enormous wealth the Vandals had collected by plundering the domains of the Romans. Belisarius arrived just in time to organize his troops, who were wandering aimlessly, collecting more booty then they could carry, while the Vandal forces were regrouping in order to counterattack.[462]

18. To Catch Bandits, First Capture Their Leader

If the enemy is strong and persistent, then take aim at the leader. If the commander falls, the rest of the army may disperse or come over to your side. This is particularly true if they are allied to the commander only by money or threats. If, however, they are allied to the leader through loyalty, then it is important to be cautious, as they may continue to fight on after his death. "Capturing the Leader" can also mean bypassing the enemy's main force to attack their headquarters or attacking the "hub" (the key point or linchpin) of their dispositions.

In Hexagram 2, the Kun diagram that contains Earth over Earth, Earth stretches to respond to Heaven, the Creative. Kun should not combat, but should complete Heaven. If the sixth weak line of the Kun hexagram (representing a weak leader) attempts to hold the position of leadership, he will be vulnerable to capture or attack and his forces will then collapse.

One story from the An Lushan rebellion in the eight century, during the Tang dynasty, is often associated with this stratagem. Zhang Xun, in battling with the forces of Yi Ziqi, one of the rebel generals, attacked Yi's positions, driving his forces back. Zhang knew this was only a partial victory. Without eliminating Yi, victory would be incomplete and the rebellion would continue. It was impossible to identify General Yi among the mass of enemy troops, so Zhang had his troops fire arrows made of rue branches. When these harmless projectiles rained down on the enemy troops, they thought that Zhang's men had run out of arrows. The enemy soldiers crowded around one man, to show him the arrows. Zhang knew that this must be general Yi. He immediately had his men shoot real arrows at the general. Yi was wounded in the eye and subsequently surrendered his troops.

19. Remove the Firewood from Under the Cauldron

When faced with an enemy too powerful to engage directly, you must first weaken him by undermining his foundation and attacking his source of power.

Remove the Firewood from Under the Cauldron is associated with Hexagram 41 (Sun, Decrease/Reduction). Mountain above the Lake. The third line has moved upward to the top, decreasing the foundation. The balance of the hexagram is weakened and the structure is unstable.

In 1991, during the Gulf War, the United States and the coalition forces carried out an air offensive against Iraq. Leaving most of Baghdad intact, they knocked out radio and television communications and destroyed the public works of the city, leaving the Iraqi capital paralyzed and unable to know what was happening with its military forces. This incapacitated Iraq's air defenses, isolating their air bases by depriving them of early warning and central command. The Iraqi ground forces were also paralyzed, because destruction of lines of supply and communication, bridges, depots, refineries, and munitions factories left them without food supplies and ammunition. This diminished Iraqi resistance and paved the way for a swift coalition victory.[463] Edward Luttwack compares this with the Allied bombing attacks against Germany in World War II. While these large-scale attacks severely damaged cities and towns, they did little to directly incapacitate the ability of the German army to fight. In Iraq, the coalition air attack minimally destroyed the towns and cities, but completely incapacitated the Iraqi armed forces in only two weeks.[464]

20. Muddle the Water to Seize the Fish

Before engaging your opponent's forces, create confusion to weaken their perception and judgment. Do something unusual, strange, and unexpected in order to arouse the enemy's suspicion and disrupt their thinking. This distracts and confuses them, so that they cannot understand your intentions or ascertain your dispositions.

Muddle the Water to Seize the Fish is associated with Hexagram 17 (Sui, Following). Thunder (movement) below and Lake (joy) above. The hard below the soft. Thunder beneath the Lake means that Thunder follows and, by following, initiates movement. This changes the orientation of the situation. Rather than using direct force, one chooses alternate routes or paths in order to prevail. Initiating movement provokes a response, allowing one to adapt and seize an opportunity. By adapting, by following, one can succeed.

Cao Cao, the commander of the Wei army in the Three Kingdoms era, employed this strategy in his confrontation with the much larger army of Yuan Shao. Cao Cao took advantage of Yuan Shao's disagreements with his advisers. Following a battle in which his troops were forced to retreat and take refuge in Guandu, Cao Cao successfully defended the city for months. Eventually grain supplies ran out and Cao Cao was soon forced to abandon the city. Cao Cao decided to seize the supply depot of the enemy. He had his men dress in the uniforms of Yuan Shao's troops and enter the depot pretending to be reinforcements sent to guard the grain. In this way he was able to pass all the sentries and attack and burn Yuan Shao's supplies. Still dressed as Yuan Shao's troops, they met the relief troops racing toward the depot. Cao Cao's men presented themselves as the remnants of the depot forces struggling back to camp. The relief forces relaxed their guard and Cao Cao's troops attacked and destroyed them. While the enemy commanders blamed one another for defeat, Cao Cao attacked their main camp. He then continued to "muddy the waters" by spreading rumors that he intended to attack cities in the rear of Yuan Shao's army, thereby cutting off his retreat. This made the enemy divide their forces, allowing Ca Cao to defeat them piecemeal.[465]

21. The Golden Cicada Sloughs off Its Skin

The cicada sheds its skin, and from a distance the skin appears to be the cicada itself. By appearing to be in one place, the cicada can secretly move to another. By creating a facade, one can get the opponent to focus on it while the real action is taking place elsewhere. The Cicada Sloughs Off Its Skin is often cited as a stratagem to be used when the enemy is more numerous than your own troops. One is advised to set out numerous flags and pennants, double the number of cooking fires at night, and raise clouds of dust to create the appearance of a larger army, so that the enemy will refrain from attacking. Ruses of this kind are also employed to retreat without being detected by the enemy.

Pi Tsai-yu, who fought against the Jurchen invaders during the Southern Sung dynasty, used this strategy in order to extricate his outnumbered forces from besieging Jurchen troops. He kept the battle flags raised in order to create the appearance of an occupied camp, but did not want to sacrifice troops by leaving some of them behind, to maintain the illusion through the usual deceptions of keeping fires burning, making noise, and raising clouds of dust. Instead he had sheep suspended so their hooves rested on the war drums. As they struggled to escape, they beat the drums, making the enemy think the camp was still occupied.[466]

The Golden Cicada Sloughs off Its Skin is associated with Hexagram 18 (Gu, Decay). There is stagnation due to the gentle movement of the lower trigram (Wind) and the rigid inertia of the upper trigram (Mountain). The lower trigram follows the upper, which is standing still. The yielding lines in both trigrams are stuck under solid lines that restrict upward movement. One cannot move ahead, so instead one must readjust and begin anew, like a cicada shedding its skin.

In Ba Gua Zhang: "Golden Cicada Sheds Its Skin" is the name of one of the Sixty-Four Hands, the third form in the Palace of Wind. It corresponds with Hexagram 48 (Jing, Well), with Water as the outer trigram and Wind as the inner. Golden Cicada Sheds Its Skin relies on blending with the opponent's force, conforming to their body movements and "leaking" around their resistance, just as Wind and Water conform and adapt to the terrain and the situation.

22. Shut the Door to Catch the Thief

If a thief is in one's house, instead of attacking him directly one can bolt or shut the door, trapping him inside while help is sought to capture him. If your opponent is weak or momentarily divided, one should take the opportunity to surround him, preventing escape so that he can be captured or neutralized. If the opponent is allowed to escape, this sows the seeds for future conflict. It is disadvantageous to pursue him if he escapes.

In the *Three Kingdoms*, the Riverland forces decide to capture Xu Zhi, a fierce fighter and troop commander in the Wei army. The Riverland leaders allow the Wei scouts to see them moving grain behind their lines, knowing that Xu Zhi will attempt to cut off their supplies as he has in the past. Xu Zhi takes five thousand men and intercepts the troops that are moving grain, who flee. Xu divides his forces. Half, led by him, pursue, and the others take the grain back toward their own lines. While Xue Zhi is in pursuit of the fleeing Riverland troops, suddenly wagons block his path and fires break out around him, trapping his troops on a narrow path. Surrounded, they are slaughtered. Xu Zhi alone escapes, only to be captured and killed later. At the same time, the troops with the grain have been surrounded and destroyed by another Riverlands force.[467]

Shut the Door to Catch the Thief is associated with Hexagram 23 (Bo, Splitting Apart/Falling Away). The Mountain is perched on a weak foundation. This threatens collapse. Rather than taking direct action, wait and let the enemy collapse so that they are trapped. Then action can be taken, and they can be neutralized.

23. Befriend Distant States While Attacking Nearby States

It is easier for nations that border each other to become enemies, while it is easier for nations separated by distance and obstacles to become allies. This dynamic can be employed as a means of dealing with enemies one by one—befriending those that are distant while eliminating nearby rivals.

The most famous example of this strategy occurred during China's Warring States Period, when the powerful state of Qin set out to take over the other states, which would unify what was then considered China. The Qin emperor was advised by one of his strategists that rather than taking what might seem to be a reasonable course of action—attacking the more distant and weaker states first—it would be better to attack a larger, closer state while allying with the more distant state. This would serve the dual purpose of putting the weaker states off guard, so they would not think they were the next target, and at the same time, isolating the real target. Additionally, the bordering state, once conquered, could become a springboard for attacking the smaller states later.

Befriend Distant States While Attacking Nearby States is associated with Hexagram 38 (Kui, Opposition/Separation). Here, opposition refers to polarity. Water (Lake) goes downward and Fire goes upward. The hexagram's strong second line assists the distant fifth weak line in defeating the fourth line, which is isolated between the two yin lines. Water and Fire are opposites. The Hexagram also implies that opposite approaches can be adopted to serve the same purpose by complementing or even integrating with each other.

24. Attack Hu by a Borrowed Path

Borrow the resources of an ally to attack a common enemy. When a small state is threatened by an enemy state, send troops to rescue it, thereby expanding one's sphere of influence. Then use the defeated state's resources to attack your ally. This temporary alliance is the "borrowed path."

Attack Hu by a Borrowed Path is associated with Hexagram 47 (Kun, Oppression/Exhaustion). Water is below the Lake. The Lake is empty, drained away or dried up. One's energy has been exhausted or drained. Here, the communication between the second and fifth line is the alliance in which the resources of the two states are combined, preventing "exhaustion." The top yin line can mean regret of past errors. In this case, the ally regrets lending aid, as now he is under attack and his resources are inadequate.

This strategy takes its name from the state of Jin's actions during the Spring and Autumn period. The Duke of Jin was intent on expanding his power. Intending to attack the state of Hu, he wanted to prevent their ally Yu from interceding. His minister hatched the following plan. First, he sent two beautiful women as gifts to the Duke of Yu, hoping that the duke's infatuation with them would cause disharmony in the kingdom (Stratagem

31: The Beautiful Woman Stratagem). Then, he bribed tribes north of Hu to attack and raid the state, causing external strife. Finally, he presented Yu with expensive gifts, while creating strife on his own border with Hu, so that Yu would think he was having problems with Hu and would not be suspicious of the gifts. When the Duke of Yu asked what he wanted in return for the gifts, the Duke of Jin asked for passage through Yu to attack Hu from the rear. Yu agreed, thinking he could profit from this and that his help would also ensure safety, by way of ingratiating himself with the more powerful Jin. The Duke of Yu even led some his own forces to aid the Jin in attacking and pillaging the Hu cities. Later, when Hu was even more weakened by attacks from tribesman from the north, the Duke of Jin asked to borrow a path through Yu a second time. Yu again agreed and this time Jin attacked and defeated the state of Hu. Afterward, as the victorious Jin armies passed back through the state of Yu, they launched a surprise attack on Yu, defeating them in turn.[468]

This stratagem is also known as "Borrow the Road to Conquer Gao." During the Three Kingdoms period, Sun Quan of the Southland attempted to use this strategy against Liu Bei and Zhuge Liang. He offered to attack the Riverlands on Liu Bei's behalf, so that he could trick Liu Bei into giving him the city of Jingzhou. As Jingzhou is on the way to the Riverlands, Sun asked Liu Bei and Zhuge Liang to greet his troops and provide them with grain and supplies when they reached the city. Zhuge Liang, however, saw through Sun Quan's plan, explaining to Liu Bei: "He's making plans that wouldn't fool a child, using the ancient ruse of 'passing through on the pretext of conquering Guo.' Their real objective is Jingzhou, not the Riverlands. They want you to come out of the city so they can nab you, 'attacking the unprepared, doing the unanticipated.'"[469]

25. Replace the Beams with Rotten Timbers

Disrupt the enemy's formations and interfere with their methods of operations. Change the rules they are used to following, go contrary to their standard training. Make them change formations frequently, in order to create opportunities to penetrate and disrupt their dispositions. Battle formations in ancient China were viewed as having two axles, a horizontal earthly axle and a vertical heavenly axle. By manipulating these axles, formations could be made to lose their integrity so that they collapsed. Replace the Beams with Rotten Timbers could also be interpreted as taking out the enemy's key support structures, thereby disrupting the integrity and cohesion of their forces and efforts.

During the Civil War, railroads were extensively used by the North to transport men and supplies. Ultimately, railroads helped Union forces win the war, "but in 1862, the dependence of Union armies on railroads proved as much curse as blessing. 'Railroads are the weakest things in war,' declared Sherman; 'a single man with a match can destroy and cut off communications.' Although 'our armies pass across and through the land, the war closes in behind and leaves the same enemy behind.'"[470] Sherman's supply lines were frequently cut by irregular troops burning bridges and water tanks, or tearing up sections of track. That Sherman learned from these experiences is evident in his march through South Carolina in 1864. He had his troops live off the country while he destroyed the Confederacy's railroads—the enemy's line of communication and supply.

Replace the Beams with Rotten Timbers is associated with Hexagram 64 (Wei Ji, Before Completion/Not Yet Fulfilled). Fire above and Water below. Fire moves upward and Water moves downward. The yang lines are like the axles of a cart. The second line represents a wheel that can become bogged down or stuck, killing the force of momentum. This can be likened to replacing the roof beam.

26. Point at the Mulberry Tree but Curse the Locust Tree

It is sometimes easier to alter an adversary's behavior by sending a message covertly through indirect means, rather than by direct attack. One way to control another, whose position prevents direct confrontation or criticism, is to send them a message by disciplining or punishing someone else.

Duke Huan, ruler of the Qi state, invited the other eight surrounding states to a conference in order to ally and establish peace. Only half of the states attended. At the conference, Huan proposed attacking the states that did not attend. The other delegates all agreed except for the Duke of Song, who left thinking that this would cause the alliance to collapse. Instead of pursuing him, Duke Huan's advisers suggested that the duke attack one of the smaller neighboring states that had not attended the conference. The other state apologized and agreed to join the alliance when Huan forces surrounded their city. This not only led the other states that had not attended the conference to also join, but sent a message to the Duke of Song, who, now isolated, knew he had no chance against the other seven states. In the end, he also joined.

Point at the Mulberry Tree but Curse the Locust Tree is related to Hexagram 7 (Shi, The Army). Here Water beneath Earth represents groundwater stored under the earth. "The Army" refers to the people. Danger is below—masses of people are a powerful force, but just as Earth holds the Water, this powerful force must be guided by discipline and obedience (represented by Earth). The strong second line is the general or commander. The yielding lines are subordinate to the general. The general must use punishment and reward correctly so they serve as examples to control his troops.

27. Feign Madness but Keep Your Balance

Feign ignorance and make no moves. Hide one's intention behind the mask of a fool, a drunk, or a madman to create confusion about your intentions and motivations. Lure your opponent into underestimating your ability until, overconfident, he drops his guard. Then you may attack. Play the fool when not ready to act, and deceive even your own forces if necessary.

Feign Madness but Keep Your Balance is associated with Hexagram 3 (Zhun, Difficulty at the Beginning). Water over Thunder symbolizes danger or difficulty at the beginning of an enterprise. It also symbolizes inchoate chaos. The upward-moving yang line is held down by yin Water. One can take action in the midst of danger, and prevail through firmness and perseverance. Everything is in motion, but still unformed and even unclear. The yang line at the bottom cannot rush ahead into danger, but must hide its true intentions until the situation or move stabilizes before moving forward.

When Sima Yi and Cao Shuang assisted Cao Fang, the heir apparent, to ascend the throne, Cao Shuang was advised not to share the military authority with Sima Yi. He had Cao Fang appoint Sima Yi to the position of imperial guardian, so that all military authority then passed from Sima Yi to himself. He immediately appointed his brothers to command positions within the army, thereby consolidating his power. Cao Shuang then appointed other followers to other key positions and indulged in a lavish lifestyle usually reserved for the emperor. Meanwhile, Sima Yi stayed out of public office on the pretext of illness and his sons also resigned from their positions.

After ten years in power, Cao Shuang woke up feeling unsettled and sent one of his men to find out whatever he could about Sima Yi. Sima Yi knew that Cao Shuang wanted to see if he was actually sick, so he lay in bed, loosened his hair, and had himself propped up on pillows. He pretended he didn't understand Cao Shuang's envoy, and appeared befuddled and hard of hearing. He told the envoy he was dying and his sons were useless. Then he toppled over in bed, breathing laboriously. Upon receiving the report of Sima Yi's condition, Cao Shuang was now confident that there was no threat to his power. Despite warnings from one of his advisers, he felt confident enough that he accompanied the emperor to visit the Wei tombs and pay respect to his ancestors, bringing with them his brothers and many important ministers. Seizing the opportunity, Sima Yi rallied his veterans, who had campaigned with him in the past, and went directly to the imperial court, where he decreed Cao Shuang a traitor before the Queen Mother. Fearing for her son's safety, she complied with Sima Yi's plan to kill the "traitors." When word of the coup reached Cao Shuang and his followers, they were helpless, as their families were in the city in Sima Yi's clutches. In the end, Cao Shuang and his brothers were executed and Sima Yi became the Prime Minister.[471]

28. Lure Your Enemy onto the Roof and Remove the Ladder

With bait and deception, lure your enemy into treacherous terrain. Then cut off his lines of communication and avenue of escape. This can be done by letting him penetrate your battle line or letting him advance into your territory, and then surrounding him. This strategy can also be understood to be one of placing your own troops in a position of desperation, where they must prevail or perish. Burning your own boats or destroying your own supplies can put your troops in such a situation.

> *When [the commander] wants to make a determined drive, he burns his boats and smashes his cooking pots.*
> —Sunzi[472]

In the fifth century, the Persians and the "White Huns" came into conflict. As the Persians advanced, approaching the lands of the Huns, the King of the Huns took his troops to the plain across which the Persians would have to pass during their invasion. His men dug a large, deep trench, leaving only a narrow strip in the center intact, ten horses wide. Over the trench he placed reeds and earth. When the Persians entered this area, the King of the Huns had his men show themselves and then retreat, taking care to ride in the safe center as they retreated. The Persians pursued and fell into the trench, where they were destroyed.[473]

Cortés employed a version of Lure Your Enemy onto the Roof and Remove the Ladder during his conquest of Mexico. Governor Velasquez of Cuba had picked Cortés to build a colony in Mexico. However, soon afterward, Velasquez suspected Cortés would not follow his orders and would seize glory for himself. He canceled the expedition, but Cortés had already assembled men and equipment and left for Mexico. He landed on the coast of what is now the state of Tabasco. Creating a base there, he allied with local tribes while negotiating with the Aztecs. Cortés knew that there were men among his contingent who were spies for Velasquez and might create trouble among his other followers; some of them had already conspired to seize a ship and escape. He also knew that the prospect of gold, combined with self-interest, would promote further divisions among his troops. He dealt with the situation by sinking his ships. Now there could be no retreat, and his men would have to fight together to prevail.[474]

    Lure Your Enemy onto the Roof and Remove the Ladder is associated with Hexagram 21 (Shi He, Bite Through). The image is an open mouth with an obstruction between the teeth. One must bite through the obstacle for the teeth to meet. Yang lines on top and bottom are lips and the fourth line is an obstruction to be ground by the "teeth" of the other lines. Another interpretation is that the fourth yang line has moved from below to the upper trigram, where it is now isolated and in a position of weakness. Its line of retreat is empty. Like the ladder, it has been removed.

29. Deck the Tree with False Blossoms

Exploit external forces so that a weak force can gain power, whether it is real or illusory. Attaching silk flowers to a dead tree can convince people that the tree is healthy. Use the illusion of strength to distract or intimidate the enemy in order to take advantage of their weak point. If possible, use external forces, advantages in terrain, and other unconventional devices to actually augment your strength.

    The classic example of this maneuver was Tian Dan's use of "fire oxen" to overcome a large army besieging a city. The defenders, led by Tian Dan, attached sharp blades to the horns of the oxen and fire brands to their tails. Released at night, through gaps in the city walls, the crazed oxen surged through the enemy camp, followed by several thousand warriors. The psychological and physical shock of the attack routed the besiegers.

    Deck the Tree with False Blossoms is associated with Hexagram 53 (Jian, Gradual Advance). Wood on top of Mountain. On the Mountain (keeping still), a tree grows slowly. It is weak but also firmly rooted in the Mountain, unlike a fast-growing plant with shallow roots. The penetration and insight of Wind and the flexibility of Wood allow one to access the stability of the Mountain. Each line in the hexagram is also likened to a wild goose flying higher and higher until it reaches the clouds in the sixth line. Movement proceeds, gradually allowing a transcendence over ordinary affairs and activities. This is a progressive growth or augmentation of strength.

30. Reverse Positions of the Host and Guest

This is a strategy of infiltration. By leading with a deceptively weak move, one can penetrate into the adversary's organization or structure, where one is subordinate or at a disadvantage, and usurp leadership. Once accepted, one can take over from the inside. Initially, pretend to be a guest to be accepted, but then develop your strategy from inside in order to take control.

In military strategy, one is a guest when attacking into the enemy's territory, and the enemy is the host. Being the guest in this case has the advantage of initiative, but the disadvantages of transporting supplies over longer distances, dealing with a potentially hostile populace and unknown terrain. If the invading army can transform these disadvantages into advantages, it becomes the host.

Reverse Positions of the Host and Guest is associated with Hexagram 53 (Jian, Gradual Advance). The development of cooperation happens slowly, over the proper course of time. It is not hasty. There must be the adaptability and pliability of Wind with the strength and firmness of the Mountain underlying it for the guest and host to reverse their positions.

The usual story told in relationship to this stratagem takes place during the Qin dynasty. Xiang Liang of the Chu state had killed a man and, with his nephew, sought asylum in the state of Wu. He became a low-level administrator there, and over time, gained the trust of the governor of Wu. Later, when the various states rebelled against the Qin, the governor of Wu decided to join the rebellion and sought the help of Xing Liang. He asked Xiang Liang and his nephew to lead an army against the Qin. Later, when meeting privately with the governor, Xiang Liang signaled his nephew and the nephew cut off the governor's head. Xiang Liang then took the seals of office and made himself governor. Those who objected were killed. Xiang Liang raised the army and attacked the Qin, eventually freeing the Chu state.

In the early tenth century the Khitans, a proto-Mongol people from the Northern Steppes who had paid tribute to the Tang dynasty, took advantage of Chinese weakness during the disintegration of the Tang. Abuaoji united the Khitan tribes, took over sections of northern China, and formed the Liao dynasty. The Song dynasty found it easier to buy off the Khitans, rather than fight them. In 1115, the Jurchens, a pastoral hunting and herding people from eastern Manchuria, united into the Jin State and attacked the Khitans. The Song Chinese allied with the Jurchen, hoping to divide the territory of the Khitans, but the alliance quickly collapsed as the Jurchen attacked captured Kaifeng and took the emperor and his family prisoner. This led to the creation of the Southern Song dynasty, as the entire north was ruled by the Jurchen. In this case the Jurchen started out as guests, but took over and became the hosts.

Another interpretation of Reverse Positions of the Host and Guest comes from the Three Kingdoms period. Huang Zhong and Fa Zhong, military commanders under Liu Bei, in seeking to dislodge the northern Wei troops from their encampment on a mountain, decided to take advantage of the volatility and aggressiveness of Xiahou Yuan, the Wei commander. Fa Zhong suggested: "We must inspire our troops to break camp and advance, bivouacking at each stage, then draw Xiahou Yuan into battle and capture him. This is what military science calls 'reversing the roles of host and guest.'"[475] One of the Wei commanders recognized the "host and guest ruse" and warned Xiahou Yuan to refrain from taking offensive action. He was ignored and the Wei troops were defeated in the engagement, and Xiahou Yuan was captured.

31. The Beautiful Woman Stratagem

The classic employment of this strategy is to send adversaries or potential adversaries beautiful women, to cause discord within their camp. This can cause the ruler to become distracted, neglecting his duties and reducing his concentration and vigilance. It can also inspire jealousy among other leaders and create intrigue among other women, including those in positions of power. However, "beautiful woman" is also a metaphor for something the opponent desires or has a weakness for. By finding out and exploiting this desire, it is possible to weaken the enemy's power and control the situation.

The Beautiful Woman Stratagem is associated with Hexagram 53 (Jian, Gradual Advance). The third yang line of the hexagram is close to the two yin lines, one above and below. This yang line is the husband who must have proper relationships with the yin lines (women around him) in order to move ahead. If his desires and weaknesses are known it is dangerous, as he can be manipulated by the yin lines.

32. The Empty City Strategy

This strategy uses deception to overcome an inferiority in strength or numbers. Deliberately make yourself defenseless in order to confuse the opponent and make them think that your weakness is a trap, that you are confident due to hidden strength. In Chinese strategy this is also known as making the insubstantial substantial. Generally this is used against clever opponents, and only in desperate circumstances.

The Empty City Strategy is often attributed to Zhuge Liang, the master-strategist of the Three Kingdoms. Zhuge Liang and a few thousand men stayed in Yang Ping to move grain and supplies while the rest of the army went on to combine forces for other operations. While half of his men were moving supplies, a scout reported the unexpected advance of a vast enemy army commanded by Sima Yi, a very able commander who had encountered Zhuge Liang in past engagements. Zhuge Liang commanded that the battle flags be hidden and the military drums silenced. The streets were swept and sprinkled with water and the gates left open. Twenty of his men, dressed as commoners, were then sent out to sweep the roadway. They were instructed to keep their heads down and appear intent only on their task. Zhuge Liang then went onto the battlements in his crane feather cloak, and, in a relaxed mood, played the zither while burning incense. When Sima Yi saw the situation, the lack of concern of the sweepers and the carefree attitude of Zhuge

Liang, he immediately pulled his army back. When questioned about his actions by his son, he responded: "Zhuge Liang has always been a man of extreme caution, never one to tempt the fates. He opened the gates because he had set an ambush. On entering we would have been trapped. You are too young to know! Hurry the retreat!"[476]

The Empty City Strategy is associated with Hexagram 39 (Jian, Obstruction/Adversity). Water on top of Mountain signifies danger (Water) ahead, while one's retreat is blocked by an obstruction (Mountain). The key to prevailing in this situation is the Mountain, waiting in the stillness, persevering and turning attention inward. The third line cannot contend with the fifth line, which is in a strong position. Rather than confronting danger, it stops, concealing the weaker, softer lines below and within. The third line is yang, so it creates an illusion of strength and hardness on the outside.

33. Turn the Enemy's Agents against Him

Undermine the opponent by creating discord among his agents and allies—his friends, allies, advisers, family, commanders, soldiers, and the general population. By upsetting the critical relationships upon which your adversary depends, you weaken his ability to contend with you. This strategy can take many forms—enemy spies can be turned and co-opted, or by feigning ignorance they can be fed false information that calls into question the motives of the opponent's closest advisers.

Maurice's Strategikon, the handbook of Byzantine military strategy attributed to the Emperor Maurice (582–602), advises:

> Suspected defectors should be told the opposite of what we intend to do, so that we may use them to deceive the enemy.
>
> By no means should we believe reports that come from deserters or defectors alone, but their reports should be checked against statements made by prisoners taken in raids, and in this way truth may be discerned.[477]

This strategy is associated with Hexagram 8 (Bi, Unity). Here Kan (Water) is over Kun (Earth). The image is one of Water flowing over the Earth, Water supported by Earth, and Water flowing through the open yin lines of the Earth. In military strategy this represents turning the agents of the enemy against him to lead him into a trap. Another way to interpret the hexagram is that the second weak line receives a summons for service to those above, particularly the strong fifth line, representing the leader. This second line represents the reliable person in the opponent's camp, whose services have been secured.[478]

The famous battle at Red Cliff, described in the *Three Kingdoms*, in which Cao Cao's fleet is destroyed by flames, is an example of a complex inter-weaving of several stratagems, including using the enemy's own agents against him. Zhou Yu, the Chief Commander of the Southland forces, and Zhuge Liang, the master-strategist aiding Liu Bei, agreed that the only way to defeat Cao Cao was by a fire attack. Although they kept the plan a secret, Huang Gai, one of the Southland commanders, had the same idea. Zhou Yu and Huang Gai concocted a plan. Huang Gai would be publicly flogged to give him credibility with Cao Cao so that he could pretend to defect. It would be witnessed by two false defectors from Cao Cao's camp that Zhou Yu was already aware of.

The next day Huang Gai disagreed with Zhou Yu in front of all the troops. Zhou Yu, enraged, accused Huang Gai of undermining morale and ordered him executed. As Zhou suspected they would, the other command-ers interceded, asking him to forgive Huang Gai's outburst. However, he insisted on punishing him, and had him flogged instead.

Later, Kan Ze, a military counselor and close friend of Huang Gai, paid him a sympathy visit. Huang Gai enlisted his aid in carrying a letter to Cao Cao, offering Huang Gai's defection and desire to join the northern forces. Kan Ze, disguised as a fisherman, rowed close to the northern camp, where he was picked up by a river patrol. Announcing his name, he asked to see Cao Cao. He then proceeded to deliver the letter and negotiate Huang Gai's defection. Cao, having received a report from his spies, laughed and ordered Kan Ze executed, saying that he saw through the "flogging to win confidence trick." As his men dragged Kan Ze away, the prisoner also laughed. Suspicious, Cao Cao called him back. Kan Ze openly made fun of Cao, saying that he wasn't really the master strategist he thought he was and cleverly pointing out what appear to be mistakes in Cao Cao's appraisal of the situation. Impressed by his fearlessness and clever argument, Cao Cao believed Kan Ze and sent him back to the Southland base to plan the time and place for Huang Gai's defection. Meanwhile, Cao Cao also sent Jiang Gan, a defector who was an old friend of Zhou Yu's, to the Southland camp to get information.

While Kan Ze and Huang Gai met with the two false defectors who had joined the Southland army, to plan the "defection," Zhou Yu received Jiang Gan, who arrived by boat. Although secretly delighted at his arrival, Zhou Yu upbraided him for his past disloyalty and alliance with Cao Cao. He had Jiang Gan conducted to a retreat house on the hill, away from the Southland army, so that Jiang Gan could not reveal the Southland plans. Meanwhile, Zhou Yu made a secret plan with Pang Tong, an adviser to the Southland armies. Once at the retreat house, Jiang Can "accidentally" met Pang Tong, who said he had come there to get away from Zhou Yu's overbearing overconfidence and intolerance. Jiang Gan offered to introduce him to Cao Cao, who appreciated the worthy adviser's opinions. Pang Tong agreed, and they escaped and went by boat to Cao Cao. Having heard of Pang Tong's brilliance, Cao Cao eagerly invited him to comment on the dispositions of the northern troops. Pang Tong complimented Cao Cao's arrangements, but commented that many of the troops were sick. He suggested that tying all the boats together would prevent the northern troops, who were not used to the constant movement of the boats, from feeling sick. Cao Cao also liked the idea, as he thought that his army would simply be able to march across the river on the linked boats. This is exactly what Pang Tong and Zhou Yu had discussed in secret would guarantee the destruction of the entire fleet in one attack by fire. If the boats were tied together, none could escape. Once Cao Cao followed Pang Tong's advice, the fire attack was carried out.[479]

34. The Self-Injury Strategy

By injuring yourself, you take advantage of the opponent's natural sus-
picions. As people do not generally injure themselves, you appear to be
a victim. This can make the enemy relax his guard, as he may no longer
consider you a threat. It can also win the opponent's trust, particularly if it
appears that the injury was caused by a mutual adversary.

In the story of the fire attack at Red Cliff (see Strategy 33: Turn the
Enemy's Agents against Him), this ploy is referred to by Zhuge Liang and
Cao Cao, who are both aware of its use as a ploy to gain the opponent's
confidence. Zhuge Liang refers to the beating of Huang Gai as "the battered
body trick."[480]

Hexagram 35

The Self-Injury Strategy is associated with Hexagram 36 (Ming Yi, Light
Suppressed/Darkening of the Light). In Hexagram 35 (Jin, Progress or
Advance), Fire is above Earth, like the sun progressing over the Earth. In
Hexagram 36, Fire has now been covered by the Earth; the strong lines are
suppressed or injured, and the weaker yin lines are in control. To prevail,
one must keep one's light, intelligence, and intent hidden, by feigning injury
and stupidity, or by pretending to be ordinary.

Hexagram 36

35. Linked Stratagems

In difficult situations, one can employ a series of interlinked strategies.
These can act as a kind of chain reaction that progressively demoralizes and
confounds the opponent. Deceptions, ruses, maneuvers, false appearance,
and disinformation can be connected like links in a chain. The complex
stratagems woven around the battle of Red Cliff (see Strategy 33: Turn the

Enemy's Agents against Him) are an example of linked strategies. In complex plans, however, if any one strategy fails, then the chain breaks and the whole scheme can fail.

Linked Stratagems is related to Hexagram 7 (Shi, The Army). Here, Water beneath Earth represents groundwater stored under the Earth. The strong second line is the general or commander. The yielding lines are the people or the troops who are subordinate to the general. He links the other lines (and strategies) together. The general is responsible for the army, and without interference he can implement complex and many-faceted plans.

36. If All Else Fails, Retreat

To preserve the troops, evade the enemy. Escape prevents defeat. The line commentary for the fourth line in Hexagram 7 (Shi, The Army) is: "The Army retreats, no blame." If one is too weak, it is better to retreat, regroup, and wait rather than to contend. This is a strategic withdrawal, which can be used as a tactic to get the opponent to overextend himself. As long as one is not defeated, there is still a chance for victory.

> *If you are fewer than the enemy in number, retreat. If you are no match for him, try to elude him. For no matter how stubbornly a small force may fight, it must in the end succumb to greater strength and fall captive to it.*
>   —Sunzi[481]

If All Else Fails, Retreat is one of the most famous of the Thirty-Six Stratagems, immortalized in the form of a Chinese idiom: "Of the Thirty-Six Stratagems, fleeing is best."

If All Else Fails, Retreat is related to Hexagram 33 (Dun, Withdrawal), which contains Heaven over Mountain. Withdrawal here refers to making a strategic withdrawal. The yin lines represent the enemy rising up. The yang lines maintain contact while retreating so that they can counterattack. Success in this case lies in retreating at the right moment. Heaven retreats before the Mountain's immobility, but by keeping the enemy (Mountain) at a distance, he is brought to a standstill. Another way to interpret this is that the yin lines represent the withdrawal. By withdrawing twice, in stages, the enemy is lured to overextend himself. The active lines represent a counterattack. In martial arts this can mean that when the hands meet one yields, absorbing the opponent's force and drawing them off-balance while at the same time borrowing their force to amplify one's own counterattack.

Notes

Introduction

1 *The Classic of Changes: A New Translation of the I Ching,* as interpreted by Wang Bi, trans. Richard John Lynn (New York: Columbia University Press, 1994), p. 10.

2 *Fathoming the Cosmos and Ordering the World: The Yijing and Its Evolution in China,* Richard J. Smith (University of Virginia Press, 2008), pp. 95–97.

3 *The Art of War,* by Sun Tzu, trans. John Minford (New York: Penguin Books, 2009), p. xxxii.

4 *Fathoming the Cosmos and Ordering the World: The Yijing and Its Evolution in China,* Richard J. Smith, pp. 92–3.

5 *The Spring and Autumn of Chinese Martial Arts: 5000 years,* Kang Gewu (Santa Cruz, CA: Plum Publishing, 1995), p. ii.

6 Ibid., p. ii.

Chapter I

7 *Sun Zi: The Art of War and Sun Bin: The Art of War* (Beijing: Foreign Language Press, Library of Chinese Classics, 1999), p. 23.

8 Ibid., p. 43.

9 *Sun Tzu: The Art of War,* trans. Samuel B. Griffith (Oxford: Oxford University Press, 1963), p. 87.

10 Ibid, pp. 88–9.

11 "The Origins of Pa Kua Chang—Part 3," *Pa Kua Chang Journal,* High View Publications, vol. 3, no. 4, May/June 1993, pp. 25–29.

12 *The Essentials of Ba Gua Zhang,* Gao Ji Wu and Tom Bisio (New York: Trip Tych Enterprises Inc, 2007), p. 329.

13 *The Propensity of Things: Toward a History of Efficacy in China,* Francois Jullien, trans. Janet Lloyd (New York: Zone Books 1999), p. 27.

14 *Liang Zhen Pu Eight Diagram Palm,* Li Zi Ming, comp. and ed., Vincent Black (Pacific Grove, CA: High View Publications, 1993), p. 12.

15 *Sun Zi: The Art of War,* p. 51.

16 *Strategy,* B. H. Liddell Hart (London: Faber and Faber Ltd., 1967; reprinted in Signet Classics, New American Library, 1974), p. xx.

17 *A Treatise on Efficacy: Between Western and Chinese Thinking,* Francois Jullien, trans. Janet Lloyd (Honolulu: University of Hawai'i Press, 2004), p. 21.

18 "Destruction and Creation," John R. Boyd (Fort Leavenworth, KS: *U.S. Army Command and General Staff College,* September 3, 1976).

19 *The Tao of Deception: Unorthodox Warfare in Historic and Modern China,* Ralph D. Sawyer, p. 13.

20 *The Propensity of Things: Toward a History of Efficacy in China,* Francois Jullien, p. 28.

21 Ibid., p. 29.

22 *Sun Tzu: The Art of War,* trans. Samuel B. Griffith (Oxford: Oxford University Press, 1963), pp. 42–43.

23 Sun Zi: The Art of War and Sun Bin: The Art of War, pp. 31–33.

24 *The Tao of Deception: Unorthodox Warfare in Historic and Modern China,* pp. 5–6.

25 *Hannibal,* Theodore Ayrault Dodge (New York: Barnes & Noble, 2005, originally published, 1889), pp. 257–261.

26 *Liang Zhen Pu Eight Diagram Palm,* p. 18.

27 *Bagua Quan Xue,* Sun Lutang, trans. Joseph Crandall (Pinole, CA: Smiling Tiger Martial Arts, 2002), p. 18.

28 Strategy: The Logic of War and Peace (revised edition), Edward N. Luttwak (Cambridge, MA: Harvard University Press, 1987, 2001, 2003), p. 113–115.

29 Sun Zi: The Art of War and Sun Bin: The Art of War, p. 7.

30 *Cambridge Illustrated History of China,* by Patricia Buckley Ebrey (Cambridge: Cambridge University Press, 1996), pp. 86–87.

31 *The Tao of Deception: Unorthodox Warfare in Historic and Modern China,* p. 344.

32 Ibid., pp. 371–372.

33 *Sun Tzu: The Art of War,* p. 97.

34 *Essentials of Xing Yi Quan,* Wang Li with Li Gui Chong and Chen Cheng Fu, trans. Huang Guo Qi.

35 *Three Kingdoms: Vol. 3,* Luo Guanzhong, trans. Moss Roberts (Beijing: Foreign Language Press, 1995), pp. 1290–94.

36 *Three Kingdoms: Vol. 1,* pp. 379–80.

37 *The Landmark Herodotus: The Histories,* ed. Robert B. Strassler (New York: Pantheon Books, 2007), pp. 631–32. *The Battle of Salamis: The Naval Encounter That Saved Greece and Western Civilization,* Barry Strauss (New York: Simon and Schuster, 2004), pp. 113–18.

38 *Sun Zi: The Art of War and Sun Bin: The Art of War,* p. 77.

39 *The Tao of Deception: Unorthodox Warfare in Historic and Modern China,* p. 340.

40 Ibid. p. 341.

41 *Outlaws of the Marsh, Vol. 2,* Shi Nai'an and Luo Guanzhong, trans. Sidney Shapiro (Beijing: Foreign Language Press, 1993), pp. 914–919.

42 *General Yue Fei*, Qian Cai, trans. T. L. Yang (Hong Kong: Joint Publishing, 1995), pp. 659–662.

43 *Ba Gua Quan Xue*, Sun Lutang, trans. Joseph Crandell (Pinole, CA: Smiling Tiger Martial Arts, 2002), 18.

44 *The Essentials of Ba Gua Zhang*, pp. 328 and 339.

45 Ibid., pp. 328 and 336.

46 *Sun Tzu: The Art of War*, p. 106.

47 *The Essentials of Ba Gua Zhang*, p. 328 and p. 332.

48 *Liang Zhen Pu Eight Diagram Palm*, Li Zi Ming, comp. and ed. Vincent Black, pp. 20–21.

49 *Strategy*, B. H. Liddel Hart, p. 327.

50 *The Essentials of Ba Gua Zhang*, p. 334.

51 *The Wiles of War:* 36 Military Strategies from Ancient China, trans. Sun Haichen (Beijing: Foreign Language Press, 1996), p. 320.

52 *The Grand Strategy of the Byzantine Empire*, Edward Luttwak (Cambridge, MA: The Belknap Press of Harvard University Press, 2009), pp. 56–8.

53 Diagram adapted from *Byzantine Cavalryman c. 900-1204*, by Timothy Dawson, illustrated by Giuseppe Rava (Oxford: Osprey Publishing Ltd., 2009), p. 27.

54 *The Attacking Hands of Ba Gua Zhang*, Gao Ji Wu with Tom Bisio, photographs by Valerie Ghent (New York: Trip Tych Enterprises LLC, 2010), p. 34.

55 *The Washing of the Spears: The Rise and Fall of the Zulu Nation*, Donald R. Morris (New York: Simon & Schuster Inc, 1965), p. 50.

56 Ibid, p. 53.

57 *Ba Gua Zhang*, Jiang Rong-Qiao.

58 *Warfare in the Classical World*, John Warry (New York: St. Martin's Press, 1980), p. 20.

59 *Patterns of Conflict*, pp. 62–63.

60 *Ba Gua Quan Zhen Chuan*, Sun Xi Kun, trans. Joseph Crandall (Pinole, CA: Smiling Tiger Martial Arts, 2000), p. 19.

61 Ibid., p. 17.

62 Ibid.   .

63 *Ba Gua Zhang*, Jiang Rong-Qiao.

64 *God's Chinese Son: The Taiping Heavenly Kingdom of Hong Xiuquan*, Jonathan Spence (New York: W. W. Norton and Company, 1996), pp.130–132.

65 Ibid., p. 132.

66 Ibid.

67 *The Seven Military Classics in Ancient China,* trans. Ralph D. Sawyer (Boulder, CO: Westview Press Inc., 1993), p. 341.

68 *Three Kingdoms: Vol. 4,* Luo Guanzhong, pp. 1823–1824.

69 *The Seven Military Classics in Ancient China,* p. 327.

70 Great Battles of the Ancient World: The Legions of Rome (Lecture 17), Garret G. Fagan (Chantilly, VA: The Teaching Company, 2005).

71 *Strategy,* pp. 329–30.

72 Ibid.

73 *Napoleon's Glance: The Secret of Strategy,* William Duggan (New York: Nation Books, 2004), p. 19.

74 *Makers of Modern Strategy: From Machiavelli to the Modern Age,* ed. Peter Paret (Princeton, NJ: Princeton University Press, 1986), p. 131.

75 *Patterns of Conflict,* ed. John C. Boyd, Chuck Spinney, and Chet Richards, pp. 34–36.

76 *The Essentials of Ba Gua Zhang,* p. 323.

77 *Patterns of Conflict,* p. 31.

78 Ibid., p. 86.

79 Ibid., p. 98.

80 Ibid., p. 87.

81 *Liang Zhen Pu Eight Diagram Palm,* Li Zi Ming, comp. and ed. Vincent Black (Pacific Grove, CA: High View Publications, 1993), p. 25.

82 *Patterns of Conflict,* p. 85.

83 *The Essentials of Ba Gua Zhang,* p. 325.

84 *Lincoln's Generals,* Gabor S. Boritt, Stephen W. Sears, Mark E. Neely, Michael Fellman (New York: Oxford University Press US, 1995), p. 24.

85 *Hannibal,* Harold Lamb (New York: Pinnacle Books, 1958), pp. 222–24.

86 *Liang Chen Pu Eight Diagram Palm,* p. 94.

87 *The Essentials of Ba Gua Zhang,* p. 333.

88 *Patterns of Conflict,* p. 151.

89 *The Essentials of Ba Gua Zhang,* p. 341.

90 *Strategy,* B. H. Liddell Hart, p. 365.

91 *Seven Pillars of Wisdom,* T.E. Lawrence (Garden City, NY: Doubleday, Duran & Co., 1926 and 1935), p. 194.

92 *The Peninsular War,* Roger Parkinson (Great Britain: Wordsworth Editions, 2000), p. 154.

93 *The Shield of Achilles: War, Peace, and the Course of History,* Philip Bobbit (New York: Random House Inc., Anchor Books, 2002), p. 301.

94 *Strategy,* B. H. Liddell Hart, p. 365.

95 *Ba Gua Zhang,* Zhang Rong-jiao, trans. by Huang Guo Qi and Tom Bisio.

96 *On Guerrilla Warfare,* Mao Tse-Tung, trans. Samuel B. Griffith (New York: Praeger Publishing, 1961, BN Publishing, 2007), p. 52.

97 *Guerrilla Warfare,* Che Guevara, trans. J. P. Morray (Lincoln, NE: University of Nebraska Press, 1985), p. 56.

98 Ibid., p. 58–9.

99 *Liang Zhen Pu Eight Diagram Palm,* p. 18.

100 *On Guerrilla Warfare,* Mao Tse-Tung, p. 104.

101 *Masters of War: Classical Strategic Thought,* Michael Handel (London: Frank Cass Publishers, 1992, 1996 and 2001), p. 278.

102 *The Essentials of Ba Gua Zhang,* p. 331.

103 Ibid., p. 339.

104 *On Guerrilla Warfare,* p. 103–104.

105 *The Essentials of Ba Gua Zhang,* p. 326.

106 Ibid., p. 327.

107 *Some Principles of Maritime Strategy,* Julian Stafford Corbett (London: Bibliobazaar, 2006), p. 102.

108 Ibid., p. 106.

109 *Some Principles of Maritime Strategy,* p. 118.

110 *A Frozen Hell: The Russo-Finnish Winter War of 1939-40,* William R. Trotter (Chapel Hill, NC: Algonquin Books, 1991), p. 132.

111 *A Frozen Hell: The Russo-Finnish Winter War of 1939-40,* pp.136–38.

112 *Sun Zi: The Art of War and Sun Bin: The Art of War,* p. 225.

113 *Sun Tzu: The Art of War,* p. 73.

114 *Armed Conflict: The Lessons of Modern Warfare,* Brian Steed (New York: Ballantine Books, 2002), pp. 56–57.

115 Ibid., p. 56.

116 *Beating Goliath: Why Insurgents Win,* Geoffrey Record (Herndon, VA: Potomac Books, 2007), p. 27.

117 *Certain to Win,* Chet Richards (Bloomington, IN: Xlibris Corporation, www.Xlibris.com, 2004), p. 73.

118 *War of the Flea: The Classic Study of Guerrilla Warfare,* Robert Taber (Washington, DC: Potomac Books, Inc., 2002), p. 20.

119 *The 33 Strategies of War,* Robert Greene (London: Penguin Books, 2006), p. 354.

120 *Swish of the Kris: The Story of the Moros,* Vic Hurley (New York: E. P. Dutton and Co. Inc., 1936), pp. 146–7.

121 *Imperial Grunts: the American Military on the Ground*, Robert D. Kaplan (New York: Random House, 2005), p. 139.

122 *Swish of the Kris: The Story of the Moros*, pp. 196–7.

123 *Imperial Grunts: the American Military on the Ground*, Robert D. Kaplan, p. 140.

124 *The Utility of Force: The Art of War in the Modern World*, General Rupert Smith (New York: Random House, Vintage Books, 2005), p. 164.

125 *Learning to Eat Soup with a Knife: Counterinsurgency Lessons from Malaysia and Vietnam*, John A. Nagal (Chicago: University of Chicago Press, 2002), p. 105.

126 *The Changing Face of War: Lessons of Combat from the Marne to Iraq*, Martin Van Creveld (New York: Ballantine Books, 2006), pp. 230–34.

127 *Cheng Family Ba Gua Palms*, Ma You Jing and Liu Jing Ru, trans. Joseph Crandall (Pinole, CA: Smiling Tiger Martial Arts, 1995), pp. 18–19.

128 *The Shorter Science and Civilization in China: 4*, Joseph Needham, abridged by Colin A. Ronan (Cambridge: Cambridge University Press, 1986), p. 170.

129 *Three Kingdoms, Vol. 4*, ch. 102.

130 *The Making of Europe: Conquest, Colonization, and Cultural Change 950–1350*, Robert Bartlett (Princeton: Princeton University Press, 1993), pp. 72–75.

131 *Combat Baguazhang Vol. One: Forms and Principles*, John Painter (Hollywood, CA: Unique Publications, 2007), p. 242.

132 *Great Battles of the Ancient World: Macedonian Military Innovations* (Lecture 15), Garret G. Fagan (Chantilly, VA: The Teaching Company, 2005).

133 *Soldiers and Ghosts: A History of Battle in Classical Antiquity*, J. E. Lendon (New Haven, CT: Yale University Press, 2005), pp. 115–126.

134 *Great Battles of the Ancient World: Macedonian Military Innovations.*

135 *Fighting Techniques of the Ancient World 3000 BC–AD 500: Equipment, Combat Skills and Tactics*, Simon Anglim, Phyllis G. Jestice, et al (New York: St. Martin's Press, 2001), p. 43.

136 Ibid., pp. 45–46.

137 *The History of the Art of War in the Middle Ages Vol. 2: 1278-1485*, Sir Charles Oman (London: Greenhill Books, 1898, 1991), p. 256.

138 *Imperial Spain 1469–1716*, J. H. Elliot (New York and London: Penguin Books Ltd., 1963, 2002), pp. 133–4.

139 *The Shield of Achilles: War, Peace, and the Course of History*, p. 114.

140 *The Thirty Years War 1618-1648*, Richard Bonney (Oxford, Great Britain: Osprey Publishing, 2002), p. 28.

141 *The Utility of Force: The Art of War in the Modern World*, General Rupert Smith, p. 39.

142 *The Shield of Achilles: War, Peace and the Course of History,* p. 152.

143 *Battle Cry of Freedom,* James M. McPherson (Oxford: Oxford University Press, 1988), p. 475.

144 *The Utility of Force,* pp. 89–90.

145 Ibid., p. 115.

146 Ibid., p. 125.

147 *Patterns of Conflict,* ed. John C. Boyd. Chuck Spinney, and Chet Richards, p. 57.

148 *Patterns of Conflict,* p. 59.

149 *Soldiers of the Dragon,* p. 83.

150 *The Utility of Force,* p. 131.

151 *Rommel's Greatest Victory: The Desert Fox and the Fall of Tobruk, Spring 1942,* Samuel W. Mitchum Jr. (Novato, CA: Presidio Press Inc. 2001), p. 30.

152 *The West Point Military Series — The Second World War: Europe and the Mediterranean,* ed. Thomas E. Griess (New Hyde Park, NY: Square One Publishers, 2002), pp. 2–6.

153 Ibid., p. 5.

154 *The Age of Napoleon,* Will and Ariel Durant (New York: Simon and Schuster, 1975), p. 247.

155 *The Western Way of War: Infantry Battle in classical Greece,* Victor David Hanson (Berkeley, CA: University of California Press, 1989), from the introduction by John Keegan, p. xii.

156 Ibid., p. 4.

157 *A History of the Art of War in the Middle Ages: from the Fourth to the Fourteenth Century Vol. 2: 1278-1485,* Sir Charles Oman (London: Greenhill Books, 1898, 1924, and 1991), p. 59.

158 *Agincourt,* Charles Kightly (Surrey, UK: Almark Publishing Co. Ltd., 1974), p. 24.

159 *Organic Design for Command and Control,* ed. John R. Boyd. Chuck Spinney, and Chet Richards, p. 15. www.chetrichards.com/modern_business _strategy/boyd/organic_design/organic_design_frameset.htm.

160 *The Changing Face of War: Lessons of Combat from the Marne to Iraq,* Martin Van Creveld, p. 143.

161 *The Utility of Force: The Art of War in the Modern World,* p. 242.

162 *Sun Zi: The Art of War and Sun Bin: The Art of War,* p. 285.

163 *Tactics of the Crescent Moon: Militant Muslim Combat Methods,* by H. John Poole (Emerald Isle, NC: Posterity Press, 2004), p. 219.

164 "Weight of Combat Gear Is Taking Toll," Ann Scott Tyson, *The Washington Post,* 2/1/09.

165 *Tactics of the Crescent Moon: Militant Muslim Combat Methods,* pp. 229–30.

166 Ibid., p. 109.

167 *How the Weak Win Wars: A Theory of Asymmetric Conflict,* Ivan Arreguin-Toft Cambridge: Cambridge University Press, 2005), pp. 186–7.

168 *Beating Goliath: Why Insurgencies Win,* p. 56.

169 *Makers of Modern Strategy: From Machiavelli to the Modern Age,* ed. Peter Paret (Princeton: Princeton University Press, 1986), p. 69.

170 Ibid., p. 83.

171 *Armed Conflict: The Lessons of Modern Warfare,* Brian Steed (New York: Ballantine Books, 2002), p. 197.

172 *The Real Explanation of Boxing Meaning,* Sun Lu-Tang, trans. Huang Guo-qi.

173 *Strategy,* p. 39.

174 *The History of the Art of War in the Middle Ages: from the Fourth to the Fourteenth Century,* Sir Charles Oman (London: Methuen & Co., 1898), p. 27–29.

175 The *Decline and Fall of the Roman Empire Vol. 4,* Edward Gibbon (London: Methuen & Co. Ltd., 1909), p. 339.

176 *The Life of Belisarius,* Lord Mahon (London: John Murray, Albemarle Street, 1829), p. 246.

177 Ibid., p. 318.

178 *The Wiles of War: 36 Military strategies From Ancient China,* pp. 189–190.

179 *The Life of Belisarius,* pp. 366–7.

180 *The History of the Art of War in the Middle Ages: from the Fourth to the Fourteenth Century,* Sir Charles Oman (London: Methuen & Co., 1898), p. 32.

181 *Strategy,* p. 53.

182 *History of the Wars: Books V and VI,* Procopius, translated H. B. Dewing (London: Biblio Bazaar, 1971 and 2007), pp. 115–17.

183 *The Life of Belisarius,* pp. 44–45.

184 *The Wiles of War,* p. 141.

185 *Belisarius and Small Force Theory,* Robert R. Leonard. Originally published in the *Armchair General.* www.jhuapl.edu/areas/warfare/papers/SmallForce-Theory.pdf.

186 *The Age of Faith,* Will Durant. (New York: Simon and Schuster, 1950), p. 116. *The Life of Belisarius,* Lord Mahon, pp. 427–8.

187 *Maurice's Strategikon: Handbook of Byzantine Military Strategy,* trans. George T. Dennis (Philadelphia: University of Pennsylvania Press, 1984), p.84.

188 Ibid., pp. 87–8.

189 *The Art of War*, Sun Tzu, trans. John Minford (New York: Penguin Books, 2009).

190 *A Treatise on Efficacy: Between Western and Chinese Thinking*, Francois Jullien, pp. 172–3.

Chapter II

191 *The Making of Strategy: Ruler, States and War*, ed. Williamson Murray, Mac-Gregor Knox, and Alvin Bernstein, p. 22.

192 *On War*, Carl von Clausewitz (London: Penguin Books, 1908 and 1982), p. 119.

193 *Makers of Modern Strategy: From Machiavelli to the Modern Age*, p. 200.

194 *On War*, pp. 118–119.

195 *Masters of War: Classical Strategic Thought*, p. 16.

196 *Some Principles of Maritime Strategy*, Julian Stafford Corbett, p. 76.

197 Ibid., pp. 75–76.

198 *Strategy*, B. H. Liddell Hart, pp. 356–357.

199 *Strategy: The Logic of War and Peace*, Edward N. Luttwak, pp. 20–28.

200 *Masters of War: Classical Strategic Thought*, pp. 165–213.

201 *On War*, p. 570.

202 *Masters of War: Classical Strategic Thought*, p. 210.

203 *The Art of War*, Sun Tzu, trans. John Minford, p. 13.

204 *On War*, p. 92.

205 Ibid., p. 94.

206 Ibid., p. 604.

207 *The Grand Strategy of the Roman Empire: From the First Century AD to the Third*, Edward Luttwak (Baltimore and London: Johns Hopkins University Press, 1976), pp. 21–25.

208 *Great Battles of the Ancient World: Reflections on Warfare in the Ancient World* (Lecture 24), Prof. Garret G. Fagan, The Teaching Company, 2005.

209 Ibid.

210 *The Art of War*, Sun Tzu, p. 3.

211 *The Making of Strategy: Ruler, States and War*, ed. Williamson Murray, Mac-Gregor Knox, and Alvin Bernstein, p. 3.

212 Ibid., pp. 535–38.

213 Ibid., pp. 542–544.

214 *The Making of Europe: Conquest, Colonization and Cultural change 950–1350*, Robert Bartlett (Princeton: Princeton University Press, 1993), pp. 85–90.

215 *The Dream and the Tomb: A History of the Crusades*, Robert Payne (New York: Stein and Day Publishers, 1984), p. 50.

216 Ibid.

217 *The Making of Strategy: Ruler, States and War*, p. 57.

218 Ibid., p. 84.

219 *The Grand Strategy of the Roman Empire: From the First Century AD to the Third*, Edward Luttwak, pp. 7–50.

220 Ibid., pp. 3–4.

221 *Sun Zi: The Art of War and Sun Bin: The Art of War*, p. 23.

222 *The Peloponnesian War*, Donald Kagan (New York: Penguin Books, 2003), pp. 1–54.

223 *Learning to Eat Soup with a Knife: Counterinsurgency Lessons From Malaysia and Vietnam*, pp. 213–14.

224 *The Black Swan: The Impact of the Highly Improbable*, Nassim Nicholas Taleb (New York: Random House, 2007), pp. 40–41.

225 *The Utility of Force: The Art of War in the Modern World*, p. 399.

226 *Strategy: The Logic of War and Peace*, Edward N. Luttwak, pp. 87–91.

227 Ibid., p. 137.

228 *The Utility of Force: The Art of War in the Modern World*, General Rupert Smith, p. 15.

229 Ibid., pp. 13–18.

230 *Strategy: The Logic of War and Peace*, p. 265.

231 *Violence, Blunders, and Fractured Jaws: Advanced Awareness Techniques and Street Etiquette*, Marc "Animal" MacYoung (Boulder, CO: Paladin Press, 1992), p. xii.

232 Ibid., pp. xii-xiii.

233 *Strategy: The Logic of War and Peace*, pp. 234–57.

234 *The Making of Strategy: Ruler, States and War*, pp. 573–74.

235 *Meditations on Violence: A Comparison of Martial Arts Training & Real World Violence*, Rory Miller (Boston, MA: Publication Center Inc., 2008), p. 30.

236 *Learning to Eat Soup With a Knife*, pp. 179–180.

237 *How the Weak Win Wars: A Theory of Asymmetric Conflict*, Ivan Arreguin-Toft (Cambridge: Cambridge University Press, 2005), pp. 3–4.

238 Ibid., p. 18.

239 *Sun Zi: The Art of War and Sun Bin: The Art of War*, p. 139.

240 Ibid., p. 17.

241 "How David Beats Goliath: When Underdogs Break the Rules," Malcolm Gladwell, *The New Yorker*, The Innovators Issue, May 11, 2009, pp. 45–46.

242 *Beating Goliath: Why Insurgencies Win*, p. 138.

243 *The Making of Strategy: Ruler, States and War*, p. 1.

244 *Battle Cry of Freedom*, James M. McPherson (Oxford: Oxford University Press, 1988), pp. 464–469. *Lee's Lieutenants: A Study in Command*, Douglas S. Freeman (New York: Simon and Schuster, 1998), pp. 246–52.

245 *On War*, Carl von Clausewitz, p. 164.

246 *On War*, p. 165.

247 *The Utility of Force: The Art of War in the Modern World*, p. 155.

248 *The Making of Strategy*, p. 645.

249 *Masters of War: Classical Strategic Thought*, pp. 246.

250 Ibid., pp. 246–47.

251 Ibid., p. 247.

252 *The Black Swan: The Impact of the Highly Improbable*, p. 157.

253 *Blink: The Power of Thinking Without Thinking*, Malcolm Gladwell (New York: Back Bay Books—Little Brown and Company, 2005), pp. 99–119.

254 *Sun Zi: The Art of War and Sun Bin: The Art of War*, p. 167.

255 *A Treatise on Efficacy: Between Western and Chinese Thinking*, p. 17.

256 Ibid., pp. 23–24.

257 *Certain to Win*, p. 84.

258 Ibid., p. 75.

259 *The Propensity of Things: Toward a History of Efficacy in China*, p. 261.

260 *The I Ching: An Illustrated Guide to the Classic of Changes* (Singapore: ASIAPAC Books, 1993), p. 61.

261 Ibid., p. 60.

262 *The I Ching: An Illustrated Guide to the Classic of Changes*, p. 61.

263 Ibid., p. 60.

264 *The I Ching: An Illustrated Guide to the Classic of Changes*, p. 60.

265 Ibid.

266 Ibid.

267 Ibid., p. 61.

268 *The Living I Ching: Using Ancient Chinese Wisdom to Shape Your Life*, Deng Ming Dao (New York: HarperCollins Publishers, 2006), p. 28.

269 *The Classic of Changes: A New Translation of the I Ching as Interpreted by Wang Bi*, p. 122.

270 Ibid., p. 121–22.

271 *Strategy*, B. H. Liddell Hart, pp. 334–335.

272 *The Shield of Achilles: War, Peace, and the Course of History*, p. 292.

273 *The Utility of Force: The Art of War in the Modern World,* Rupert Smith, p. 320.

274 *The Numerology of the I Ching: A Sourcebook of Symbols, Structures and Traditional Wisdom,* Alfred Huang (Rochester, VT: Inner Traditions International, 2000), p. 89.

Chapter III

275 *The Making of Strategy: Ruler, States and War,* p. 645.

276 *The Classic of Changes: A New Translation of the I Ching as Interpreted by Wang Bi,* p. 25.

277 *Patterns of Conflict,* John C. Boyd, p. 141.

278 Ibid., p. 176.

279 *Organic Design for Command and Control.*

280 Ibid., p. 16.

281 Ibid., p. 23.

282 *Certain to Win,* p. 89.

283 *Musashi's Book of Five Rings,* Miyamoto Musashi, trans. Stephen F. Kaufman (Rutland, VT, Tokyo: Tuttle Publishing, 1994), p. xv.

284 *Sun Zi: The Art of War and Sun Bin: The Art of War,* p. 27.

285 *Karate & Qi: The Origin of Ki and the Depth of Thought,* Kenji Ushiro (Japan: Aiki News, 2008), p. 135.

286 *Meditations on Violence: A Comparison of Martial Arts Training & Real World Violence,* p. 39.

287 Ibid., p. 38.

288 老僧托钵

289 劈拳

290 推磨掌

291 *Bagua Qian Xue,* Sun Lutang, trans. and ed. Joseph Crandall (Pinole, CA: Smiling Tiger Martial Arts, 2002).

292 *Bagua Quan Zhen Chuan* (the Genuine Transmission of Ba Gua Quan), Sun Xikun, trans. and ed. Joseph Crandall (Pinole, CA: Smiling Tiger Martial Arts, 2000).

293 滚, 鑽, 爭, 裹

294 劲力

295 *Ba Gua You Shen Zhang: Eight diagram Swimming Body Palm,* Wang Shu-jin, trans. and annotated Marcus Brinkman and Bradford Tyrey, insiderasia .com/gaostylebagua.com, pp. 6–7.

296 *Bagua Quan Xue,* p. 15.

297 定式

298 老八掌

299 *Ba Gua Linked Palms,* Wang Shujing, trans. and commentary Kent Howard and Chen Hsiao-Yen (Berkeley, CA: Blue Snake Books, 2009), pp. 3–5.

300 *Masters of War: Classical Strategic Thought,* pp. 247–8.

301 *The Black Swan: The Impact of the Highly Improbable.*

302 Zhou Cang is a character in the *Romance of the Three Kingdoms.* He swore his loyalty to General Guan Yu and was appointed be General Guan's saber carrier. A skilled boatman, his talents were critical in the success of Guan Yu's water attack at the Battle of Fancheng.

303 In the *Romance of the Three Kingdoms,* Zhang Fei is one of Liu Bei's generals. He is fierce and brave, but also impetuous and rash.

Chapter IV

304 *Sunzi: The Art of War and Sun Bin: The Art of War,* p. 281.

Chapter V

305 *Moltke on the Art of War, Selected Writings,* ed. Daniel J. Hughes (New York: Random House Publishing, 1993), p. 124.

306 *The Laws of Change: I Ching and the Philosophy of Life,* Jack M. Balkin (Branford, CT: Sybil Creek Press, 2002 and 2009), pp. 10–11.

307 *On War,* p. 121.

308 *Masters of War: Classical Strategic Thought,* pp. 51–2.

309 *The Art of Action: How Leaders Close the Gaps Between Plans, Actions and Results,* Stephen Bungay (Boston: Nicholas Brealey Publishing, 2011), pp. 44–5.

310 Ibid., pp. 47–9.

311 Ibid., pp. 85–87.

312 *Science, Strategy and War: The Strategic Theory of John Boyd,* Frans P. B. Osinga (Oxford: Routledge, 2007), p. 210.

313 Ibid., pp. 212–13.

314 Ibid., p. 218 and 228.

315 *The Art of Action: How Leaders Close the Gaps Between Plans, Actions and Results,* Stephen Bungay, p. 95.

316 *The Laws of Change: I Ching and the Philosophy of Life,* Jack M. Balkin, p. 19.

317 Ibid., p. 21.

318 For a more extensive list, see *Chinese Leadership Wisdom: From the Book of Changes,* by Mun Kin Chok (Hong Kong: Chinese University Press, 2006), pp. 5–7.

319 *Chinese Leadership Wisdom: From the Book of Changes,* Mun Kin Chok, p. 157.

320 *The Classic of Change: A New Translation of the I Ching,* interpreted by Wang Bi, p. 243.

321 *The Classic of Change: A New Translation of the I Ching,* p. 9.

322 *The Art of Action: How Leaders Close the Gaps Between Plans, Actions and Results,* pp. 47–9.

323 *Chinese Leadership Wisdom: From the Book of Changes,* Mun Kin Chok, p. 32.

324 *War: Ends and Means,* Angelo Condevilla and Paul Seabury (Washington, DC: Potomac Books, 2006), p. 70.

325 *16 Strategies: The Art of Management,* Alan Chong (Singapore: Asiapac Publications, 1995). "'Managerial Grid' and Zhuge Liang's 'Art of Management': Integration for Effective Project Management," Low Sui Pheng and Ben S. K. Lee, in *Management Decision* 35/5 [1997], pp. 382–391.

326 *Rework,* Jason Fried and David Heinemeier Hansson (New York: Crown Business, 2010), pp. 19–20.

327 "The Prusso-German School: Moltke and the Rise of the General Staff," Hajo Holborn, in *Makers of Modern Strategy: from Machiavelli to the Nuclear Age,* ed. Peter Paret (Princeton: Princeton University Press 1986), 289.

328 *The Art of Action,* pp. 198–203.

329 *Certain to Win,* p. 84.

330 Ibid., p. 84.

331 *Making Things Happen: Mastering Project Management,* Scott Berkun (San Francisco: O'Reilly Media, 2008), p. 75.

332 *Rework,* p. 20.

333 *Making Things Happen,* p. 73–75.

334 *Certain to Win,* pp. 108–112.

335 *99 Idea Killers.* Designed by Rapp Y Collins, Inc. (A Doyle-Dane Bernbach Co., Innovation Labs Inc., 1980).

336 "'Managerial Grid' and Zhuge Liang's 'Art of Management.'"

337 *Sun Tzu's the Art of War plus the Art of Management: Strategy for Leadership,* Gary Gagliardi (Seattle: Clearbridge Publishing, 1992 and 2004), pp. 146–47.

338 *The Art of Action: How Leaders Close the Gaps Between Plans, Actions and Results,* Stephen Bungay, pp. 130–31.

339 *Rework,* p. 37.

340 *Making Things Happen: Mastering Project Management,* p. 166.

341 *The Art of Action,* p. 214.

342 *The Righteous Mind: Why Good People Are Divided by Politics and Religion,* Jonathan Haidt (New York: Vintage Books, 2012), p. 341.

343 Ibid., p. 105.

344 *The Classic of Change: A New Translation of the I Ching,* interpreted by Wang Bi, p. 329.

345 *Chinese Leadership Wisdom: From the Book of Changes,* Mun Kin Chok, p. 234.

346 *The Laws of Change: I Ching and the Philosophy of Life,* Jack M. Balkin, p. 345–46.

347 *The I Ching: or Book of Changes,* Richard Wilhelm and Cary F. Baynes, pp. 124–5.

348 *Transforming Emotions with Chinese Medicine: an Ethnographic Account from Contemporary China,* Yanhua Zheng (Albany, NY: SUNY Press, 2007).

349 Ibid., p. 41.

350 *The Righteous Mind,* p. 61.

351 Ibid., pp. 104–105.

352 *Essentials of Tai Chi And Qigong* (Transcript Book), David-Dorian Ross (Chantilly, VA: The Great Courses, 2014), p. 334–5.

353 *The Organization of Behavior,* Donald Hebb (New York: Wiley & Sons, 1949), p. 70.

354 *The Laws of Change: I Ching and the Philosophy of Life,* p. 352.

355 *The Silent Transformations* by Francois Jullien (Calcutta, India: Seagull Books, 2011), p. 76.

356 *The Classic of Change: A New Translation of the I Ching,* p. 206.

357 *The Silent Transformations,* pp. 76–79.

358 *The Classic of Change: A New Translation of the I Ching,* p. 215.

359 The mnemonic phrase is usually attributed to Carla Shatz at Stanford University. en.wikipedia.org/wiki/Hebbian_theory.

360 *The Silent Transformations,* pp. 126–7.

361 *Sun Tzu: The Art of War,* trans. John Minford, p. 19.

362 *The 4 Hour Workweek,* Tim Ferris (New York: Crown Publishers, 2007), p. 51.

363 *Strategy: The Logic of War and Peace,* Edward N. Luttwak, p. 67.

364 *Vital Nourishment: Departing from Happiness,* Francois Jullien, trans. Arthur Goldhammer (New York: Zone Books, 2007), p. 108.

365 Ibid., p. 25.

366 *The 4 Hour Workweek,* pp. 51–2.

367 *Sun Tzu: The Art of War,* trans. John Minford, p. 28.

368 *Vital Nourishment: Departing from Happiness,* Francois Jullien, p. 9.

369 *Huang Di Nei Jing:* Chapter 1, "A Complete Translation of the Yellow Emperor's Classics of Internal Medicine and Difficult Classic (Nei-Jing and Nan-Jing)," Henry C. Lu (Vancouver: International College of Traditional Chinese Medicine, 2004).

370 *Vital Nourishment,* p. 31.

371 *Chinese Leadership Wisdom from the Book of Change,* p. 387.

372 *Joint Operational Warfare: Theory and Practice,* Milan N. Vego (Newport, RI: Naval War College, Government Printing Office, 2009), p. 16.

373 *Vital Nourishment,* p. 109.

Appendix I

374 *History of the Wars: Books VI and VII,* Procopius, trans. H. B. Dewing, p. 127.

375 *Strategy: The Logic of War and Peace* (revised edition), Edward N. Luttwak, p. 1.

376 *The Prince,* Niccolo Machiavelli, trans. George Bull (London: Penguin Books, 1961 and 1999), p. 73.

377 *The Art of War,* Sun Tzu, trans. John Minford, p. 11.

378 *The Tao of Organization: The I Ching for Group Dynamics,* Cheng Yi, trans. Thomas Cleary (Boston and London: Shambhala, 1995), p. 12.

379 *Beating Goliath: Why Insurgents Win,* Geoffrey Record, p. 26.

380 *On the Origins of War and the Preservation of Peace,* Donald Kagan (New York: Doubleday, 1995), pp. 252–260.

381 *Sun Zi: The Art of War and Sun Bin: The Art of War,* p. 103.

382 *The Life of Belisarius,* Lord Mahon, pp. 268–270.

383 *Sun Zi: The Art of War and Sun Bin: The Art of War,* p. 141.

384 *On the Origins of War and the Preservation of Peace,* Donald Kagan, pp. 73–4.

385 *A Greater Than Napoleon: Scipio Africanus,* by B. H. Liddell Hart (New York: Biblio & Tannen Booksellers and Publishers Inc., 1927 and 1976), pp. 83–84.

386 *Sun Zi: The Art of War and Sun Bin: The Art of War,* pp. 4–5.

387 *A Greater Than Napoleon,* p. 24.

388 Ibid., p. 25.

389 *Mastering the Art of War,* Zhuge Liang and Liu Ji, p. 93.

390 *Maurice's Strategikon: Handbook of Byzantine Military Strategy,* p. 81.

391 *The Story of Civilization Part XI: The Age of Napoleon,* Will and Ariel Durant (New York: Simon and Schuster, 1975), p. 247.

392 *Mastering the Art of War,* Zhuge Liang and Liu Jin, p. 67.

393 *Sun Zi: The Art of War and Sun Bin: The Art of War,* p. 21.

394 *The Life of Belisarius,* p. 261.

395 *Sun Zi: The Art of War and Sun Bin: The Art of War,* p. 19.

396 Ibid., pp. 43–45.

397 *The Life of Belisarius,* p. 263–4.

398 *The Story of Civilization Part XI: The Age of Napoleon,* p. 247.

399 *Sun Zi: The Art of War and Sun Bin: The Art of War,* pp. 19–20.

400 *Sun Zi: The Art of War and Sun Bin: The Art of War,* p. 151.

401 *On War,* pp. 405–6.

402 Ibid., p. 405.

403 *Sun Zi: The Art of War and Sun Bin: The Art of War,* pp. 19–20.

404 *Makers of Modern Strategy: From Machiavelli to the Modern Age,* p. 485.

405 *The Art of War,* Zhuge Liang, trans. Tom Bisio.

406 *The 33 Strategies of War,* Robert Greene (London: Penguin Books, 2006), p. 93.

407 *Mastering the Art of War,* p. 85.

408 Ibid., p. 79.

409 Ibid., p. 81.

410 *The Shield of Achilles: War, Peace, and the Course of History,* p. 178.

411 *On the Origins of War and the Preservation of Peace,* Donald Kagan (New York: Doubleday, 1995), p. 568.

412 *Our Oriental Heritage: The Story of Civilization: Vol. 1,* Will Durant (New York: Simon & Schuster, 1935 and 1963), pp. 440–45.

413 *The Age of Reason Begins,* Will and Ariel Durant (New York: Simon and Schuster, 1961), p. 33.

414 Ibid., p. 32.

415 Ibid., p. 8.

416 Ibid., p. 8.

Appendix II

417 *Three Kingdoms: Vol. 2,* Luo Guanzhong, p. 681.

418 *Cognitive Strategy from the Romance of the Three Kingdoms,* Check Teck Foo, Chinese Management Studies vol. 2, no. 3, 2008 (Emerald Group Publishing Ltd.), p. 172.

419 *Sun Zi: The Art of War and Sun Bin: The Art of War,* p. 17.

420 *Three Kingdoms: Vol. 2,* p. 680.

421 *Knowing Words: Wisdom and Cunning in the Classical Traditions of China and Greece,* Lisa Raphals (Ithaca, NY: Cornell University Press, 1992), pp. 140–141.

422 *Three Kingdoms: Vol. 2,* pp. 717–19.

423 *Three Kingdoms: Vol. 2,* Chapter 85, pp. 1513–18.

424 *Cognitive Strategy from the Romance of the Three Kingdoms,* p.179.

425 *Knowing Words: Wisdom and Cunning in the Classical Traditions of China and Greece,* by Lisa Raphals, p. xii.

426 *The Art of War.*

427 *Mastering the Art of War,* Zhuge Liang and Liu Jin. Translated by Thomas Cleary (Boston: Shambhala Publications Inc., 2005), p. 74.

428 *Organic Design for Command and Control,* pp. 32–34.

429 *Mastering the Art of War,* pp. 91–2.

430   *The Art of War.*

431   "'Managerial grid'" and Zhuge Liang's 'Art of management,'" p. 382.

432   *The Art of War.*

Appendix III

433   *Sun Zi: The Art of War and Sun Bin: The Art of War,* pp. 282–3.

434   *Sun Zi: The Art of War and Sun Bin: The Art of War,* pp. 296–7.

435   *Liang Zhen Pu Eight Diagram Palm,* Li Zi Ming, p. 90.

436   *Maurice's Strategikon: Handbook of Byzantine Military Strategy,* p. 81.

437   *16 Strategies: The Art of Management,* Zhuge Liang, trans. Alan Chong (Singapore: ASIAPAC Books, 1995 and 2000), pp. 16–27.

438   *The Essentials of Ba Gua Zhang,* Gao Ji Wu and Tom Bisio, p. 328.

439   *A Modern History of Tanganyika,* John Iliffe (Cambridge: Cambridge University Press, 1979), p. 243.

440   *The Cambridge History of Africa: Vol. 7, 1905-1940,* John Donnelly Fage, A. D. Roberts, Roland Anthony Oliver (Cambridge: Cambridge University Press, 1986), p. 666.

441   *A Modern History of Tanganyika,* p. 244.

442   *Cambridge Illustrated History of China,* Patricia Buckley Ebrey (Cambridge: Cambridge University Press, 1996), p. 129.

443   *Sun Zi: The Art of War and Sun Bin: The Art of War,* pp. 40–41.

444   *The Age of Napoleon,* Will and Ariel Durant (The Story of Civilization: Vol. XI), pp. 108–109.

445   *The Essentials of Ba Gua Zhang,* p. 325.

446   *The Essentials of Ba Gua Zhang,* p. 337.

447   *The Essentials of Ba Gua Zhang,* p. 342.

448   *Three Kingdoms: Vol. 2,* Luo Guanzhong, pp. 850–70.

449   *The Book of Stratagems: Tactics for Survival and Triumph,* Harro Von Senger, trans. by Myron B. Gubitz (New York: Viking, 1991) p. 130.

450   *Sun Zi: The Art of War and Sun Bin: The Art of War,* p. 67.

451   *Sun Zi: The Art of War and Sun Bin: The Art of War,* p. 99.

452   *Three Kingdoms: Vol. 3,* pp. 1340–1372.

453   *The Utility of Force: The Art of War in the Modern World,* Rupert Smith, p. 237.

454   *The 33 Strategies of War,* Robert Greene, p. 154.

455   *History of the Wars: Books III and IV,* Procopius, trans. H. B. Dewing, p. 147.

456   *Hannibal,* Theodore Ayrault Dodge (New York: Barnes & Noble, 2005, originally published, 1889), pp. 201–16. *Hannibal,* Harold Lamb, pp. 68–80.

457   *The Wiles of War,* Sun Haichen, p. 125.

458 *Three Kingdoms: Vol. 2*, pp. 1891–1900.

459 *The Wiles of War*, p. 133.

460 *The Life of Belisarius*, Lord Mahon, pp. 44–45.

461 *Maurice's Strategikon: Handbook of Byzantine Military Strategy*, p. 81.

462 *History of the Wars: Books III and IV*, Procopius. Trans. H. B. Dewing, pp. 101–105.

463 *Strategy: The Logic of War and Peace*, Edward N. Luttwak, pp. 185–6.

464 Ibid., pp. 186–7.

465 *Three Kingdoms: Vol. 1*, Luo Guanzhong pp. 495–508.

466 *The Tao of Deception: Unorthodox Warfare in Historic and Modern China*, Ralph D. Sawyer, pp. 364–5.

467 *Three Kingdoms: Vol. 4*, pp. 1977–79.

468 *The Wiles of War*, pp. 214–19.

469 *Three Kingdoms: Vol. 2*, pp. 969–70.

470 *Battle Cry of Freedom*, James M. McPherson (Oxford: Oxford University Press, 1988), p. 515.

471 *Three Kingdoms: Vol. 4*, pp. 1934–53.

472 *Sun Zi: The Art of War and Sun Bin: The Art of War*, p. 91.

473 *History of the Wars: Books I and II*, Procopius, trans. H. B. Dewing, pp. 24–26.

474 *The 33 Strategies of War*, Robert Greene, pp. 42–3.

475 *Three Kingdoms: Vol. 3*, p. 1279.

476 *Three Kingdoms: Vol. 4*, pp. 1737–38.

477 *Maurice's Strategikon: Handbook of Byzantine Military Strategy*, p. 82.

478 *The Wiles of War*, p. 303.

479 *Three Kingdoms: Vol. 2*, pp. 815–49.

480 *Three Kingdoms: Vol. 2*, p. 821.

481 *Sun Zi: The Art of War and Sun Bin: The Art of War*, p. 19.

Bibliography

Anglim, Simon, and Phyllis G. Jestice, et al. *Fighting Techniques of the Ancient World 3000 BC–AD 500: Equipment, Combat Skills and Tactics.* New York: St. Martin's Press (Amber Books Ltd.), 2001 and 2006.

Arreguin-Toft, Ivan. *How the Weak Win Wars: A Theory of Asymmetric Conflict.* UK: Cambridge University Press, 2005.

Balkin, Jack M. *The Laws of Change: I Ching and the Philosophy of Life.* Branford, CT: Sybil Creek Press, 2002 and 2009.

Bartlett, Robert. *The Making of Europe: Conquest, Colonization, and Cultural Change 950–1350.* Princeton: Princeton University Press, 1993.

Berkun, Scott. *Making Things Happen: Mastering Project Management.* San Francisco: O'Reilly Media, 2008.

Black, Jeremy. *Cambridge Illustrated Atlas: Warfare Renaissance to Revolution 1492–1792.* Cambridge: Cambridge University Press, 1996.

Black, Jeremy editor. *The Seventy Great Battles in History.* London: Thames and Hudson, 2005.

Blofield, John, trans. *I Ching: The Book of Changes.* New York: E.P. Dutton and Co. Inc., 1968.

Bobbitt, Philip. *The Shield of Achilles: War, Peace, and the Course of History.* New York: Random House Inc., Anchor Books, 2002.

Bonilla, Gabriel. "The Bocage." http://cghs.dadeschools.net/normandy/bocage/overcame.htm.

Bonney, Richard. *The Thirty Years War 1618–1648.* Oxford: Osprey Publishing, 2002.

Boritt, Gabor S., Mark E. Neely, Stephen W. Sears, and Michael Fellman. *Lincoln's Generals.* New York: Oxford University Press US, 1995.

Boyd, John R. "Destruction and Creation." Fort Leavenworth, KS: *U.S. Army Command and General Staff College*, September 3, 1976.

Boyd, John R., Chuck Spinney, and Chet Richards. "Organic Design for Command and Control." 2005. Available at: www.chetrichards.com/modern_business_strategy/boyd/organic_design/organic_design_frameset.htm.

Boyd, John R., Chuck Spinney, and Chet Richards. *Patterns of Conflict.* 2005. Re-creation of the last briefing given by Col. Boyd. Available at: www.d-n-i.net/boyd/patterns.ppt.

Bungay, Stephen. *The Art of Action: How Leaders Close the Gaps Between Plans, Actions, and Results.* Boston: Nicholas Brealey Publishing, 2011.

Carfano, James Jay. *GI Ingenuity: Improvisation Technology and Winning WWII.* Westport, CT: Praeger Security International (Greenwood Publishing Group, Inc.), 2006.

Chang, Stephen T. *The Integral Management of Tao: Complete Achievement.* Reno, NV: Tao Publishing, 1988, 1991.

Check Teck Foo. "Cognitive Strategy from the Romance of the Three Kingdoms." *Chinese Management Studies* vol. 2, no. 3, 2008. Emerald Group Publishing LTD: 171–82.

Cheng Yi. *The Tao of Organization: The I Ching for Group Dynamics.* Trans. Thomas Cleary. Boston and London: Shambhala, 1995.

Citino, Robert. *The Path to Blitzkrieg: Doctrine and Training in the German army 1920–1939.* London: Lynne Rienner Publishers, 1999.

Clausewitz, Carl von. *On War.* London: Penguin Books, 1908 and 1982.

Clausewitz, Carl von. *On War.* Trans. Michael Howard and Peter Paret. Princeton: Princeton University Press, 1976.

Condevilla, Angelo and Paul Seabury. *War: Ends and Means.* 2nd ed. Washington, D.C.: Potomac Books, 2006.

Corbett, Julian Stafford. *Some Principles of Maritime Strategy.* London: Bibliobazaar, 2006 (first published 1911).

Crandall, Joseph and Helin Dong, trans. "In His Own Words: Sun Lu Tang's Single Palm Chang." *Pa Ku Chang Journal* vol. 5, no. 5, July/August 1995. Pacific Grove, CA: High View Publications.

Crawford, Amy. "The Swamp Fox Elusive and Crafty, Francis Marion Outwitted British Troops During the American Revolution." Smithsonian.com, July 1, 2007.

Dawson, Timothy. *Byzantine Cavalryman c. 900–1204.* Illus. Giuseppe Rava. Oxford: Osprey Publishing LTD, 2009.

Deng Ming-Dao. *The Living I Ching: Using Ancient Chinese Wisdom to Shape Your Life.* New York: HarperCollins, 2006.

Dennis, George T, trans. *Maurice's Strategikon: Handbook of Byzantine Military Strategy.*, Philadelphia: University of Pennsylvania Press, 1984.

Dodge, Theodore Ayrault. *Hannibal.* New York: Barnes & Noble, 2005 (originally published 1889).

Duggan, William. *Napoleon's Glance: The Secret of Strategy.* New York: Nation Books (Avalon Publishing Group Inc.), 2004.

Durant, Will. *The Age of Faith: The Story of Civilization: Vol. IV.* New York: Simon & Schuster, 1950.

Durant, Will. *Our Oriental Heritage: The Story of Civilization: Vol. 1.* New York: Simon & Schuster, 1935 and 1963.

Durant, Will and Ariel. *The Age of Reason Begins: The Story of Civilization: Vol. VII.* New York: Simon & Schuster, 1961.

Durant, Will and Ariel. *The Age of Napoleon: The Story of Civilization: Vol. XI.* New York: Simon & Schuster, 1975.

Ebrey, Patricia Buckley. *Cambridge Illustrated History of China.* Cambridge: Cambridge University Press, 1996.

Elliot, J. H. *Imperial Spain 1469–1716.* London and New York: Penguin Books Ltd., 1963 and 2002.

Fagan, Garret G. *Great Battles of the Ancient World: The Legions of Rome (Lecture 17).* Chantilly, VA: The Teaching Company, 2005.

Fagan, Garret G. *Great Battles of the Ancient World: Macedonian Military Innovations (Lecture 15).* Chantilly, VA: The Teaching Company, 2005.

Fagan, Garret G. *Great Battles of the Ancient World: Reflections on Warfare in the Ancient World (Lecture 24).* Chantilly, VA: The Teaching Company, 2005.

Fage, John Donnelly, A. D. Roberts, and Roland Anthony Oliver. *The Cambridge History of Africa: vol. 7, 1905–1940.* Cambridge: Cambridge University Press, 1986.

Ferris, Tim. *The 4-Hour Workweek.* New York: Crown Publishers, 2007.

Freeman, Douglas S. *Lee's Lieutenants: A Study in Command.* New York: Simon & Schuster, 1998.

Fried, Jason and David Heinemeier Hansson. *Rework.* New York: Crown Business, 2010.

Friezer, Karl-Heiz. *The Blitzkrieg Legend: The 1940 Campaign in the West.* Annapolis, MD: US Naval Institute Press, 2005.

Gagliardi, Gary. *Sun Tzu's The Art of War plus The Art of Management: Strategy for Leadership.* Seattle: Clearbridge Publishing, 1999, 2004.

Gao Ji-wu and Tom Bisio. *The Essentials of Ba Gua Zhan.* New York: Trip Tych Enterprises Inc, 2007.

Gibbon, Edward. *The Decline and Fall of the Roman Empire Vol. 4.* London: Methuen & Co. Ltd. 1909.

Gibson, David J. *Napoleon and the Grande Armée: Military Innovations Leading to a Revolution in 19th Century Military Affairs.* The Napoleon Series, 1995–2004. www.napoleonseries.org/military/organization/c_rma.html.

Gladwell, Malcolm. *Blink: The Power of Thinking Without Thinking.* New York: Back Bay Books, Little Brown and Company, 2005.

Gladwell, Malcolm. "How David Beats Goliath: When Underdogs Break the Rules." *The New Yorker,* The Innovators Issue, May 11, 2009, 40–49.

Govinda, Lama Anagarika. *The Inner Structure of the I Ching: The Book of Transformations.* San Francisco, New York: Wheelwright Press and John Weatherhill Inc., 1981.

Greene, Robert. *The 33 Strategies of War.* London: Penguin Books, 2006.

Griess, Thomas E., ed. *The West Point Military Series—The Second World War: Europe and the Mediterranean.* New Hyde Park, NY: Square One Publishers, 2002.

Guderian, Heinz Panzer Leader. Cambridge, MA: Da Capo Press, 1996 (first published in 1952).

Guevara, Che. *Guerrilla Warfare.* Trans. J. P. Morray. Wilmington, DE: Scholarly Resources Inc., 1997. First published by University of Nebraska Press, 1985.

Haidt, Jonathan. *The Righteous Mind: Why Good People are Divided by Politics and Religion.* New York: Vintage Books, 2012.

Handel, Michael. *Masters of War: Classical Strategic Thought.* 3rd edition. London: Frank Cass Publishers, 1992, 1996, and 2001.

Hart, B. H. Liddell. *Strategy.* London: Faber and Faber Ltd., 1967. Reprinted in Signet Classics, New American Library, 1974.

Hebb, Donald. *The Organization of Behavior.* New York: Wiley & Sons, 1949.

Herodotus. *The Landmark Herodotus: The Histories.* Robert B. Strassler, ed. New York: Pantheon Books, 2007.

Huang, Alfred. *The Numerology of the I Ching: A Sourcebook of Symbols, Structures, and Traditional Wisdom.* Rochester, Vermont: Inner Traditions International, 2000.

Huang Pu-min, Xiao Da-wei, and He Xiao-dong. *The Three Strategies of Huang Shigong and Questions and Replies Between Tang Taizong and Li Weigong.* Beijing: Military Science Publishing House, 2004.

Hughes, Daniel J, ed. *Moltke on the Art of War: Selected Writings.* New York: Random House, 1993.

Hurley, Vic. *Swish of the Kris: The Story of the Moros.* New York: E. P. Dutton and Co. Inc., 1936.

The I Ching: An Illustrated Guide to the Chinese Classic of Changes. Singapore: ASIAPAC Books PIE LTD, 1993, 2002.

Iliffe, John. *A Modern History of Tanganyika.* Cambridge: Cambridge University Press, 1979.

Javary, Cyrille. *Understanding the I Ching.* Boston: Shambhala Publications, 1997.

Jiang Rong-Jiao. *Ba Gua Zhang.* Trans. Huang Guo Qi and Tom Bisio.

Jullien, François. *The Propensity of Things: Toward a History of Efficacy in China.* Trans. Janet Lloyd. New York: Zone Books, 1999.

Jullien, François. *The Silent Transformations.* Calcutta, India: Seagull Books, 2011.

Jullien, François. *A Treatise on Efficacy: Between Western and Chinese Thinking.* Trans. Janet Lloyd. Honolulu: University of Hawai'i Press, 2004.

Jullien, François. *Vital Nourishment: Departing from Happiness.* Trans. Arthur Gold-hammer. New York: Zone Books, 2007.

Kagan, Donald. *On the Origins of War and the Preservation of Peace.* New York: Doubleday, 1995.

Kagan, Donald. *The Peloponnesian War.* New York: Penguin Books, 2003.

Kang Ge-wu. "The Origins of Pa Kua Chang—Part 3." *Pa Kua Chang Journal.* High View Publications: Vol. 3, No. 4, May/June 1993. 25–29.

Kang Ge-wu. *The Spring and Autumn of Chinese Martial Arts: 5000 Years.* Santa Cruz: Plum Publishing, 1995.

Kaplan, Robert. *Imperial Grunts: The American Military on the Ground.* New York: Random House. 2005.

Keegan, John. *The Face of Battle.* New York: The Viking Press, 1976.

Keegan, John. *A History of Warfare.* New York: Alfred A, Knopf, 1994.

Keegan, John. *The Second World War.* New York: Viking Penguin, 1989.

Krippendorff, Kaihan. *The Art of the Advantage: 36 Strategies to Seize the Competitive Edge.* UK: The Penguin Group, 2003.

Lamb, Harold. *Hannibal.* New York: Pinnacle Books, 1958.

Lawrence, T. E. *Seven Pillars of Wisdom.* Garden City, NY: Duran & Co., 1926 and 1935.

Lendon, J. E. *Soldiers and Ghosts: A History of Battle in Classical Antiquity.* Yale University, 2005.

Leonard, Robert R. "Belisarius and Small Force Theory." Originally published in the Armchair General. www.jhuapl.edu/areas/warfare/papers/SmallForce -Theory.pdf.

Liu Jing Ru and Ma You Jing. *Cheng Family Ba Gua Palms.* Trans. Joseph Crandall. Pinole, CA: Smiling Tiger Martial Arts, 1995.

Li Zi Ming, Liang Zhen Pu. *Eight Diagram Palm.* Compiled and edited by Vincent Black. Pacific Grove, CA: High View Publications, 1993.

Low Sui Pheng and Ben S. K. Lee. "'Managerial Grid' and Zhuge Liang's 'Art of Management': Integration for Effective Project Management." *Management Decision Journal* 1997, vol. 35, issue 5. Emerald Group Publishing LTD. 382–391.

Lu, Henry C., trans. *A Complete Translation of the Yellow Emperor's Classics of Internal Medicine and Difficult Classic (Nei-Jing and Nan-Jing).* Vancouver: International College of Traditional Chinese Medicine, 2004.

Luo Guanzhong. *Three Kingdoms: Vol. 1-4.* Trans. by Moss Roberts. Beijing: Foreign Language Press, 1995, 2007.

Luttwak, Edward. *The Grand Strategy of the Byzantine Empire.* Cambridge, MA: The Belknap Press of Harvard University Press, 2009.

Luttwak, Edward. *The Grand Strategy of the Roman Empire: From the First Century AD to the Third.* Baltimore and London: Johns Hopkins University Press, 1976.

Luttwak, Edward. *Strategy: The Logic of War and Peace.* Cambridge, MA: Harvard University Press (Belknap Press), 1987, 2001, 2003.

Lynn, Richard John, trans. *The Classic of Changes: A New Translation of the I Ching, as interpreted by Wang Bi.* New York: Columbia University Press, 1994.

Machiavelli, Niccolo. *The Prince.* Trans. George Bull. London: Penguin Books, 1961 and 1999.

MacYoung, Marc "Animal." *Violence, Blunders, and Fractured Jaws: Advanced Awareness Techniques and Street Etiquette.* Boulder, CO: Paladin Press, 1992.

Mahon, Lord. *The Life of Belisarius.* London: John Murray, Albemarle Street, 1829.

Mao Tse-Tung. *On Guerrilla Warfare.* Trans, Samuel B. Griffith. New York: Praeger Publishing, 1961.

Mao Tse-tung. "Selected Works of Mao Tse-tung: Vol. IX (1937)." Maoist Documentation Project/Brian Basgen Maoist Documentation Project (2000); Reference Archive (marxists.org), 2000. www.marxists.org/reference/archive/mao/works/1937/guerrilla-warfare/index.htm.

McPherson, James M. *Battle Cry of Freedom.* New York and Oxford: Oxford University Press, 1988.

Miller, Rory. *Meditations on Violence: A Comparison of Martial Arts Training & Real World Violence.* Boston: YMAA Publication Center Inc., 2008.

Milne-Tyte, Robert. *Armada.* Wordsworth Military Library. Hertfordshire, England: Wordsworth Editions, 1988.

Mitchum, Samuel W. Jr. *Rommel's Greatest Victory: The Desert Fox and the Fall of Tobruk, Spring 1942.* Novato, CA: Presidio Press Inc., 2001.

Morris, Donald R. *The Washing of the Spears: The Rise and Fall of the Zulu Nation.* New York: Simon & Schuster Inc, 1965.

Mun Kin Chok. *Chinese Leadership Wisdom: From the Book of Changes.* Hong Kong: Chinese University Press, 2006.

Murray, Williamson, MacGregor Knox, and Alvin Bernstein, eds. *The Making of Strategy: Ruler, States and War.* New York, Cambridge: Cambridge University Press, 1994 and 2008.

Musashi, Miyamoto. *Book of Five Rings.* Trans. Stephen Kaufman. Rutland, VT and Tokyo: Tuttle Publishing, 1994.

Musashi, Miyamoto. *A Book of Five Rings.* Trans. Victor Harris. New York: The Overlook Press, 1974.

Nagal, John A. *Learning to Eat Soup with a Knife: Counterinsurgency Lessons from Malaysia and Vietnam.* Chicago: University of Chicago Press, 2002.

Needham, Joseph. *The Shorter Science and Civilization in China: 4.* Abridged by Colin A. Ronan. Cambridge: Cambridge University Press, 1986.

Ni Hua-Ching. *I Ching: The Book of Changes and the Unchanging Truth.* Santa Monica, CA: Seven Star Communications, 1983 and 1994.

Oman, Sir Charles. *A History of the Art of War in the Middle Ages: from the Fourth to the Fourteenth Century.* London: Methuen & Co., 1898.

Oman, Sir Charles. *The History of the Art of War in the Middle Ages Vol 2: 1278–1485.* London: Greenhill Books, 1898, 1991.

Osinga, Frans P. B. *Science, Strategy, and War: The Strategic Theory of John Boyd.* Oxford: Routledge, 2007.

Painter, John. *Combat Baguazhang Vol. One: Forms and Principles.* Hollywood, CA: Unique Publications, 2007.

Paret, Peter, ed. *Makers of Modern Strategy: From Machiavelli to the Modern Age.* Princeton: Princeton University Press, 1986.

Parkinson, Roger. *The Peninsular War.* Great Britain: Wordsworth Editions, 2000.

Payne, Robert. *The Dream and the Tomb: A History of the Crusades.* New York: Stein and Day Publishers, 1984.

Peers, C. J. *Soldiers of the Dragon: Chinese Armies 1500 BC–AD 1840.* Oxford: Osprey Publishing, 2006.

Poole, H. John. *Tactics of the Crescent Moon: Militant Muslim Combat Methods.* Emerald Isle, NC: Posterity Press, 2004.

Procopius. *History of the Wars: Books I and II.* Trans., H. B. Dewing. London: BiblioBazaar, 1971 and 2007.

Procopius. *History of the Wars: Books III and IV.* Trans., H. B. Dewing. London: BiblioBazaar, 1971 and 2007.

Procopius. *History of the Wars: Books V and VI.* Trans., H. B. Dewing. London: BiblioBazaar, 1971 and 2007.

Procopius. *History of the Wars: Books VI and VII.* Trans., H. B. Dewing. Cambridge, MA: Harvard University Press, Loeb Classical Library, 1924 and 2006.

Qian Cai. *General Yue Fei.* Trans, T. L. Yang. Hong Kong: Joint Publishing. 1995.

Raphals, Lisa. *Knowing Words: Wisdom and Cunning in the Classical Traditions of China and Greece.* Ithaca, NY: Cornell University Press, 1992.

Record, Geoffrey. *Beating Goliath: Why Insurgents Win.* Sterling, VA: Potomac Books, 2007.

Richards, Chet. *Certain to Win.* Bloomington, IN: Xlibris Corporation, 2004. www .Xlibris.com.

Ritsema, Rudolf and Shantena Augusto. *The Original I Ching Oracle: The Pure and Complete Texts with Concordance.* London: Watkins Publishing, 2005.

Ross, David-Dorian. *Essentials of Tai Chi and Qigong.* Chantilly, VA: The Great Courses, 2014.

Sawyer, Ralph D., trans. *The Seven Military Classics in Ancient China.* Boulder, CO: Westview Press Inc., 1993.

Sawyer, Ralph D. *The Tao of Deception: Unorthodox Warfare in Historic and Modern China.* New York: Basic Books, 2007.

Secter, Mondo. *I Ching Clarified: A Practical Guide.* Rutland, VT, and Tokyo: Charles E. Tuttle Company Inc., 1993.

Sheppard, Alan. *France 1940: Blitzkrieg in the West.* Oxford: Osprey Publishing, 1990.

Shi Nai'an and Luo Guanzhong. *Outlaws of the Marsh, Vol. 1–3.* Trans. Sidney Shapiro. Beijing: Foreign Language Press, 1993.

Smith, General Rupert. *The Utility of Force: The Art of War in the Modern World.* New York: Random House, 2005.

Smith, Richard J. *Fathoming the Cosmos and Ordering the World: The Yijing and its Evolution in China.* Charlottesville and London: University of Virginia Press, 2008.

Spence, Jonathan. *God's Chinese Son: The Taiping Heavenly Kingdom of Hong Xiuquan.* New York: W. W. Norton & Company, 1996.

Spence, Jonathan. *The Search for Modern China.* New York: W. W. Norton & Company, 1990.

Steed, Brian. *Armed Conflict: The Lessons of Modern Warfare.* New York: Ballantine Books, 2002.

Strauss, Barry. *The Battle of Salamis: The Navel Encounter That Saved Greece and Western Civilization.* New York: Simon & Schuster, 2004.

Sun Haichen, trans. *The Wiles of War: 36 Military Strategies from Ancient China.* Beijing: Foreign Language Press, 1996.

Sun Lu-tang. *Bagua Quan Xue.* Trans., Joseph Crandall. Pinole, CA: Smiling Tiger Martial Arts, 2002.

Sun Lu-tang. *Xing Yi Quan Xue: The Study of Form-Mind Boxing.* Trans., Albert Liu; ed., Dan Miller. Pacific Grove, CA: High View Publications, 1993.

Sun Tzu. *The Art of War.* Trans., John Minford. New York: Penguin Books, 2009.

Sun Tzu. *The Art of War.* Trans., Samuel B. Griffith. Oxford: Oxford University Press, 1963.

Sun Xikun. *Bagua Quan Zhen Chuan.* Trans. and ed., Joseph Crandall. Pinole, CA: Smiling Tiger Martial Arts, 2000.

Sun Zi: The Art of War and Sun Bin: The Art of War. Beijing: Foreign Language Press (Library of Chinese Classics), 1999.

Taber, Robert. *War of the Flea: The Classic Study of Guerrilla Warfare.* Washington, DC: Potomac Books Inc., 2002.

Taleb, Nassim Nicholas. *The Black Swan: The Impact of the Highly Improbable.* New York: Random House, 2007.

The Thirty-Six Military Strategies, Wengu Chinese Classics and Translations. www.afpc.asso.fr/wengu/wg/wengu.php?l=intro.

Trotter, William R. *A Frozen Hell: The Russo-Finnish Winter War of 1939–40.* Chapel Hill, NC: Algonquin Books, 1991.

Tyson, Ann Scott. "Weight of Combat Gear Is Taking Toll." *The Washington Post,* 2/1/09.

Ushiro, Kenji. *Karate & Qi: The Origin of Ki and the Depth of Thought.* Japan: Aiki News, 2008.

Van Creveld, Martin. *The Changing Face of War: Lessons of Combat from the Marne to Iraq.* New York: Ballantine Books 2006.

Vego, Milan N. *Joint Operational Warfare: Theory and Practice.* Newport, RI: Naval War College, Government Printing Office, 2009.

Verstappen, Stefan H. *The Thirty-Six Strategies of Ancient China.* South San Francisco, CA: China Books, 1990.

Von Senger, Harro. *The Book of Stratagems: Tactics for Triumph and Survival.* Trans. Myron B. Gubitz. New York: Viking Penguin, 1991.

Wang Shu-jin. *Ba Gua Linked Palms.* Trans. and commentary, Kent Howard and Chen Hsiao-Yen. Berkeley CA: Blue Snake Books, 2009.

Wang Shu-jin. *Ba Gua You Shen Zhang: Eight Diagram Swimming Body Palm.* Trans. and annotation, Marcus Brinkman and Bradford Tyrey. insiderasia.com /gaostylebagua.com.

Wang Yang and Sandifer, John. *The Authentic I Ching.* London: Watkins Publishing, 2003.

Warry, John. *Warfare in the Classical World.* New York: St. Martin's Press, 1980.

Wilhelm, Helmut. *Change: Eight Lectures on the I Ching.* Princeton: Bollingen Series Princeton University Press, 1960, 1990.

Wilhelm, Richard. *Lectures on the I Ching: Constancy and Change.* Princeton: Bollingen Series Princeton University Press, 1979.

Wilhelm, Richard and Cary F Baynes. *The I Ching: or Book of Changes.* New York: Bollingen Series XIX, Princeton University Press, 1950, 1990.

Zakaria, Fareed. *The Post American World.* New York: W. W. Norton & Company, 2008.

Zheng, Yanhua. *Transforming Emotions with Chinese Medicine: An Ethnographic Account from Contemporary China.* Albany, NY: SUNY Press, 2007.

Zhuge Liang. *16 Strategies: The Art of Management.* Trans., Alan Chong. Singapore: ASIAPAC Books, 1995 and 2000.

Zhuge Liang and Liu Jin. *Mastering the Art of War.* Trans., Thomas Cleary. Boston: Shambhala Publications Inc., 2005.

Index

About the Author

TOM BISIO is the founder of New York Internal Arts, and Internal Arts International, which teach and promote the Chinese Internal Arts of Ba Gua Zhang and Xing Yi. He is also the cofounder of Zheng Gu Tui Na, an organization that teaches traditional Chinese medicine skills worldwide. A practitioner of acupuncture and traditional Chinese medicine, for twenty-five years Bisio headed a clinic in New York City specializing in trauma and Chinese sports medicine. Bisio is the author of the popular book on healing, *A Tooth From the Tiger's Mouth*. He has also written and collaborated on a number of books on martial arts.